Foster Children

of related interest

Fostering Now
Messages from Research
Ian Sinclair
ISBN 1 84310 362 1

Foster Carers
Why They Stay and Why They Leave
Ian Sinclair, Ian Gibbs and Kate Wilson
ISBN 1 84310 172 6

Foster Placements
Why They Succeed and Why They Fail
Ian Sinclair, Kate Wilson and Ian Gibbs
ISBN 1 84310 173 4

Fostering Adolescents
Elaine Farmer, Sue Moyers and Jo Lipscombe
ISBN 1 84310 227 7

Developing Adoption Support and Therapy
New Approaches for Practice
Angie Hart and Barry Luckock
ISBN 1 84310 146 7

Trauma, Attachment and Family Permanence
Fear Can Stop You Loving
Edited by Caroline Archer and Alan Burnell
for Family Futures
ISBN 1 84310 021 5

Supporting Parents
Messages from Research
David Quinton
Foreword by the Right Honourable Margaret Hodge, Minister for Children,
Young People and Families
ISBN 1 84310 210 2

Supporting South Asian Families with a Child with
Severe Disabilities
Chris Hatton, Yasmeen Akram, Robina Shah, Janet Robertson and
Eric Emerson
ISBN 1 84310 161 0

Parenting in Poor Environments
Stress, Support and Coping
Deborah Ghate and Neal Hazel
ISBN 1 84310 069 X

Foster Children

Where They Go and How They Get On

*Ian Sinclair, Claire Baker, Kate Wilson
and Ian Gibbs*

Jessica Kingsley Publishers
London and Philadelphia

First published in 2005
by Jessica Kingsley Publishers
116 Pentonville Road
London N1 9JB, UK
and
400 Market Street, Suite 400
Philadelphia, PA 19106, USA

www.jkp.com

Library of Congress Cataloging in Publication Data
Foster children : where they go and how they get on / Ian Sinclair ... [et al.].-- 1st American ed.
   p. cm.
Includes bibliographical references and index.
ISBN-13: 978-1-84310-278-6 (pbk.)
1. Foster home care--Great Britain. 2. Foster children--Great Britain. I. Sinclair, Ian, 1938-
HV887.G7F67 2005
362.73'3'0941--dc22

                          2005008614

British Library Cataloguing in Publication Data
A CIP catalogue record for this book is available from the British Library

ISBN-13: 978 1 84310 278 6
ISBN-10: 1 84310 278 1

Printed and Bound in Great Britain by
Athenaeum Press, Gateshead, Tyne and Wear

Contents

ACKNOWLEDGEMENTS   6

1. Introduction   7

2. Movements and Destinations: An Overview   29

3. Outcomes and Going Home   43

4. Going Home: What Makes A Difference?   70

5. Adoption: Who is Adopted and How Do They Do?   91

6. Adoption: What Makes A Difference?   107

7. Foster Care: Can It Offer 'Permanence'?   127

8. Foster Care: Does It Feel Like A Family?   149

9. Leaving Foster Care   171

10. Living Independently: What Makes A Difference?   187

11. Tara's Story: A Case Study   217

12. Alistair's Story: A Case Study   226

13. A Common Explanation?   234

14. Conclusion   250

APPENDIX 1: SAMPLING BIAS IN SWEEPS 1 AND 2   269

APPENDIX 2: SOME KEY VARIABLES   273

REFERENCES   278

SUBJECT INDEX   284

AUTHOR INDEX   285

Acknowledgements

This project has achieved what success it has through the efforts of many people.

We are grateful to our funders, the Department of Health, and to the officials within the department, particularly Carolyn Davies, Helen Jones and Caroline Thomas, who made us feel that we had a potentially exciting contribution to make.

Within our unit we have relied heavily on the help of Claire Skidmore and Suzy Alcock who spent countless hours on the telephone to social workers and other social services staff gathering information and leads on the latest known destinations of the children and young people in the study. Lorraine Wallis and Penny Williams carried out the majority of interviews for the case studies and did so with exemplary skill, persistence and empathy. Mike Stein and Jim Wade read the manuscript in whole or in part and their criticism was always constructive and to the point.

We owe a major debt to the authorities who took part in the project. Our efforts to track down the destinations of foster children gave us an unusual but nevertheless real insight into the difficulties under which social services departments labour. This increases our respect for the willingness of aftercare workers, foster carers, information officers, family placement social workers and social workers to help us and complete our questionnaires. We thank them for enabling the research to take place and for the generosity with which they took part.

Outside these formal organisations we have relied on the collaboration of adoptive parents, birth parents and current and former foster children. Their willingness to respond to our questionnaires and take part in our interviews made the project possible. From their responses we gained, we hope, some understanding of their situations and of the way they faced them. Many of the situations were sad. Despite this we found that our interviews increased our respect for those involved. We are very grateful to them all.

Chapter One

Introduction

We have listened to children and know that they have very clear ideas about what they want and need. Getting to live in the right place, not being moved around, and settling down so that they can fulfil their potential is vital. (Jacqui Smith (former Minister of State for Health) Department for Education and Skills 2001, p.2)

Introduction

This book is about what happens to foster children. The children studied were first contacted at the beginning of 1998.[1] They were then followed up 14 months later in 1999. The primary purpose of this earlier research[2] was to discover how successful foster placements could be defined and measured and how more of them might be produced. This new book takes up the story of these 596 children from 1999 and continues it till January 2001. This time the focus is not on their foster placements but on their 'three-year careers'.

The book arises from concerns about the outcomes of these careers, about the explanations for these outcomes and about the feasibility of changing them. We wanted to know if the children 'got to the right place'. If so, did they settle there and 'fulfil their true potential'? Would these outcomes have been better if they had gone somewhere else, or more support had been provided where they actually went? How feasible would it have been to bring this about? How far did the outcomes reflect their experience in the previous foster placement?

Against this background, the book concentrates on three major sets of issues.

Overall outcomes

- What kind of placements (e.g. adoption, birth family) do the children have now?
- How far do these provide a 'permanent' home in which they settle and thrive?
- Allowing for the fact that placements take different, but overlapping, kinds of children, do some kinds of placement have better outcomes than others?

Distribution

- What are the initial differences between children who go to different kinds of placement?
- What explains this distribution?
- Does there appear to be scope for modifying it?

Specific placement outcomes

- Within specific kinds of placement are there differences in the quality of the placement process, the security of the placement or the outcomes achieved?
- What explains these differences?
- Does there seem to be scope for improvement in these respects?

These issues structure the research. The next sections describe some of the research background to them. They also foreshadow a dilemma that will be central to much of the study.

The assumptions behind the research

It is the common assumption that the state is not a satisfactory 'corporate parent'. On past evidence children in the care system move frequently, more often than they themselves want, their educational outcomes are poor, and they have a high prevalence of mental ill-health. Those that graduate from the care system often face lonely, unstable and difficult lives. They make up a surprisingly high proportion of those in the prison system and those sleeping rough on the streets.[3] So it seems that the care system fails to compensate for – may even exacerbate – the problems of those who enter it.

A natural response to this conclusion is that children are better off at home. This sentiment informed the 1989 Children Act. As the government explained in a subsequent report:

> Central to the philosophy of the Act is the belief that children are best looked after within the family with both parents playing a full part and without resort to legal proceedings. (Department of Health 1993, p.3)

This belief was reflected in a number of duties required of local authorities in the 1989 Act. The most relevant to the current study required local authorities to give support to children and their families; to ensure contact with parents whenever they looked after a child away from home; and to return these children to their families unless this was against their interests.

In practice it is not always in a child's interests to return home. So what happens to those who do not do so? In 1998, the year in which we first contacted our sample, the government responded to their difficulties by launching its initiative *Quality Protects*.[4] Its driving idea was that vulnerable children should be 'securely attached to carers capable of providing safe and effective care for the duration of childhood'. Consistently with this objective, government priorities for children in public care have emphasised 'permanence'. Legislation, targets and guidance have promoted permanence through adoption, the introduction of 'special guardianship', the reduction of turnover in foster care and better support for those graduating out of the care system.[5] Such permanence will, it is assumed, imply better upbringing for children in public care – the fruits of which should be apparent in better educational performance and better development.[6]

This emphasis on adoption, guardianship and leaving care implies a concern with long-term care and with alternatives to the birth family. In this way it may be seen as striking a slightly new balance in the inevitable tensions between what may be good for the child, what he or she may want, and the rights of parents and child to a family life. This dilemma is essentially moral and political. Research cannot resolve it. Nevertheless research can outline the nature of the dilemma and suggest possible solutions to it. For example, it can explore attitudes among participants to adoption, or ways of enabling children to return home with less risk. What so far has it had to say?

Some relevant past research

The studies carried out just before the 1989 Children Act (for example, Rowe 1985) were predominantly concerned with children entering the care system. They assumed that the obvious – and usually better – alternative to being looked after by the state was *return to birth family.*[7] Contact was seen as the key to enabling a child to return home and strongly promoted for this reason. Voluntary admissions were seen as preferable to compulsory ones, at least partly because they too were associated with rehabilitation. The sharp drop in the likelihood of return home the longer a child remains in the care system was used as an argument for planning, purposeful social work, and energetic attempts to return a child home as soon as he or she is admitted. Arguably this research had a major influence on the thinking behind the Children Act 1989.

This committed set of studies paid little attention to a body of work which only dubiously supports this enthusiasm for returning looked-after children to their homes. Thus there is at least some evidence that:

- The children's educational and behavioural difficulties antedate their arrival in the care system. The latter may not cure them (Aldgate *et al.* 1992) but it arguably does not cause them either (Essen, Lambert and Head 1976; Lambert, Essen and Head 1977).

- Among children who enter the care system those who stay longer tend to do better in various ways – being more likely to thrive psychologically (Hensey, Williams and Rosenbloom 1983) and physically (King and Taitz 1985) if younger, and less likely to be involved in 'delinquent activity' if older (Minty 1987; Zimmerman 1982).

- Children who return from residential care to poor or disharmonious homes often do badly there[8] (Quinton and Rutter 1988; Sinclair 1971), although they may do comparatively well away from home (Sinclair 1971, 1975).

In general, and in keeping with current policy, research suggests that *adoption* offers the best chance of good outcomes for vulnerable children (Bohman 1971, 1996; Maugham, Collishaw and Pickles 1998; Maugham and Pickles 1990; St Claire and Osborne 1987; Tizard and Rees 1975; Triseliotis and Russell 1984). This picture, however, is by no means clear. Adoption in most studies has meant adoption at a very young age. It is not obvious that its superiority will hold for children adopted from highly disturbed backgrounds or who are older. One study notoriously found that children adopted from the 'at-risk register' were more disturbed and less satisfactorily parented than children who were fostered or at home (Gibbons *et al.* 1995). Another study found that breakdowns were as likely among teenage children placed for adoption as they were for those who were fostered long-term (Fratter *et al.* 1991), a pattern which a review suggests is common (Sellick and Thoburn 1996).

In practice some looked-after children will not be adopted or able to return home. *Long-term foster care* is a third major 'permanent' option and one which is of particular interest to this study. It likewise is hedged with uncertainties. On the face of it, it is a 'limbo' placement. Difficult to define, but nevertheless apparently ubiquitous (Lowe *et al.* 2002), it offers not a 'forever family' but rather a recognition that a return home is no longer planned. On the surface the commitment is ambiguous and tentative – a home while the child behaves or as 'long as it is needed' or until they take the initiative and go home in their teens.[9] Despite these uncertainties many children do commit to their foster carers and their foster carers to them (Schofield *et al.* 2000; Sinclair, Wilson and Gibbs 2004; Thoburn, Norford and Rashid 2000). Here too therefore is an option whose possibilities need to be taken seriously and evaluated.

A key question is how these foster children fare in the longer term. Foster care offers a 'time-limited' form of permanence. It needs to be evaluated not on its own but rather as part of a career. In practice the UK literature on foster care has, like our last study, tended to focus on the foster placement *per se* and in particular on breakdown (Berridge and Cleaver 1987; Farmer, Moyers and Lipscombe 2004; Fenyo, Knapp and Baines 1989; George 1970; Napier 1972; Parker 1966; Sinclair and Wilson 2003; Trasler 1960). Even studies of intensive foster care (Hazel 1981; Shaw and Hipgrave 1983, 1989; Walker, Hill and Triseliotis 2002) tend to concentrate on events during fostering.[10] There is, however, life after foster care and foster care needs to prepare children for it. Earlier research on residential work (Allerhand, Weber and Haug 1966; Sinclair 1971, 1975) suggests that while a residential home has a major impact on the behaviour of children in it, its influence is often short-lived. The issue of whether the effects of foster care are similarly temporary is clearly an important one. It is not an issue on which research has focused.

In general therefore research has not provided many conclusive results on the 'long-stay' children who seem to be the focus of much current policy. We still do not know how many of them would do better if they were adopted, returned home, fostered long-term or dealt with in some 'intermediate way' such as through a residence order.

This book is concerned with these issues. In the course of it we will examine:

- differences in outcomes between those in the main seven destinations (home, adoption by strangers, adoption by carer, remaining with the index (original 1998) foster carer, foster care by other carer, residential care, independent living)

- the factors which were present in 1998 and which predict these different outcomes

- whether type of placement seems to affect outcomes after allowing for the child's characteristics and situation in 1998.

In this way we explore how far foster care either offers satisfactory long-term care itself or provides good stepping stones to other forms of placement which do. We may also cast light on the central dilemma of how far long-stay children can safely return to their homes.

Distribution

The policy agenda raises issues of distribution between different types of placement as well as outcome. It may, for example, be better for children to be adopted. If so, what prevents more of them being dealt with in this way? Here, too, research has provided less help than it might, particularly over those children who are looked after for a long time.

The late 1970s and early 1980s saw a number of studies concerned with process and the factors that determined the destinations of children entering the care system (Rowe 1985). With some exceptions[11] these studies focused on admissions to the care system and with the probability or otherwise of return home. In 1989 Rowe, Hundleby and Garnett published a major account of children's moves into, within and out of the care system. More recently Bullock, Good and Little (1998) followed up 463 children entering social services departments for a period of two years. Taken together these studies showed a system much concerned with movement.[12] Children came and went rapidly, leaving behind them a small 'core' of long-stay children who themselves move within the system and take up the great majority of places.[13]

These studies raised the question on which we have already touched. 'What kind of stability does the care system offer to different groups of children who are in foster care and do not rapidly return home?' They showed that it certainly offered stability to some (Rowe *et al.* 1984), that any kind of long-term stable career was probably rare, particularly if the child entered when aged ten or over (Garnett 1992), and that the likelihood of adoption was strongly related to age. As already described, however, the main question on which these researchers focused was how to enable more children to go home. It is only recently, for example, that a study has particularly focused on the differences between those children for whom there are plans for adoption as against long-term fostering (Lowe *et al.* 2002).[14]

In contrast to these earlier studies our own research has concentrated on a group of children who were in the system on a particular date. Such a 'cross-sectional' sample reflects the way the resources in the foster care system are used. Typically its children have stayed in the system for some considerable time.[15] As far as we know the destinations of such a British sample have not been studied before.

In the course of the book we will consider among other things:

- which children go home
- which children are adopted by their carers and which by 'strangers'
- which children go into residential care
- which children stay in foster care
- the differences between those who stay with one foster carer and those who move to another
- the differences between those on residence orders and others in foster care
- the differences between those leaving foster care at 16 plus and those staying on.

In each case we try to establish the differences between the groups being compared and, as far as we can, the reasons why one group ends up in one kind of placement and the others in a different one.

Outcomes within specific placements

Outcomes within placement include 'final outcomes' (e.g. child's educational status) and what might be called 'process outcomes' – the feelings of those involved about the way the placement was reached and is currently working.

Process outcomes are a proper concern of much British research. Irrespective of where children are, the process of how they got there matters to them, their families and others who look after them. So too does the way the placement is currently working. Previous studies of adoption, return home, and leaving care have covered the processes involved.[16] There have also been consumer studies of foster children. In general the latter have either been small – some of the most valuable are autobiographical accounts (e.g. Arden 1977; Fever 1994; Moore 1990) – have had rather low response rates (e.g. Fletcher 1993), are American (e.g. Festinger 1983) or come from some time ago (Kahan 1979; Page 1977; Timms 1973; Van der Waals 1960).

The present study should help to confirm or modify the picture these other studies have painted. Against this background the book will examine:

- how birth parents view the process of return home and the help they receive

- how adoptive parents view the process of adoption and the help they receive

- how foster carers view the transitions of their foster children from foster care

- how children experience foster care and where they want to be in future

- how young people and foster carers view their transitions to independent living.

Our work on 'final outcomes' may make a more unusual contribution. In the course of our research we have been able to gather detailed information on the behaviour and well-being of foster children while they are in placement. We can then use this to see whether characteristics of the placement (e.g. quality of foster care) predict success in subsequent placement after allowing for a rating of child difficulty, and whether subsequent events in the new placement (e.g. support from social workers) appear to alter what would have been predicted. This advantage has not been available to other British studies. Internationally such prospective follow-up studies have also been rare. Instead researchers have often concentrated on atypical samples – for example, those who do not move or those whose stability of life makes them easier to locate (Festinger 1983; Meier 1965, 1966; for review and critique see Maluccio and Fein 1985).

Against this background we will be examining:

- the degree to which the quality of prior foster care affects well-being in subsequent adoptive or home placements or on leaving care
- the extent of support available in each placement type and its apparent effects after allowing for the child's characteristics as measured in foster care
- the degree to which former foster carers provide support after the child has left and the effects of this.

Guiding ideas of the research

Our research aims required us to think about the following questions:

- What constitutes a good outcome?
- What variables are likely to influence outcome?
- Under what conditions is a good foster care outcome likely to ensure a good outcome in a subsequent setting?

We had ideas about the plausible answers to these questions. These guided our research, determining the variables we chose to measure and the analyses we undertook.

First, we thought that *variables likely to determine outcome* would have to do with certain characteristics of the child together with the characteristics of three key arenas:

- the foster or other home in which they were
- their relationship with members of their birth family
- their school or work.

These broad hypotheses came from our previous work on this sample. They concerned the groups of factors that predicted foster care breakdown over 14 months. They were also in keeping with longitudinal studies of community samples. Vulnerable children escape from difficulty or otherwise through a combination of their own genetic inheritance, their family and their schooling (see e.g. Sampson and Laub 1993; Werner 1989). Appropriate early schooling may also be a treatment intervention which prevents later trouble (Schweinhart, Barnes and Weikart 1993).

In addition the hypotheses were suggested by our analysis of foster care. As we saw it foster care has the following *basic characteristics:*

- Foster care is family care. Factors which are called into play in ordinary family life – for example, rivalry between siblings or the love shown by parents – are likely to be important.

- Foster care involves separation from birth family and often results from abuse. The consequences of separation and abuse are likely to be important. So too is the relationship between birth and foster families.

- Foster care is socially devised and temporary.[17] The bureaucratic, temporary and legally constrained nature of foster care is likely to affect both its outcomes and the way it is experienced.

This analysis suggests that two particular characteristics of the child are likely to be important. The first of these is 'what the child wants'. Children who are or have been in foster care are vulnerable to split loyalties (e.g. to their birth family, their adoptive family or their foster family). Our previous work suggested that if they do not want to be where they are, the placement is unlikely to succeed (Sinclair and Wilson 2003).

A second key factor is 'attachment status' and the way this is handled. Foster children have inevitably experienced separation. This is likely to heighten their difficulties over attachment. Prior to this they are likely to have experienced some form of abuse, usually from a parental figure. A possible consequence is that the threat of abuse arouses a heightened desire to get closer to the parental figure who is also the source of threat – a situation which is said to predispose to 'disorganised attachment'. In any event the temporary and apparently partial commitment of foster care means that the child may be quick to perceive threats of rejection.[18]

Our ideas about what constitutes a good outcome came partly from the literature on *permanence*. The antecedents of permanency planning in England lay in the discovery of 'drift' in the care system (Rowe and Lambert 1973). The idea was that children were entitled to a family life. What was needed was a process which within a reasonable time-span would ensure that they got it. Those who developed the theory (Maluccio, Fein and Olmstead 1986) were aware that a full family life was not possible for all children. Nevertheless, they believed that placements with birth families, relatives or adoption were more likely to provide what was good about a family than long-term fostering. Fostering in turn was more likely to provide this experience than residential care.

These ideas about permanence assumed more than we wished to assume in this study. For example, it seemed to us conceivable that long-term foster care might in certain circumstances provide a 'better' kind of permanence than either adoption or birth family. For this reason we wanted to define 'permanence' as it were in the abstract, so that one could ask of any kind of placement how permanent it was. In approaching this issue we distinguished between the following:

- *Objective permanence* – this would occur when a child had a stable placement, which was likely to last for their childhood, and would provide back-up and if needed accommodation after the age of 18.

- *Subjective permanence* – this would be high if the child conceived of their family as their own, if they felt they belonged to it, and conversely if they did not feel excluded by it.

- *Enacted permanence* – this would be high if all concerned behaved as if the family was a lasting unit: for example, if the child was included in family occasions (e.g. weddings and holidays), if the carers went the 'extra mile' in fighting for what the child needed, if the child was prominent in family photographs, called their carers mum and dad and played their own part in making the family work (e.g. doing the washing up).

- *Uncontested permanence* – this would be high if a *modus vivendi* had been reached between the families involved but low if, for example, a child felt torn between two families or one was trying to set her or him against the other.

Permanence, however defined, is in part an end in itself and in part a means to other ends. These other ends were, as we saw it, those promoted by the looked-after children system. In particular we were concerned with:

- school performance/involvement in work
- the avoidance of abuse
- mental health
- relationships with others
- social behaviour (e.g. involvement or otherwise in anti-social actions).

We expected that these 'outcomes' would both influence and be influenced by the degree to which a child was settled in a placement. For example, children who were unhappy at school would be less likely to be settled and vice versa. Of equal interest were the long-term effects of having a settled or 'permanent' placement. Here our ideas were influenced by the research on residential work cited above. We expected the effects to be in many cases 'latent'. Those who learn French at school may only speak it later in the company of French speakers. In a similar way we expected that the lessons of previous foster care would be more likely to be enacted if the new environment called them forth and supported them. Children returning to similar environments to those which had generated their original problems might be expected to respond as they had originally done.

These ideas guided our research. They could also be modified by our results. If validated we thought that they could inform principles for practice.

Method

Our basic sample consists of 596 children in foster care at the beginning of 1998 in seven local authorities. This section describes the information available on the sample, the way we used it and its limitations.

Our main information for sweeps 1 (1998) and 2 (1999) was provided by postal questionnaires. Table 1.1 sets out the details. In addition we carried out 24 case studies and collected postal questionnaires from 150 children aged eight or over.

To this information, sweep 3 (2001) added information from the local authority on the current location of the child. We also sought information from the following sources:

- the child's current or most recent social worker – all cases
- current carer – all cases except those where the child was in residential care or independent living (i.e. birth family, adoptive parents, foster carer)
- the previous foster carer – all cases except for those currently in foster care
- the child or young person – all cases except those where the child had been adopted or was living with their birth family and where it was thought difficult to ask the child to comment on their current circumstances.

Table 1.2 sets out the details of the sweep 3 questionnaires, the number of replies obtained and the response rate of the relevant population this represents. As can be seen there were considerable variations in the response rates of the different groups, which varied from 82 per cent (adoptive parents) to 26 per cent (birth parents).

Table 1.1 Source and response rates to postal questionnaires

Source	Responses	Contents
Sweep 1 (1998)		
Foster carer	495 (83%)	Details of foster family, carer's perception of placement process, plans, contact with birth family, support received and carer's approach to fostering and child's personality, behaviour and progress
Social worker	416 (70%)	Placement history, reasons for placement, prior abuse, abilities, plans, work done by social worker, contact with family, worker's perception of carer, child's behaviour, personality and progress
Link worker*	492 (83%)	Perception of carer and outcome of case
Sweep 2 (1999)		
Foster carer	504 (85%)	Outcome, whether disrupted, contacts with family, measures of personality and problems if still in foster care, views of progress and outcome, lessons to be learnt
Social worker	337 (57%)	Outcome, views of progress and lessons
Link worker	462 (78%)	Outcome, views of progress and lessons

*Social workers who work with the foster carers rather than the child are now sometimes called 'supervising social workers'. At the time of the research they had various titles including 'link worker' and 'family placement social worker' which are the names used in this book.

As outlined in Appendix 2 these response rates had much to do with the methods used to gain access to the different groups. In general where we were dependent on field social workers to make the initial contact (birth parents, foster children in one area, and some young people living independently) the response rates were very much lower.[19] Appendix 1 discusses the issue of the bias introduced by these varying response rates. Our general conclusion is that there is remarkably little serious bias. Those who reply to the questionnaire seem to differ from non-responders in the ability of their past or present social worker to spend time on the research rather than in their own personal experiences and characteristics.

Table 1.2 Response rates to postal questionnaires: sweep 3

Source	Potential respondents	Responses
Social workers	596	356 (60%)
Current foster carers	231	183 (79%)
Last foster carer	365	227 (62%)
Adoptive parents	90	74(82%)
Birth parents	96	25 (26%)
Young person living independently	116	48 (41%)
Foster child	231	126 (55%)
Young person in residential care	22	6 (27%)

Information available: case studies

We carried out 30 case studies, based wherever possible on interviews with key stakeholders – carer, social worker and child. The aim was again to understand how the child came to be in their current position, how they seemed to be doing in the eyes of all concerned and what seemed to have brought this about.

In those cases where the child was adopted or with birth family we tried to interview the previous foster carer as well as the parent. Interviews with the social worker were by telephone and those with other respondents face to face. The interviews were free-flowing and followed no set order. However, the interviewers were given an interview guide which set out the key areas they should cover.

We selected the cases on the grounds that they fulfilled criteria outlined below and the social workers, birth families, adopters and foster carers or – in the case of those in independent living – young people had agreed to co-operate. We did not approach the children directly but through their parents, foster carers or social workers. Some children chose not to be interviewed or used forms of non-verbal communication which meant that we could not usefully interview them given our available resources. We included these cases in our sample.

In selecting the sample we used the information already available to divide the cases into three groups – those going well, those apparently not going well and an intermediate group. It was not possible to make this division for adoption where all cases appeared to be going well. Similarly we had no case with a residence order that was clearly 'not going well'. With these exceptions we ensured at least one case in each of these classes in each of our target groups. We also wanted to ensure variety in terms of age, sex and ethnicity and that at least some of the sample were regarded by our respondents as 'disabled'.[20]

We list below the number of case studies undertaken in the different categories:

Adopted by carer	2
Adopted by 'stranger'	2
Independent living	6
Residence order	4
Birth family	6
Fostered	10

Within these we carried out 87 interviews with the following:

Adoptive parent(s)	4
Birth parent	6
Foster carer (current or last)	28
Young person	5
Child	15
Social worker	29

We did not attempt interviews with children who were aged less than five, who explicitly or implicitly showed they did not want to be interviewed or who had no verbal communication. We did, however, spend time with a child in two further cases.

We achieved, in our eyes, enough variation. The sample included six children whose ethnicity was not British, a spread of ages from the youngest to the oldest (5 to 18 plus) and a roughly even split between the sexes. We deliberately included rather more children (n=12) who could be said to be disabled than would have occurred naturally in the sample as a whole.

Analysis

We used three main methods of analysis.

Our primary method was *statistical*. The aim here was to describe (e.g. destinations of sample), to relate outcomes to information from sweep 1, and to draw tentative causal inferences. Thus we tried to predict particular outcomes (e.g. psychological state) at sweep 3 using sweep 1 information and then to see whether events subsequent to sweep 1 (e.g. adoption) could be said to have modified this outcome for better or worse. This provides a tentative answer to such questions as 'Does trial at home typically produce better or worse outcomes than would have occurred if the child had remained in foster care or been adopted?'

A difficulty with this method was that the relevant samples often became small. Our sample was large and most of our response rates were good. Nevertheless some information (e.g. on the child's 'strengths and difficulties' as measured by the Goodman scale – Goodman 1994) was not available on children under the age of three at sweep 1. Moreover response rates were not 100 per cent and analyses which involved information from more than one source reduced numbers severely.[21] For example, analyses that were restricted to children over three and required data from both social workers and foster carers at sweep 1 typically reduced sample size by around 55 per cent. Size was then further reduced by the size of the sweep 3 sub-sample considered and its response rate.

We tackled this difficulty in various ways. A key method was to produce what we called 'composite variables'. Where we have had information on the same variable from more than one source we have tried to combine information so that we can use the variable even where one of the sources is missing. An obvious example is 'breakdown'. We had information on placement breakdown from foster carers, social workers, and family placement social workers. We adopted the convention of assuming that a case had 'broken down' if any of these disparate sources said that it did.[22]

Our second method involved *qualitative analysis*. Our questionnaires gave plenty of scope for respondents to express opinions, as to why things had turned out the way they had and what they liked and did not like about the process. What they wrote was often incisive and insightful. However, not everyone writing about a given case chose to answer the open-ended questions and those that did would often make different, although not necessarily contradictory, points. We wished neither to ignore their insights nor to give undue weight to the pungent phrase. We have followed a rule of trying to represent the key points made, of noting where points were disputed, and of trying to locate the insights within a broader framework so that apparently different points could be seen as flowing from the same basic situation.

Our third method was *case analysis*. Our case studies provided us with a wealth of material and explanations for outcome as seen from different perspectives. In addition they allowed information to be put in the context of an individual's history. For example, it may become apparent that a child is prone to feel the odd one out. This tendency may be revealed in what the child says (for example, in the vivid accounts which some gave of being ignored in the context of their family). It may also be apparent in the foster carer's account. It can be put together with other information (for example, to the effect that the child's placement breakdowns tend to follow the arrival of another child in the placement) to provide a plausible account of the reason for which the breakdown takes place. Again we tried to ensure that these explanations were located within a broader framework capable of encompassing the variety of outcomes experienced.

In general we aimed to 'triangulate' these three types of approach so that the explanations yielded by one are at least compatible with, and at best reinforced by, those yielded by others. To return to the example just given, the idea that 'being an odd one out' is a key theme in foster care may be suggested by case studies, reinforced by what children and foster carers say in their questionnaires, and reinforced again by statistical analyses that predict outcome on the basis of some measure of 'felt exclusion'. This ideal is not always – or even commonly – realised in this book. It is the approach we have used as far as we can.

Limitations

Like all studies this one has its limitations.

First, the study is 'observational'. We did not try to introduce changes in a controlled way. This limits our ability to make confident assertions about cause and effect. We make these statements with appropriate caveats. Experimental research is needed if many of our conclusions are to be tested.

Second, we do not deal with the possible effects of differences between social services departments or with the effects of 'micro-level' organisational differences (e.g. in the attitude of team leaders). The reason is partly lack of numbers[23] and partly lack of the relevant data.

Third, we have made little reference to children from ethnic minorities. This partly stems from lack of numbers. The sample was not sufficiently large to provide separate analyses for children whose families came originally from, say, China, South Asia, Somalia or the Caribbean. These groups are themselves highly diverse but we were reduced to classifying all those with a 'non-UK' ethnic origin as a single group for statistical analysis. We routinely included this variable in analyses but it did not yield significant differences. Our case studies made clear the complexity of the issues surrounding ethnicity and fostering. They also showed many of the fundamental issues do not differ by ethnic group. Rejection and separation are difficult irrespective of ethnicity.[24]

Shape of the book

The book is shaped by the destinations to which children go. Chapter 2 provides an overview – outlining the proportions going to different destinations, the quality of environment these seem to provide, and the reasons for them. This chapter introduces a key dilemma. It suggests that while foster care may well provide a satisfactory environment it generally does so for only a restricted period of time. Subsequent environments, other than adoption, appear less positive.

The remaining chapters explore this dilemma. Chapters 3 to 10 deal in order with returns to birth families, adoption, remaining in foster care and independent living. Each of these chapters seeks to explain why the children were in these particular kinds of placements, to compare outcomes with other appropriate comparison groups and to say something of how the participants experienced the process. In this way they inform discussion of whether there is scope for changing the children's careers or improving the outcomes associated with particular placements. Chapters 11 to 13 describe two cases in some detail and explore how far their outcomes illustrate the findings presented elsewhere in the book. Chapter 14 summarises the evidence on the dilemma and suggests ways in which it might be reduced.

Difficulties for the reader

This book relies on case material, reports of what children and adults said or wrote, and statistical analysis. All this material is central to the argument. However, readers are likely to differ over which parts they find accessible or conversely hard to follow.

Those who are used to statistics may feel that we have provided too little detail. We have tried to cater for their needs in two ways. First, we have provided footnotes which do offer more detail. Second, we always try to make it clear what kind of analysis we have done.[25]

Other readers may find the statistics hard to follow. We have tried to write sentences in such a way that they make sense if the technical statistics are omitted. For example, we might write that foster children are significantly more likely to be adopted if they are first looked after when aged less than five ($p<0.001$). This sentence continues to make sense if the word 'significantly' and the bracket are omitted. In practice most of the technical statistics are concerned with how likely it is that a finding would be repeated if similar research was done on a sizeable sample elsewhere.[26]

Conclusion

The book describes a three-year follow-up of 596 children. It compares the outcomes of different kinds of placement and seeks to understand the distribution of children between these placements. It is particularly concerned with differences in the outcomes of those who go home and those who do not. The book also examines the reasons for differences in outcome within placements. To do this it uses a wide variety of different sources of data and a combination of statistical and qualitative methods.

The research has been guided by ideas about what counts as a successful outcome in foster care (particularly the achievement of 'permanence') and what is likely to make for successful outcome. The latter includes factors connected with the individual child (in particular what they want and their attachment status), the foster family, the birth family and the child's school. A particular interest is the relationship between a child's situation at one point in time (e.g. in a foster family) and their subsequent life in a different environment.

A key dilemma raised by the study is the limited nature of the 'permanence' typically offered by foster care. Much of the book is concerned with ways in which this dilemma might be addressed either through changing the 'careers' typically followed by foster children or by changing the support available in the placements to which they go.

Notes

1. We aimed to describe the sample as at 1 January 1998. The questionnaires took some time to come in. Some of the information may therefore have related to a slightly later date (e.g. March 1998). Similar considerations apply in later sweeps. However, we have not found that date of questionnaire return is related to outcomes.

2. A still earlier study in 1997 surveyed foster carers to discover what support they wanted and whether additional support might affect whether they continued to foster. The children in the present study were all fostered by foster carers involved in our 1997 survey. Some data from this original study (e.g. on whether these were lone carers) were included in the present study. For details of both studies see Sinclair, Gibbs and Wilson 2004 and Sinclair, Wilson and Gibbs 2004.

3. For recent summaries of the relevant literature see Stein 2002; Wilson *et al.* 2004. For a number of key articles on education of children in care see Jackson 2001. Official reports (e.g. Health and Social Services Committee 1998; Utting 1997) commonly list disturbing statistics on these matters.

4. The momentum for this initiative probably came from scandals in the care system rather the long-term outlook for looked-after children. The skilfulness of the title lies in its ability to link the negative agenda of reducing scandal to the positive one of promoting quality.

5. 'Leaving care' might seem the antithesis of 'permanence'. In practice, however, the guidance accompanying the Leaving Care Act (2000) emphasises the desirability of children staying on in foster care if appropriate. The strong emphasis on improving life for those 'moving on' should also reduce any sense that the previous time in the care system is simply an antechamber to a 'doomed' and potentially unsettled life.

6. From the official point of view the key dimensions of development are those specified in the 'Looked After Children' system (see Parker *et al.* 1991; Ward 1995). Success in these endeavours is seen as involving wider agendas. It should reduce social exclusion. It may require an inter-agency approach.

7. This is not entirely fair. Rowe (1985) explicitly notes that there is insufficient evidence to determine which children should enter the care system and which should remain at home. Nevertheless the prevailing assumption in the studies she quotes is that it is in the children's interest to return, that the vast majority will do so anyway and that return is therefore something for which social workers should vigorously work. These studies were carried out a time when certain groups of children (e.g. those admitted because of delinquency, poor school attendance or environmental circumstances) were entering the care system much more frequently than they do today. The assumption that looked-after children do better at home may have been more plausible then than it is now.

8. Children removed from appalling conditions by contrast often do surprisingly well away from home, a point made, albeit not totally consistently, by studies of children brought up by animals, locked alone in rooms, chained to radiators or in other appalling conditions (e.g. Koluchova 1976; Skuse 1984). Similarly children removed from very poor institutional care can show a surprising degree of recovery. These effects seem to depend on which area of recovery is considered, the age and genetic inheritance of the child at the time of the change of environment, and the quality of environment to which the child goes (e.g. Rutter and the ERA study team 1998; Skeels and Harms 1948). Recovery also seems common when children are displaced through war (Rathbun, Di Virgilio and Waldfogel 1958; Rathbun *et al.* 1965).

9. For a discussion of these and related points see Schofield *et al.* 2000.

10. American studies are rather more forthcoming in this respect. There have been studies of the effects of treatment foster care (Chamberlain 1990, 1998a, 1998b; Chamberlain

and Reid 1991; Chamberlain, Moreland and Reid 1992; Reddy and Pfeiffer 1997), as well as of skills training in foster care (Cook 1994) and numerous studies of the relevance of intervention at home while the child is in foster care (family reunification studies).

11. Rowe and her colleagues' own (1984) study focused on a sample of long-stay children in foster care. It was, however, cross-sectional and concerned less with the process whereby children reached this state than with the experience of being there. Vernon and Fruin's (1986) study included longer-staying children as well as new entrants in their sample and was concerned with process as we define it. Their study, however, was predominantly concerned with factors affecting return home.

12. Rowe and her colleagues (1989) asked social workers about the reasons for placement. It turned out that many reasons were concerned with holding the child temporarily and in an emergency, allowing time for assessment or preparing her or him for other events such as adoption or independent living.

13. A recent study (Packman and Hall 1998) showed that only 10 per cent of a sample of children voluntarily accommodated were still looked after two years later. Bullock and his colleagues (1998) found that 20 per cent of all those admitted (i.e. compulsorily or voluntarily) were 'separated from their families' two years later. This included nearly 3 per cent who were adopted.

14. Rowe and her colleagues (1989) did document moves among long-stay children. However, their design focused on movements. They did not collect data on those children who did not move during the two years of their study.

15. In 1998 71 per cent of our sample of 596 children had spent more than a year in the care system in their current 'episode of being looked after'. This was comparable to national figures at the time.

16. See, for example, Thomas et al. (1999) for views of adopted children on the process of adoption; Bullock, Little and Millham (1993) for views of parents, children and social workers on return home; and Biehal et al. (1995) for accounts of the process of leaving care.

17. Foster children do not live in their foster families as a right, and they have opportunities to damage them by bringing complaints. Foster children may fear unwanted removal or be refused a removal that they did want. They may find that their lives are hedged around and constrained by regulations in a way in which other children's lives are not.

18. For research on foster care from an attachment perspective, together with related literature, see Downes (1992) for adolescents and Schofield et al. (2000) for children under 12.

19. This effect was seen most starkly in relation to foster children where the response rate in the area which used social workers to make the approach was approximately a third of that in the highest responding area and half the response rate in the sample as a whole where the child was approached via their foster carer.

20. There is no internationally agreed definition of this word. Respondents also differed over what they counted as 'disability'. In general, however, children were seen as disabled if they had intellectual or physical impairments which were not adequately compensated by social provisions.

21. In most cases the likelihood of response by one source on a child was unrelated to the likelihood of response by another. The combination of two 80 per cent response rates therefore reduced the overall response rates to around 64 per cent.

22. This particular rule introduces a possible bias. Other things being equal the greater the number of respondents the greater the chance that one will state that a placement has broken down. In practice there was almost no difference in the proportions of break-downs by number of relevant questionnaires returned and the predicted association was not significant. 'Difficult children' seemed to attract slightly more questionnaires and if this was taken into account the slight association between breakdown and number of questionnaires was further reduced. Composite variables carry their dangers of which we have tried to be aware.

23. This may seem strange in a study involving 596 children. In practice, however, place-ment choice was heavily influenced by age. Thus the effects of organisation had to be tested after allowing for this. It was sometimes apparent that one or two out of our seven authorities were pursuing distinct policies (e.g. over the use of residence orders). However, the numbers were too small and the degrees of freedom too many for this to be shown statistically.

24. For example, one South East Asian girl had a very unhappy placement with a West Indian family. She later had a far more successful one with a family closely matched with her own in terms of religion and ethnicity. The success of this latter placement seemed to have to do both with the degree of matching and also with factors in the second place-ment which would have made for success in placements involving white children and carers as well.

25. For example, the text may not make clear whether in carrying out an analysis we have combined categories. In such cases we quote the degrees of freedom. We do not generally quote degrees of freedom where, for example, we are cross-tabulating age and whether at home.

26. This is only partly a matter of technical statistics. It also requires a judgement of whether the sample we drew essentially 'represents' foster children in other situations. If it does not, inferences from our findings, however statistically significant, are hazardous.

Chapter Two

Movements and Destinations: An Overview

...my foster carers are the only family I had coz I haven't a family that cares about me...now I am alone...I was unhappy because I've moved around too much and every time I settled in somewhere I had to move again. So I didn't bother settling in anywhere coz I didn't know if they would move me again or not. But what I can say, it's one of them things that happen. I was happy in some ways. Don't worry about that. (Foster child who had left care)

The whole time of being fostered has made me be the person I am today. The carers brought me in as one of their own. We've grown that close over the years, it's like they are my real parents. (Foster child who had left care)

Introduction

Foster care can be variously experienced. For some it seems to offer a permanent home. For others it is a temporary and unstable resting place before entry into a sometimes uncertain world. Policy efforts to encourage adoption and special guardianship assume that the latter is too often the case. This chapter begins our examination of foster care for this sample, assessing the stability it offered and the degree to which it was an antechamber to a better supported future.

The chapter takes an overview of the sample as a whole. We look first at where the children were three years after our first contact with them. We then consider how stable their placements were and at how far, on the simplest criteria, the children could be said to have achieved some kind of permanent family home. Finally we look at the quality of their new placements and environments as judged by the children's social workers and their current or former foster carers.

As we will see these outcomes were strongly related to age.[1] Older children were not adopted: younger ones did not go into independent living. So we need to take account of age in explaining their current location and the degree of 'permanence' achieved.

Method and measures

The task of identifying the current location of the sample was onerous and time-consuming. We began with the local authority information systems. However, we checked these through the child's current or last social worker, team leaders, leaving care workers and teams, adoption and fostering sections, and current and previous foster carers. Our date for identifying the child's location was January 2001 and we asked for information as at that date.[2]

Where the children were

Table 2.1 gives the placement of the children three years after we first surveyed them. In looking at these figures it should be remembered that our sample consisted of those who were in foster care at a particular point in time. They represent this population, not the population of those entering foster care over a period. The latter would contain many more short-stay foster children, and, by a similar token, many more who returned home.

As can be seen just under four out of ten children in our sample were still in foster care. Six out of ten of these were still with their previous foster carer. The remainder of the sample were distributed between other outcomes in roughly similar proportions. Fifteen per cent were adopted (around a quarter of these by the original carer). One in six (17%) were with their birth families. A similar proportion (18%) were living independently. Small numbers were either in residential care (4%) or lost to the sample (7%). In most of the 'lost' cases this was because we could not trace where they were but some were withdrawn from the sample by the local authority. Two of these were known to have died.

The likelihood of a child achieving these placements obviously varied by age. The differences here were striking.

Adoption was reserved for young children. Three-quarters of those who were aged less than two when we first learnt of them were adopted. So too were four out of ten of those aged between two and four. By contrast this was

Table 2.1 The child's placement in January 2001

Placement	n	%	Average age (yrs) at sweep 1
With index foster carer*	144	24.2	9.93
With new foster carer	89	14.9	9.26
Adopted by index carer	21	3.5	3.45
Adopted by other	69	11.6	2.41
In residential care	23	3.9	11.38
With birth family	102	17.1	8.36
Independent living	107	18.0	16.13
Other	2	0.3	13.50
Lost track	29	4.9	11.76
No longer in sample	10	1.7	8.60
Total	596	100.0	9.72

*Index foster carer refers to the person who was fostering the child at the start of the study.

true of only one in nine of those aged between five and ten. Only one child over this age was adopted.

Long-stay foster care was largely used for the middle age group – those aged between 2 and 14 in 1997. For most of these children age had ruled out adoption and independent living was not an option. None of those aged under two at first encounter were now in foster care. By contrast foster care was being used for 35 per cent of those then aged between two and four, for 64 per cent of those between five and ten and for 61 per cent of those between 11 and 14. Only 12 per cent of those who were then over 15 were still living with someone who had been their foster carer. At this age the almost inevitable course of events seems to be that the child moves on from foster care.

Independent living was naturally reserved for older children. This was much the most likely outcome for those who were 15 or over when we first met them. Two-thirds of them were living on their own,[3] with a partner or with friends. By contrast only one in twenty of 11 to 14-year-olds (14 to 17-year-olds in 2001) were living independently in this way.

Box 2.1

The case studies suggested that adoption is really only seen as an option when a child is young. Where attempts at maintaining a family carry on beyond a certain point it ceases to be considered as a choice. This is so even in families where other children have been removed and adopted.

Karin's mother suffered chronically from schizophrenia and refused medication for herself and hospital treatment for Karin who needed it. Attempts at containing the situation collapsed when Karin's social worker saw Karin in her pram, waxen and to all appearances dead. Observation at a family centre showed that the mother did not interact with the baby at all. Karin had survived by being propped in a corner with a bottle and occasionally fed by her four-year-old brother. The social worker and concerned grandparents agreed that adoption was the only possibility. The mother did not contest the freeing order.

Angela's mother had learning difficulties. Her eldest daughter started to be looked after at a few months. Her son was removed at birth and subsequently adopted. Angela, however, was kept at home on the at-risk register for seven years. At the age of 12 she was abused by a lodger and went into the care system. There was no question then or subsequently that she might be adopted and she returned home at 17 at her mother's insistence.

The fourth major option – return to family – was almost equally used throughout the age range. Among those aged less than 14 around a fifth of the children were at home on follow-up. Among those aged 15 to 17 at first contact the proportion dropped to 9 per cent. At this age it was slightly more likely that the young person would remain with a foster carer.

Other options were rare and confined to the older age ranges. Residential care was used for those who were aged between 6 and 14 at sweep 1, accounting for 7 per cent of this age group. Prison, secure accommodation and death accounted between them for four young people.

Objective permanence and stability

The need for stability is a key theme of the literature on 'permanence' (Maluccio *et al.* 1986). Measures of turnover are key performance indicators in the government initiative *Quality Protects*. As noted in Chapter 1, we do not consider such 'objective permanence' the only criterion for counting a placement as permanent. Nevertheless it is arguably a necessary one.

An indication of the likely stability of these placements is provided by figures on the proportions of those who were in different kinds of placements at sweep 2 (1999) and still there at sweep 3 in 2001 (see Table 2.2).

Table 2.2 Location at sweep 3 by measures of stability

Placement	n	Breakdown (%)	Three or more moves (%)
With index foster carer	144	5	2
With new foster carer	89	53	36
Adopted by index carer	21	0	0
Adopted by other	69	9	25
In residential care	23	87	63
With birth family	102	40	28
Independent living	107	42	51
Lost track	29	26	52
Total	584*	30	28

*Two 'others' and ten 'lost to sample' cases are omitted. In five cases there is no information on whether the case broke down or not.

By far the most stable placement was adoption. Forty-eight children (89%) of those who were in adoptive placements in 1999 were still in them in 2001. Of those who were not, one was with the index foster carer, one in independent living and one with their birth family. Three had been lost to the sample and were, in all probability, still with their adoptive parents. In contrast to the above, only 61 per cent of those who had gone home (by 1999) were said to be with their families, and only just over half (54%) of those in their index foster placement were still there.

These results were similar to those we obtained using two different measures of 'stability'. One of these measures, 'breakdown', essentially measured whether any of our questionnaire returns said that a placement of any kind had broken down at any point between 1998 and 2001. The

Box 2.2

The case studies illustrated the widespread assumption that foster care was a care arrangement which did not last beyond 18.

Keith's foster carers were willing to keep him beyond his 18th birthday but wanted financial support to do this. Keith's social worker would only agree if the arrangement approximated to supported lodgings. Keith had to agree to do his own washing, cooking and so on. The foster carers said that as Keith had been used to treating their house as his home the proposed arrangement was unrealistic. Keith moved out to sleep on a friend's mother's sofa.

Lara came into the care system before the age of five because of a 'horrendous combination of neglect and sexual abuse'. According to the social worker there was a long history of such things in her extended family, a relative with a history of sexual abuse was found to be targeting her in foster care and her mother and her grandmother were conniving at it. She was now 16 years old and had been looked after continuously but had had 'five or six placements – two years is probably her limit'. She had no intention of returning home. Arrangements for her to enter the armed services had run into problems and the issue of her remaining with the foster carers was obliquely raised:

> She said 'I'd like to get a flat when I'm 18.' I said 'fine'. She said 'I will come back and visit you, you know.' I said 'I don't have a problem with that Lara. I'm doing my best for you, I can't do any more.' (Lara's foster carer)

And so with the issue of staying on effectively unexplored the 'natural assumption' of moving on was allowed to rest.

second, 'three moves', measured whether the child had had three or more moves in the period.[4] Both measures are influenced by the information available and in particular by whether we had a social worker's questionnaire.[5] For reasons given in Note 5 at the end of the chapter our figures underestimate the 'true' extent of movement and breakdown in the sample as a whole. We do not, however, think that this bias invalidates our comparisons between 'high and low movers'.

Despite these difficulties the measures do show large differences in stability between the different placement groups. Disruptions are comparatively high among those who are fostered but not in their index placement, those with their birth family and, particularly, among those now in residential care. A high level of movement is characteristic of those in independent living, those who have been lost to the sample, and those in residential care. Around a quarter of those who return home or are adopted by strangers have also had three or more placements.

Obviously the current location should not be seen as 'causing' a given level of instability. Rather those who have unstable careers tend to gravitate towards certain outcomes. Adoption and placement with index foster carer, almost by definition, show a high level of stability on both measures. Other placements attract more children with unstable careers. This is particularly so with residential care.

Differences between those with stable careers and others

Age was strongly associated with instability. Of those who were aged 16 or over and still with their index carer at sweep 2 just over one in four (27%) were still there two years later. Most (around 80%) of the remainder were in independent living.

Those aged between 10 and 14 at sweep 1 were less likely to leave the care system. Less than a quarter did so, almost always going to their families. The main reason for instability in this age group was disruption. Just under half (48% of them) were said by at least one of our sources to have had at least one placement which disrupted between 1998 and 2001.

We explored the relationship between age and permanence. Our definition of permanence took no account of whether the child 'felt permanent' – as we will see many of them did not – or of whether the placement was soon likely to end. Nevertheless it is a fair assumption that 'objective permanence' as defined above is related to other desirable characteristics such as 'subjective permanence' and future placement stability.

'Permanence' in this sense was most likely to be available in the younger age groups. It was achieved by:

- 82 per cent of those aged less than 2 years
- 70 per cent of those aged between 2 and 4 years
- 52 per cent of those aged between 5 and 10 years
- 24 per cent of those aged between 11 and 14 years.

As can be seen, and despite the crudity of our definition, the results demonstrate a clear trend. Very young children – those aged under two when first encountered – were most likely to achieve 'objective' permanence as we defined it. Eighty-two per cent of them did so. The proportions doing so drop steadily with age.[6] Less than half those aged 11 to 14 in 1998 achieved permanence in this sense.

Apart from age, a number of other factors had a significant but less marked impact on the chance of permanence:

- being with the same foster carer as at first contact
- being adopted
- having moved to a birth family by first follow-up, were still with their family two years later and were not said to have had a disruption over the three years.

Age is not the only variable related to permanence. It is, however, the most important one. Other variables only become relevant within particular age groups. Among those of school age in 1998 the variables which predicted movement and lack of stability were those which predicted breakdown in our first study – particularly rejection and lack of a child-oriented carer (see Sinclair and Wilson 2003; Sinclair, Wilson and Gibbs 2004).

Adequacy of current placement

We asked the social workers whether the child's current situation was 'satisfactory' and 'safe' and whether it offered enough money and material things. In reply to each question the social workers were asked to reply 'yes' (e.g. situation was safe), 'to some extent' or 'no'. Nine per cent of the children with birth families and 17 per cent of those in independent living were said to not have adequate material resources. Elsewhere in these questions the answer 'no' was almost never used.[7]

The proportions where the social workers qualified their answers did, however, vary dramatically by placement. As can be seen from Table 2.3, adoption, almost invariably, and fostering, in the great majority of cases, were rated as satisfactory in all respects. Residential care, birth families and independent living were seen as fully safe in less than half the cases. Material provision for those in independent living was particularly likely to be seen as less than fully satisfactory.

The contrasts were particularly marked if all three criteria were considered together. Eighty-six per cent or more of those adopted or in index foster placements were seen as well placed in all three respects. By contrast the same

---

Box 2.3

Frequency of moves raised the issue of broken attachments. Attachment issues were a *leitmotiv* of the case studies. They arose in reported conversations (e.g. in Lara's discussion of whether she should get a flat), in the behaviour of foster children (Keith, on learning that he could not stay with his foster carers, did major damage to their car and then stayed out all night drinking a bottle of vodka; Karin's brother, who was adopted with her, began stealing because he believed that his grandmother's failure to send him a present meant she did not love him any more), in jealousy, and in either 'compulsive self-reliance' (a determination to hide feelings, as found perhaps with Lara) or a propensity to follow the carer around. There were accounts of harrowing arrivals and departures (Karin's siblings had to be forced into the adopters' car when they came to take them away). Partings called back painful memories which the children might blank out or obsessively recall:

> I think they've shut him out of that part of their life, because they can remember, he was the younger child, and they can just remember bloody babies, and [the] ambulance, and police, and taking him out of the house. (Carer describing reaction of siblings to contact with adopted brother)

> What I can't really get out of my head is that a long time ago when me and Dannielle were [unclear] to King's Park, and we came back and we saw police cars outside... So I went down, and I called the policeman off my dad, because I didn't want him to go. So I was running after the police car, because I wanted to get my dad out. And then suddenly these police ladies took us to hospital, because I didn't want to go, so they pulled me along on my neck, to check. (Different child describing recurrent memory)

---

was true for less than two-thirds of those in subsequent foster placements and less than a third of those in residential care,[8] with birth families or in independent living.

These perceptions can be compared with those of the last foster carers of those who were no longer in foster care. Here we asked questions about the situation to which the young person moved immediately from the foster home (by contrast we asked social workers about the current situation or immediate past if they were unaware of this).

Table 2.3 Location by social worker's view of situation

Current placement	Adequacy of current situation				
	Materially adequate (%)	Safe (%)	Satisfactory (%)	All three (%)	n
With index foster carer	88.2	95.4	92.0	85.9	91
With new foster carer	82.4	86.8	71.2	62.7	52
Adopted by index carer	100.0	100.0	100.0	100.0	14
Adopted by other	97.8	97.9	97.9	93.3	48
In residential care	64.7	38.9	36.8	23.5	19
With birth family	46.3	49.1	56.1	31.5	57
Independent living	29.2	47.9	58.0	21.3	50
Total	71.6	76.2	75.4	61.4	335

Source: Social worker questionnaire 2001. Full totals vary (material adequacy 317, safe 329, satisfactory 335) and include 'other' and 'lost track'. Numerical row totals are for 'satisfactory'.

Adoption was again the placement which was seen most positively. We had replies on 44 children who left for adoption. Almost invariably they were seen as going where they would be loved, safe, get proper guidance and feel they belonged.

These replies contrasted sharply with the similar number of returns (n=45) for birth families. In two-thirds of these cases the carers felt the children would feel they belonged. However in less than half these cases were the carers sure the child would be loved. In less than a third were they sure the child would be safe. In a quarter they said he or she would not be. In less than a tenth did they feel sure he or she would get proper guidance.

The replies on the 27 going to independent living were also unenthusiastic – more so in relation to love where fewer than one in eight were thought likely to get it.

The small number of children going to residential care from foster care (n=13) were thought likely to get guidance, to be safe but also to be most unlikely to get love.

Although they referred to different periods of time these replies from the social workers and former foster carers were significantly correlated even if not very strongly so.[9] More important, it is apparent that both carers and social workers have strong reservations about the settings, other than adoption, to which a high proportion of foster children move.[10]

Box 2.4

All the adopted children in our case studies seemed to us to be in family situations where they were loved and supported by their carers. Things were much more varied where children returned home or lived independently. Those who have already featured in this chapter had difficulties to contend with.

- Angela returned to a home where her mother pressed her for reasons of her own to have a baby by her step-father. The household was extremely interested in sex and the interviewer had difficulty in directing the interview away from it.

- Keith was living without obvious security in a friend's mother's house.

- Lara was living with her foster carer. The assumption was that she would move out but she was not showing much sign of doing this successfully.

Conclusion

Only 40 per cent of those in foster care at sweep 1 were still there three years later. There seemed to be three main reasons for this apparent instability. First, there were assumptions that children who were very young should be adopted or returned home. This group were much more likely than others to achieve what we called 'objective permanence'. Second, there was, if not an assumption, at least a pervasive practice that older children moved on at 18 or before.

Third, the intermediate group – those aged between 4 and 14 when we first met them – were apparently seen as appropriate for foster care. They were, however, vulnerable to disruptions, particularly in their teenage years, and so they moved between placements, to residential care, and back to their homes. In these ways placement histories and placement stability were strongly related to age.

The effect of these movements could be, in theory, good or bad depending on the environments to which the children moved. Social workers and foster carers generally saw foster care and adoption as providing secure, safe placements. However less than a third of the placements with birth families were seen by social workers as being fully safe, materially adequate and satisfactory. Less than a quarter of those in residential care or in independent living met the same criteria. The views of foster carers about these placements were, if anything, even more negative.

Viewed over three years foster care therefore offers less permanence than might be hoped. Objective permanence is rarely on offer. Children under the age of ten had some prospect of stability in the immediate future. This might not, however, last in their teenage years. If it did, it still seemed to be customary that they moved out of their foster carer's home at the age of 18. And when they moved on the quality of the environment offered seemed to leave much to be desired.

The extent of movement between placements raises in an acute form the issues of attachment of children to different families, the disturbed attachment patterns to which their histories give rise, and the relationship between families involved in sequential placements. It also raises the question of how far the emotional capital accumulated through the relationships between foster carers and children may be squandered by the operation of the system. These are issues which we return to, particularly in our concluding chapter.

Summary of Chapters 1 and 2

1. Foster care generally offers only a limited form of permanence and that only to children between the ages of 4 and 14.

2. After foster care, adoption is the only placement option seen by social workers and carers as offering a fully satisfactory environment: birth families, residential care and independent living are not generally seen as providing this.

3.   Contributions to resolving these problems could involve increasing the degree of permanence offered by foster care, increasing the proportion adopted, and improving support after foster care – particularly to those returning home or going into independent living.

4.   The remainder of the book is relevant to the feasibility and implications of these different 'solutions'. In this way it builds on a design which allows the outcomes of different kinds of placements to be compared, the reasons for making these placements to be explored and practice within placements to be assessed.

Notes

1.   Unless otherwise specified age in this book refers to age at sweep 1 (1998) when we first contacted the child. In general the children will be three years older at sweep 3.

2.   We did not complete our tracing until September 2001. Respondents may have answered questions on the basis of later information. Comparison of responses against date of receiving questionnaire does not suggest that this produced serious bias.

3.   This includes those living in hostels and lodgings. For more detailed information see Chapters 9 to 13 which cover various aspects of independent living.

4.   A child was counted as having moved three or more times if: the social worker at second follow-up said that they had had three or more placements; or a young person in independent living said that they had had two or more moves since leaving foster care; or it was possible to deduce that the young person had had three or more moves from knowledge of their location at the first and second follow-ups.

5.   Where there was a social worker questionnaire 32 per cent of the sample appeared to have moved three or more times and 35 per cent to have had a placement breakdown. The comparable proportions in the rest of the sample were 20 per cent and 22 per cent. The social worker figure may still underestimate moves since social worker questionnaires were rather less likely to be returned in two 'high moving' groups – independent living and 'location not known'. Allowing for this a more likely estimate of proportion moving three or more times would be around 40 per cent. This assumes that all those 'lost to sample', and at least 70 per cent of those in independent living, moved three times (a conservative estimate from questionnaires returned).

6.   These findings hold good irrespective of sex.

7.   The overall proportions were 4 per cent (not materially adequate), 3 per cent (not satisfactory), 2 per cent (not safe).

8.   The main comparison between foster care and residential care remains Colton's study (1988). He found the environment in residential care less satisfactory on a number of counts but was not able to show differences in outcome. Sinclair and Gibbs (1998) found

very high levels of misery, bullying, running away and re-offending among residents of children's homes (nearly four out of ten had considered killing themselves in the previous month and 40 per cent of those entering the homes without a previous conviction or caution acquired one if they stayed six months). This research raised the question of why such an expensive provision had such apparently poor outcomes. The rather gloomy ratings given to the quality of residential care in this study reinforce this question and the related one of whether the level of residential care can be reduced.

9. The correlations between the social worker adequacy ratings and the carers' replies on love, belonging, safety and guidance were significant with two exceptions ('safe' with 'satisfactory' (sw) and 'guidance' with 'material adequacy'.) Other correlations varied from 0.51 ($p<0.001$) to 0.22 ($p=0.026$).

10. The strong association between current setting and age meant that the latter was the major predictor of a placement that was inadequate on the criteria listed above. Adoptive placements take young children and are satisfactory on all criteria, whereas independent living (commonly seen as 'inadequate') is restricted to older young people.

Chapter Three

Outcomes and Going Home

A: I asked [the first social worker] when, I were only young... I must have been about four/five. I said, 'Can I have some tablets to make me a good girl?' and she just laughed at me, she literally laughed in my face...and then I started crying...
Q: So that early on really you knew that things weren't right sort of stuff?
A: I knew it weren't but nobody else did. (Foster child)

I don't think [my sister] ever has been really happy, really. She's just... I think that some children just want to be alone, like, with their mum and dad – their own mums and dads, and you could tell she wanted to live with my mum from an early age, but my mum just abused her, really. But she still went back for more. (Foster child)

I love my mum to bits, but no. I didn't want to be at home. Not because I don't like my mum, it's because of how...she's special needs, and I just don't live that lifestyle any more. I think I probably would have wanted to go back to my mum when I was younger, but not now, because of the way she lives. (Foster child)

Introduction

In our last chapter we looked at a simple measure of the quality of the children's and young people's environment at follow-up. In this chapter we examine a number of other measures of outcome. In each case we describe how the outcome varied between different destinations and try to explain differences in it.

As will be seen a key factor in this explanation is commonly whether or not the child went home. Over the three years 162 children (27% of the sample) were known to have returned home at some stage. For ease of identification we describe this group as 'tried at home'. Just under two-thirds of them (n=102) were believed to be still there. The chapter explores how the 162 children did. It also compares them with other children who did not return home.

As we saw in the introduction, the literature on return home speaks with a divided voice. In both the USA and the UK most studies in this area have treated return home and remaining there as virtually the only outcomes of value.[1] By contrast there is evidence that care plans which are based on a return home are more liable to change than others (Harwin *et al.* 2001). Moreover some studies have suggested that return home is associated with outcomes which are on a number of criteria 'worse'.

Two particular concerns are: the extent of re-abuse among those who return which seems higher than those expected among children who remain in foster care (Barth and Berry 1994; Ellaway *et al.* 2004; Farmer and Parker 1991; Runyan and Gould 1985; Terling 1999); and the apparently 'worse' social and behavioural outcomes of those who return or spend less time in foster care (Minty 1987; Taussig, Clyman and Landsverk 2001; Zimmerman 1982). For example, a recent American study (Taussig *et al.* 2001) followed a group of 6 to 12-year-old foster children for six years. Children who had returned home had higher arrest rates and worse school grades. The authors concluded: 'Reunification status was a significant predictor of negative outcomes in 8 out of 9 regression equations after controlling for time 1 behaviour problems, age and gender.'[2]

The last chapter reinforced these concerns. Both foster carers and social workers clearly saw the home environment as on average 'worse' on the criteria used than those found in foster care and adoption. This chapter takes up the story by exploring the apparent consequences of trial at home – whether or not this led to remaining there – for the children's behaviour and development. At this stage in the book the prognosis must be pessimistic. Not only have we found the new environments to be discouraging, there is also some evidence that children who have spent longer in the care system and who have had (like many of our sample) previous returns do worse on return than others (Farmer and Parker 1991).

Method

In general our analysis relates outcomes to information on the children when we first had information on them in 1998 (sweep 1). We test routinely whether our outcomes were related to our 1998 information on:

- child's age, sex
- Goodman score – a measure of disturbance (see Goodman 1994)
- foster carer's 'parenting score' and 'child orientation score'
- rejection score (how child and carer were getting on)
- school experience (whether happy there, involvement of educational psychologist)
- contact with birth family and whether anyone prohibited from contact.

As described in Chapter 1 these analyses were based on the findings of our first study.[3] The variables selected were those which our previous work suggested had robust relationships with outcomes. Appendix 2 gives details on how we defined and measured them.

The outcomes with which we were concerned were:

- re-abuse
- changes in Goodman score
- school adjustment
- problems in social behaviour
- overall ratings.

We describe these outcomes and then try to explain them.

Re-abuse

We asked the social workers whether the child had been abused since they first entered the sample in 1998. We also asked them to state the kinds of abuse involved (emotional, physical, sexual and through neglect) and to grade the strength of the evidence for it.[4]

According to the social workers, flagrant instances of re-abuse were rare. In only 1 per cent of cases did they note strong evidence for sexual re-abuse. The figure was slightly higher (2%) for physical abuse and higher still for neglect (4%) and emotional abuse (5%). Overall there was strong evidence for

---

Box 3.1

Only one child out of the case studies (Lorna) was said definitely to have been abused since 1998. Clearly she had a difficult time both in the care system and on return home. According to Lorna:

> ...there were one time when I were a right...bitch, sorry, I'm swearing, but I were a right bitch with her and she [foster carer] grabbed hold of me and lifted my face up like that and pulled my hair, pulled my hair back, I used to have long hair, pulled my hair back so I couldn't like look away or owt and she spoke to me, she had a right go at me and then when she'd finished she let go and pushed me, so. That's what she were like.

There followed a period in residential care when Lorna was according to her own account away more than she was present and according to the social worker did this with her mother's connivance and with individuals of unsavoury reputations. She returned home to her mother whose earlier ways of controlling her including cutting her wrists in front of her and demanding the police took her away. Her mother confirmed that the rows continued:

> I've said she's got to go, I've told her to pack her bags and get out, I don't know, duck, what will happen, I don't honestly know. No.

---

some form of re-abuse in 8 per cent of the cases for which we had a social worker questionnaire.

Suspicion of abuse was much more common. There was said to be 'some evidence' of sexual re-abuse in 4 per cent of cases, of neglect in 6 per cent, of physical re-abuse in 8 per cent and of emotional abuse in 13 per cent. Overall there was 'some evidence' of at least one kind of abuse in 16 per cent of cases. Thus in a nearly a third of the cases there was at least a suspicion that the child had been re-abused.

Location and source of abuse

Children were most likely to be seen as re-abused if they were in residential care, with their birth families or with new foster families (see Table 3.1). It does not, of course, follow that the abuse took place in these locations. The young person may have moved to a new location because of prior maltreatment. As we shall see, however, there is evidence that much of the abuse did have to do with the children's families.

Table 3.1 Placement by evidence of re-abuse since 1998

Placement at Jan 2001	Evidence of re-abuse			
	None (%)	Some (%)	Strong (%)	n
With index foster carer	87.9	7.7	4.4	91
With new foster carer	65.4	23.1	11.5	52
Adopted by index carer	85.7	7.1	7.1	14
Adopted by other	88.9	2.2	8.9	45
In residential care	52.6	36.8	10.5	19
With birth family	60.7	31.1	8.2	61
Independent living	78.8	13.5	7.7	52
Other	100.0	–	–	1
Lost track	33.3	33.3	33.3	3
Total	75.7	16.3	8.0	338

We asked the social workers to comment on the abuse. According to them a minority of incidents were either such as might have occurred to any child (e.g. abuse at school or by a stranger in the street) or reflected the children or young people's way of life and the friends and partners to whom they looked for support:

> Physically and sexually. [Mixing with] homeless people he became involved in lifestyle. Neglected as he was living on the streets – emotionally as his family did not want anything to do with him.

> Young person abused within relationships with boyfriends.

In general, however, re-abuse could be divided between incidents that had to do with the care system and others that had to do with the child's birth family.

Occasionally the 'abuse' seemed essentially related to the 'care experience' rather than to specific foster carers:

> In previous residential placement Cathy was bullied and physically abused by another older resident.

> The search for child's 1) adopters, 2) long term carers, 3) short term carers (10 placements July–November 1998) was so unsuccessful (social worker

involved was extremely diligent) that emotional damage and neglect cannot be ruled out.

Just under 20 per cent of the comments referred to abuse by foster carers or (in one case only) adopters. A small number of these seemed to be clear-cut cases of abuse:

> Sexual abuse at index placement. Emotional abuse and neglect with mother.

> Foster parent hit Damian and neglected him emotionally.

More common were comments which suggested poor practice (particularly excessive discipline or rejection) which might not have been seen as abusive if it had occurred within the context of the child's own family:

> Previous foster carers rejected the child – unable to cope with what was primarily adolescent behaviour. Boundaries were set so tight it was inevitable that the child would 'push' these. Foster carers not prepared to negotiate or discuss any compromise – insisted the child was moved with one month's notice.

> The child's birth mother has been inconsistent in maintaining contact which has had a very confusing and detrimental effect. Rejection by long term carers who led him to believe they wished to adopt him.

Other comments concerned allegations which were investigated without conclusion. The result was no further action, although the child was sometimes moved and the carers sometimes resigned later:

> Child made allegation against a former foster carer – investigated but no further action.

> Child had an injury to the side of his face. Unable to substantiate whether injury caused by carers or other. However child was moved to new foster placement where he lived until placed with his prospective adopters.

The majority of comments, around six out of ten, referred to re-abuse connected with the child's birth family. Sometimes the abuse was directly associated with contact either because contact gave the opportunity for abuse or because the unreliability of the contact was itself seen as abusive:

> Friend of mother during contact at home.

> Emotionally abused by birth father's partner – blatantly saying she does not want her to visit and making life very difficult. Contact now ceased.

Much more commonly the abuse was seen as occurring on return home:

> Witness to father abusing a friend of his sister – also severely neglected.

> Returned to birth home on placement with parents regs. Seven children. Somewhat chaotic conditions. May witness adult drunkenness/verbal aggression. Occasionally may be left to fend for himself.

The effect of such events and circumstances could be compounded by the need to remove the child:

> Following return home mother failed to meet basic needs and exposed him to risks of neglect and possible harm from partner. The failure of rehabilitation caused extreme distress to child.

In these cases birth families were seen by social workers as having a direct and obvious association with re-abuse.

Explaining re-abuse: contact with birth family and return home

In terms of our standard set of variables and analysis the only variable that predicts re-abuse is weekly contact with a relative. Reported re-abuse is more likely where this occurs. A possible explanation is that contact both exposes the child to the risk of re-abuse and is associated with return home. The latter in turn increases the risk of re-abuse.

This finding would be in keeping with our previous work (Sinclair, Wilson and Gibbs 2004). This showed that in certain cases placement breakdown was more common where at least one member of the family was, according to the foster carers, forbidden contact. This effect was limited to cases where, according to the social worker, there was strong evidence of prior abuse. In such cases placement breakdown was three times more likely where access was unrestricted for all family members than in cases where there was a restriction. Other studies (particularly Farmer *et al.* 2004 and, to a lesser extent, Cleaver 2000) have also emphasised the degree to which contact with particular family members may be detrimental as well as beneficial to children.

We examined whether similar relationships held when the outcomes of interest were re-abuse. The results were similar. *Where there was strong evidence of prior abuse:*

- re-abuse was significantly more likely if no one was forbidden contact (some evidence 20% v. 11% and strong evidence 14% v. 0%, chi square=10.41, df=2, $p<0.001$)

- breakdown over three years was significantly more likely (25% v. 40%, chi square=4.95, $p=0.026$)

'Trial at home' was similarly associated with re-abuse. There was said to be strong evidence of abuse in 11 per cent of the cases where we knew that the child went home at some stage. There was some evidence in a further 31 per cent of cases. The comparable figures for those who at no stage went home were 7 per cent and 10 per cent.[5] Statistically the difference between the two groups is very highly significant (chi square=25.69, df=2, $p<0.001$).

In summary, trial at home, frequent contact with family, and uncontrolled access in cases where there was strong evidence of prior abuse were all associated with re-abuse. Other variables – for example, our measures of the quality of the foster home – were not associated with re-abuse.

Changes in the Goodman score

Our main measure of mental health was the Goodman score which foster carers had completed at sweep 1 (see Table 3.2). Adoptive parents or, if the child had not been adopted, the current or most recent foster carers were asked to complete the Goodman questionnaire covering the period 'over the last six months' or 'when he or she was last with you'. We explored whether the children changed on this score. We subtracted this score from that at sweep 1. Given their sources the scores cannot reflect the impact of settings other than adoption or fostering. On average the mental health of the sample improved on this measure (t=3.38, $p<0.001$ on a paired t test). This finding is encouraging. Can we say which children were most likely to change?

Explaining changes in the Goodman score

The best combination of predictors of positive change from our usual list of variables comprised: the Goodman score at sweep 1 ($p<0.001$) (the higher the score, i.e. the more perceived difficulties, the greater the positive change), having a lone carer ($p=0.052$), low evidence of abuse prior to placement ($p=0.016$), low rejection by carers score ($p=0.013$) – see Table 3.2.

The 'good effect' of having a high initial difficulties score is best seen as a 'statistical artifact'. Those with high scores have more scope for improvement and are more likely to have been measured initially when going through a temporary bad patch. There is no obvious explanation for the apparently good impact of having lone carers. This should probably be regarded as a chance finding unless it is repeated in subsequent research. The important associations are with rejection at sweep 1 by foster carers and prior abuse.

Table 3.2 Current placement by Goodman score at sweep 1

Current placement	Mean	n	Standard deviation
With index foster carer	16.32	109	7.40
With new foster carer	19.82	61	6.94
Adopted by index carer	9.25	8	5.67
Adopted by other	15.06	18	7.62
In residential care	18.50	14	5.49
With birth family	15.60	55	6.60
Independent living	14.51	66	8.05
Other	21.50	2	16.26
Lost track	15.31	13	6.28
No longer in sample	20.00	2	4.24
Total	16.35	348	7.46

Anova $F=3.347$; $df=9$; $p<0.001$

In practice the strong associations with changes in our mental health score have to do with experience after the first survey. Rejection at sweep 1 and prior abuse seem to have their impact on changing mental health *through re-abuse*, rather than directly.[6] The major predictor of deteriorating mental health was our measure of rejection at sweep 3. This rejection may reflect increasing Goodman score or produce it. Either way it is strongly associated with it.[7]

A possible explanation for these findings is that worsening mental health commonly reflects emotional abuse in the form of rejection. Prior abuse may be associated with rejection by abusive relatives (e.g. on contact visits) or make a child more sensitive to any rejection that exists in the foster home. Subsequent re-abuse is also experienced as rejection and associated with worsening mental health. There may also be 'vicious circles' as worsening mental health makes a child more difficult and more likely to be rejected.

Box 3.2

The most marked improvement on the Goodman score among the case study children who went home was Kelvin's. Brought up in a chaotic home he started to be looked after at the age of nine when his anger against a new step-parent proved unmanageable. He then spent four years with firm, kindly, strongly Christian foster carers with the plan that he return to his own father eventually. The father supported the placement and Kelvin eventually returned to him when the foster carers moved and a trial with his own mother broke down.

The greatest deterioration on this score was Lorna's. Her early troubles included her mother's breakdowns, the departure of her father to a new girlfriend, the long-standing bitterness between her mother and father, her father's alleged preference for her sister and (possibly) sexual abuse. Despite this and a traumatic removal to foster care Lorna's Goodman score at sweep 1 was moderate. Its increase accompanied deterioration in relationships in the placement.

The Goodman scores and our measures of relationship

We carried out a very similar analysis on our two measures of 'stoicism' and 'childlike attachment'.[8] The results for both were similar.

- The children who became less stoical were young and more stoical to start with. At sweep 3 their carers were less rejecting and more child-oriented.[9]

- Children whose childlike attachment reduced were more attached in this way at sweep 1 and less likely to have been 're-abused' or rejected by their carers at sweep 3.[10]

These two 'attachment' variables have a strong and potentially important relationship with the Goodman score. Taken together they account for 52 per cent of the variation in it.[11]

Change in the Goodman score also correlates 0.42 ($p<0.001$) with change in the childlike attachment score and 0.32 ($p<0.001$) with change in the stoicism score.[12] The key question is whether these correlations represent cause and effect. In other words does the resolution or exacerbation of problems in attachment drive changes in the mental health score? Over the course of the research we came to believe that the answer to this question was probably 'yes'.

One prediction that we made was that unusually high 'disturbed attachment scores' should lead to a deterioration in mental health on follow-up. By 'unusually high' we meant higher than their mental health scores implied. Conversely those with 'unusually low' disturbed attachment scores should improve on their mental health scores. In other words a good or poor attachment score should, as it were, drag the Goodman score in its direction. This prediction was strongly supported in the case of childlike attachment.[13] It was not supported at all for stoicism.[14]

This finding played only a minor part in our growing conviction of the key importance of attachment in explaining outcomes.[15] More important in this respect were the qualitative material and the pattern of statistical findings throughout the study. These suggested to us that there was a chain of reactions. Children who displayed a high degree of anxious attachment were difficult for carers. These carers might then react by trying to keep their emotional distance from the child. The children themselves could experience this as rejection. This experience could lead to a general worsening in the child's mental health and hence further difficulties.

Box 3.3

Most of the examples of attachment we will give come from case studies where there were often complicated, ambivalent relationships. However, many of the issues surfaced in perhaps the most straightforward case where two young children were placed because of their mother's sudden severe illness. The foster carer described their arrival:

> They were very clingy, to each other, you know, wouldn't go anywhere without each other, and I just, I think, they were very tired, and very bewildered children, and didn't know what was going on, really... And I think when they came to me, they actually they seriously thought their mum would die...they did take a little bit of settling down at bedtimes... Sometimes I would wake up in the middle of the night and find [the girl] sat on the end of my bed! [laughs] Like a little stray.

Visits to hospital were not entirely reassuring, as the boy discussed with the interviewer:

Q: And what was that like, going to see her in hospital?

A: I was very happy.

Q: So it was good to see her, and know she was there?

A: Yeah.

Q: Yes. Was it scary as well?

A: Yeah.

Q: Did she have a lot of tubes going into her, and that kind of thing?

A: Yeah. I don't like the butterfly clip that they put on her hand – it scares me.

The mother was discharged after six weeks but in a wheelchair and needing a great deal of care. As a result return home took much longer than had been expected. Over this time the boy became attached to the foster carer and cried when he left. Subsequently the carer had to go and collect him one night as he would not settle without seeing her. The situation was resolved by continuing contact and occasional holidays with the carer which his mother thought appropriate.

Box 3.4

As noted earlier the most marked deterioration in the Goodman score was Lorna's. Her carer described classic symptoms of childlike attachment which began soon after arrival:

> ...but everywhere I went, if my husband was in there and I went in there to have a private word she would follow me. If I went out with the dog, sometimes I'd want to go out to get away...she was quite suffocating basically and one had no privacy, you know. I'd go out with the dog and I'd turn round and she'd be there with me.

The foster carer reacted by creating space for herself – marking out time when Lorna was not allowed to be with her and making her bedroom out of bounds. Lorna experienced this as rejection:

A: They treated me all right to begin with but then when I started to get on with 'em and stuff they just threw me away, if you know what I mean.

Q: That's what it felt like?

A: Mm, they just pushed me away totally. So they were like... I couldn't speak to 'em or anything.

Lorna could not comfortably return to her mother who had previously rejected her and was to do so again. Nor could she get her attachment needs assuaged by the foster carers. In this she contrasted with Kelvin who was both accepted by his foster carers and encouraged in his relationship with his father to whom he wished to return.

School adjustment

Children who return home are likely to face educational problems. They may need to change schools, something which is likely to give them academic problems and mean they have to find new friends. They may also come from deprived neighbourhoods. In such cases their new schools may face greater difficulties than old ones. Finally, their parents are likely to have a number of problems on their mind. They may have less time to spend encouraging school attendance and helping with school work than adoptive parents or foster carers. For all these reasons foster children returning home might be expected to do rather worse at school than those who remain in foster care.

In testing these hypotheses we would ideally have liked to collect data from the schools and to include national examination tests and results. In practice we did not have the resources for this. We were therefore dependent on various ratings.

Our two main ratings were concerned with:

- educational performance: rated from 1 (well below average for ability) to 4 (well above average for ability)
- participation in school: rated from 1 (rarely attends or takes part) to 4 (takes part in a wide range of activities).

We had ratings for present and earlier educational performance.[16] We also calculated a change rating – a measure of the degree to which the child's school adjustment had improved relative to our measures of prior adjustment (see Table 3.3).

Table 3.3 Prior and current school adjustment by placement

Placement	Prior school adjustment (mean)	School adjustment now (mean)	Change (mean)	n
With index foster carer	2.38	2.98	0.61	84
With new foster carer	2.24	2.74	0.51	54
Adopted by index carer	3.05	3.07	0.02	15
Adopted by other	2.69	3.20	0.51	30
In residential care	2.31	2.42	0.12	13
With birth family	2.55	2.59	0.04	27
Total	2.45	2.88	0.43	223

Note: Table is restricted to those who are of school age, less than 16 and have ratings at both points in time.

Our ratings suggest that educational adjustment had improved. The difference between prior and current adjustment was very highly significant ($t=7.31$; $df=222$; $p<0.001$, paired t test).

Despite this general improvement the change seemed to be greater in some placements than others.

- Prior educational adjustment was lowest for residential care and those moving to a new placement and highest for those who were subsequently adopted by their own carers ($F=2.82$; $df=5, 217$; $p=0.015$).
- Current adjustment was highest among those adopted by others or by index carers ($F=4.19$; $df=5, 217$; $p<0.001$).

- All those with foster carers or adopters made sizeable improvements except for those adopted by their own carers who started from a high base.

- By contrast there was no improvement for those who went to birth families or into residential care (F=2.93; df=5, 217; $p=0.014$).

Explaining school adjustment

Educational adjustment at sweeps 1 and 2[17] along with age accounted for 45 per cent of the improvement at school. (The higher the initial score the less the improvement. The reasons for this 'regression to the mean' must by now be familiar.) Unsurprisingly older children were less likely to show marked positive change. The other variables in our model were not associated with this outcome.

We did, however, find that changes in adjustment were negatively associated with going home ($p<0.01$).[18] A variety of analyses[19] failed to shake the overall conclusion. The school adjustment of children who are tried at home improves less – in fact it does not improve on average at all.

This evidence suggested that the home environment of our sample could affect their school adjustment. We further tested this hypothesis by looking at two measures of home quality: child orientation (a score based on questions answered by foster carers and adopters), and carer quality (based on ratings by social workers and available for foster carers, adoptive parents and birth parents). Social worker ratings of carer quality were on average far lower for those at home than for those in other settings. In addition the analyses showed the following:

- Child orientation at sweep 1 was after allowing for age significantly associated with prior school adjustment ($p=0.006$). It was almost significantly associated with current adjustment ($p=0.06$) but this association only held if the child remained in the same environment (i.e was fostered or adopted by the index carer).

- Carer quality at sweep 1 was not significantly associated with either measure.

- Measures of both variables at sweep 3 were, after allowing for age, significantly associated with current school adjustment (carer quality $p=0.003$ and child orientation $p=0.016$).

- Both sweep 3 measures were significantly associated with change in education adjustment after allowing for age, prior school adjustment and whether tried at home ($p<0.01$ in both cases).

These findings suggest that home environment (carer quality and child orientation) does indeed affect school adjustment in this sample. Carer quality is lower for children at home. Understandably they do less well at school.

Box 3.5

School appeared in the case studies variously: as a source of practical difficulty, a place were children where bullied or, as the carer saw it, got in with the wrong crowd, a source of pride and achievement, and a source of counselling and support. Some children's school performance seemed to improve when in foster care and deteriorated thereafter.

Social behaviour

We asked the social workers a variety of questions about the children's social behaviour over the past three years. We asked similar questions of the current or last foster carer, adoptive parents and birth families. Four questions to the young people in independent living (about drugs, alcohol, trouble with police and unplanned pregnancy of self or partner) covered some similar ground.

We used these data to create 'composite variables'. A child was for example said to have difficulty with drugs if there was evidence from any sweep 3 source that this had been the case over the past three years.[20]

Table 3.4 describes the frequency of these problems by location. It is restricted to those who were aged at least eight when they first entered the sample and were therefore at least 11 by 2001.

A striking feature of Table 3.4 lies in the high percentage of difficulties displayed by those who went home. This finding could have various explanations.[21] Whatever the reason, those who return to their homes seem to be at least as difficult as those who are in residential care.

Explaining difficulties in social behaviour

We tried to predict difficulties in social behaviour among those who were aged eight or over when we first met them. The best combinations of predictors varied with the variable being considered. Four of the outcome variables

Table 3.4 Difficult social behaviour by placement

	Truant (%)	Running away (%)	Self-harm (%)	Police problems (%)	Drink/ drugs (%)	Aggression (%)	Sex problems (%)	Involuntary pregnancy (%)	Mean	n
With index foster carer	35	23	23	23	15	55	25	8	1.88	89
With new foster carer	47	32	9	21	15	57	25	2	1.85	53
In residential care	68	58	32	79	47	84	63	0	3.68	19
With birth family	80	56	40	56	56	71	49	36	4.28	45
Independent living	35	27	27	33	48	45	33	31	2.44	84
Total	46	33	25	34	34	57	34	18	2.4	30

Note: Table based on those aged 11 or over in 2001. The total includes children adopted by index carer (2) or by other (3), other (1) and whereabouts unknown (7).

were strongly related to two variables from sweep 1 – whether the child was, according to the foster carer, unhappy at school, and whether he or she had seen an educational psychologist. These four were:

- truant – predicted by a combination of unhappy at school (p=0.01) and seen educational psychologist (p=0.02)

- running away – predicted by a combination of unhappy at school (p=0.03) and seen educational psychologist (p=0.03)

- trouble with police – predicted by a combination of unhappy at school (p<0.001) and seen educational psychologist (p=0.02)

- trouble with drink or drugs – predicted by age (p=0.004), and unhappy at school (p=0.002).

Three variables were predicted by a combination of variables variously relating to school, foster carer, and contact with home, all as measured at sweep 1:

- violence or aggression – predicted by a combination of age (p=0.024), Goodman score (p<0.001), carer low on child orientation (p=0.053)

- problems related to sexuality – predicted by a combination of being female (p=0.024), high disturbed score (p=0.01), carer low on child orientation (p=0.018), unhappy at school (p=0.021), no family member forbidden contact (p=0.042)

- self-harm – predicted by a combination of unhappy at school (p=0.02) seen educational psychologist (p=0.001), weekly visits from relatives (p=0.01).

One variable – unplanned pregnancy of self or partner – was only related to age.

In order to simplify our analysis we added the variables listed above to create a 'problem behaviour score'. We then tried to predict this score using variables which were significant predictors of one or more of its component variables. The most efficient predictor from our 'standard set' turned out to involve a combination of two variables – Goodman score and unhappiness at school.

We added 'tried at home' to this combination of variables. In this model return home was a much stronger predictor than either of the others (t=4.81; p<0.001).[22] We then added 'current school adjustment'. It proved a very strong predictor. If we took this into account only school adjustment and trial at home had significant associations with problem behaviour.[23]

The most efficient predictor that we found consisted of four variables – current school adjustment ($p<0.001$), return home ($p<0.001$), child's stoicism measure in 1998 ($p<0.001$) and child's childlike attachment measure in 1998 ($p=0.016$). To put things in more familiar language, children did 'worse' in terms of social behaviour, if they had difficulties in relating to others, were not getting on well at school and had had at least some time at home since the first survey.

These findings suggest that trial at home does tend to produce difficult social behaviour. Its influence, however, is probably modified by the child's school. The latter may have a significant impact on its own account. Conceivably school acts as a kind of machine which, depending on how it is set, may turn disturbed attachments into difficult social behaviour or modify their effects.

Box 3.6

The case studies suggested that the chains of cause and effect between school and home are indeed complicated. Lorna described her situation at school as follows:

Q: What about school and stuff, could you talk to anybody at school?

A: No, I used to be picked on all the time at school.

Q: You weren't happy there?

A: All the time but then…I thought, well stuff this, I'm not letting them stand here and hit me and all that so I beat one of the ringleaders, cos there were two, there were this Peter Bond and Jenny Hicks, well I beat that Jenny Hicks up and then they were still picking on me but they like beat it down a bit…and then…I beat her up again, I had a fight with her again and I beat her up.

A fairly dire threat to Peter Bond seems to have completed this act of deterrence and she was left alone. So Lorna's troubles at home may have made her vulnerable at school. Her mother's preoccupations may have made it difficult to pick these difficulties up. The lesson she learnt was that you had to stick up for yourself and violence pays.

Overall rating

We asked the foster carers and the social workers to make an overall rating of how the child was currently doing. We gave them three options – 'very well', 'as well as could be expected' and 'not very well'. As can be seen from Table 3.5 their views varied quite sharply depending on the placement. In general both sets of workers felt that foster care and adoption placements were going well and were pessimistic about the other ones. This contrast between foster care and placements other than adoption was particularly marked when the ratings were made by foster carers.

Despite these differences in perception there were highly significant correlations between the ratings made by foster carers and those made by social workers.[24]

Table 3.5 Success ratings by differences in placement

Current placement	Social worker (% full success)	Current carer (% full success)	Previous carer (% full success)	Most pessimistic (% full success)
Index carer	75% (88)	77% (115)	n/a	66% (136)
New foster carer	47% (53)	72% (71)	n/a	52% (77)
Adopt by carer	93% (14)	95% (19)	n/a	90% (20)
New adopter	92% (48)	91% (53)	78% (46)	75% (69)
Residential care	28% (18)	n/a	36% (11)	33% (21)
Family	46% (55)	n/a	19% (47)	25% (71)
Independent	38% (58)	n/a	20% (69)	22% (91)
Total	59% (339)*	77% (258)*	36% (178)*	50% (491)*

*Includes 'lost track' and 'other'

Explaining differences in overall ratings

We created a composite score for the overall ratings. The case was said to be a 'success' if neither social worker nor foster carer said that it had gone less than very well. Those who did 'best' on this score were younger ($p=0.002$), female ($p=0.046$) and less disturbed children ($p=0.002$) whose foster carers were child-oriented at sweep 1 ($p=0.017$).[25]

In keeping with the results discussed earlier, trial at home was negatively associated with outcome (composite score) after allowing for our predictor variables ($p<0.001$).

Thus children do 'better' in terms of this outcome if they are younger, easier, and, perhaps, girls and if they have child-oriented carers. Irrespective of whether they have these advantages they do 'worse' if they go home.

Box 3.7

In three of the six case studies where children returned home they did so to situations that were marginally, if at all, different from those they had left. Their homes were variously obsessed by sex, or managed by a person whose frail mental health made it very difficult for them to cope with the child's needs. All the mothers involved seemed, to a greater or lesser extent, to see their children through the prism of their own urgent needs.

In three others there had been sharp changes. In one a violent man had moved out. In another the mother had partially recovered from a very severe physical illness. In the third the child moved to his father rather than his mother and step-father with whom he did not get on.

In the last three cases it was fair to say that some of the underlying problems had been removed (albeit probably not through the intervention of social services). In the first three cases the most that could be said was that the children wanted to be at home and were older and presumably better able to look after themselves.

Conclusion

A broad generalisation from this chapter is that what matters is not the environment in which children were at sweep 1 but rather where they were at sweep 3. There were consistent associations between outcomes and our measures of parenting at sweep 3. We found very few between outcomes and our measures of parenting at sweep 1. Where we did find them, they were often explained by the fact that the child was still in the same environment.

There were, of course, exceptions to this rule of the primacy of the current environment. Children did seem to carry with them their difficulties in relating to others. Moreover those who were happy at school at sweep 1 were doing better in a variety of ways at sweep 3 (in part, perhaps, because they were still at the same school). These findings have implications for 'rational targets' for intervention. The good that kindly foster carers can achieve may often be limited to the time the child spends in placement. Anything that can be done to enhance the child's adjustment at school or improve her or his ability to relate to others may pay longer-term dividends.

The findings are also relevant to the central conclusion of this chapter which relates to the effects of return home. If the children's current environments are so important, their experience on their return to their families is likely to be paramount. The literature on 'permanence' sees placement with a birth family as the ideal. In keeping with that view our last chapter treated 'remaining at home for two years' as evidence of a permanent placement. Despite this strong professional preference, the present chapter shows that the children who returned home did not do well. They were more likely than others to suffer re-abuse. Their social behaviour and educational performance were 'worse'. Their placements were less likely to be rated as going well. These findings held when we controlled for what we knew of them in foster care.[26]

The most likely explanation for these findings is that the children had left home because their families were problematic and generally returned to families that had not changed much. A variety of evidence supports this explanation:

- Research on residential care suggests that where children return to disharmonious or unsatisfactory homes their new environments have a strong negative impact on their behaviour (Allerhand *et al.* 1966; Quinton and Rutter 1988; Sinclair 1971, 1975).[27]

- The main English research in this area (Bullock *et al.* 1993; Farmer and Parker 1991) suggests that the key problems of birth families tend to remain despite their child's absence in the care system.

- At sweep 3 birth parents were rated by social workers as providing poor quality parenting. Our case studies suggest that this often included rejection of the child. In the sample in general, rejection was associated with deterioration or lack of improvement in mental health in general and our attachment-related scores in particular.

- 'Poor quality' parenting at sweep 3 was associated with lack improvement in school performance. School in turn seemed to have an important influence on difficult social behaviour.

- Birth parents were the most likely source of previous abuse and re-abuse. The latter in turn seemed to be a strong correlate of deterioration in mental health.

So it is likely that it was the child's family on return which brought about these poor results.

These findings may suggest that foster children should not go home. This conclusion would go beyond the evidence. The reasons for attempting rehabilitation in at least some cases remain strong. As we will see in the next chapter, the children who returned home wanted to do so. Many parents want them back. Both sides have a right to a family life. Even if they are prevented from returning for a time, many will do so eventually as their placements break down or they themselves reach adulthood. Expense alone would make it impossible to keep in the care system all children whose return was in any way risky.

What the findings should do is to alert all concerned to the major hurdles that have to be overcome if contact and return home are to be satisfactorily handled. This realisation may lead to a re-appraisal of extreme positions in favour of contact and rehabilitation. Some foster children are desperate to go home. There are then issues about how this can be safely managed. However, many, probably most, children in our study did not want to go home. Some complained that their requests to be removed from home had been ignored for too long. Many, probably most, wanted to see more of their families. Nevertheless some did not want to see particular members of their family and felt they were pressurised to do so. In cases where there was strong evidence of previous abuse, unrestricted access for all family members was associated with breakdown and further abuse. Thus some foster children will probably fare best with a compromise. They do not return home, they see a lot of their families, but contact is promoted with due regard for safety and the children's views.

In other cases rehabilitation will no doubt continue to be tried. In achieving this the data (including data from the case studies) suggest a need to pay attention to what are likely to be the key drivers of outcome – quality of parenting and school and the effect of these on abuse, difficult social behaviour and attachment status.

Overall the findings suggest that:

- There is a need for authoritative and proactive management of contact and for active management of risk among those who return home.

- Foster carers need to be able to respond to the sometimes suffocating attachment behaviour of their foster children without either pushing them away or setting up a conflict of loyalties with the birth families.

- Anything that can be done to improve the quality of parenting among parents to whom the child returns should improve results.

- Intervention with the school may be at least as important when the child is at home as it is coming to be thought while the child is in foster care.

We return to some of these issues in the next chapter. In the meantime the most general lesson of this chapter may concern the goals of work with foster children. The aim may not be simply to get the child home, almost at any cost, or alternatively to write home off. There may be many accommodations between these positions – for example, children may be happily based with foster parents but nevertheless see their birth parents on a reasonably regular and satisfying basis. Work may therefore be needed to reduce the sharpness of the dilemma (home or away). This could be done by improving the quality of home, or by developing 'shared parenting' or by enabling the child and birth parents to come to a *modus vivendi* – the past is understood and possibly forgiven, relationships are healed but this does not require that child and parents live together.[28]

Notes

1. For example, the important study by the Dartington unit (Bullock *et al.* 1993) defines 'success at reunion' as 'remaining at home and avoiding a precipitate breakdown' (p.81). Later analyses are based on rather wider definitions of 'success' (Bullock *et al.* 1998). However, neither this study nor the related study by Farmer and Parker (1991) were able to compare outcomes for those returning home with those for children continuing to be looked after.

2. Relevant British studies include the work of Hensey *et al.* (1983), King and Taitz (1985) and Minty (1987). Hensey *et al.* studied children received into care from an at-risk register. Those who returned home were much less likely to have a satisfactory outcome judged on a composite criterion including re-abuse and educational progress. King and Taitz used a similar design and came to similar conclusions in relation to height and weight. Minty (like Zimmerman 1982) compared children who spent varying lengths of

time in the care system and found that those who spent longer were typically less delinquent. (A possible difficulty in interpreting these last results is that children who are looked after for reasons connected with abuse may enter the system earlier and be less likely to return than those who enter because their families are finding them difficult to control. The latter group, almost by definition, may be more likely to become delinquent.) In contrast to these studies the most widely quoted British work on return from care has not been comparative and has relied on ratings of the outcome (Bullock *et al.* 1993, 1998; Farmer and Parker 1991). This results in a more optimistic picture of return.

3. Contact with an educational psychologist was related to 'good outcomes'. Prohibitions on contact with particular family members were associated with good outcomes but only where there was strong evidence of prior abuse.

4. It may be clear that an alleged act would constitute abuse but not whether it has occurred. In other cases agreed 'facts' may or may not constitute abuse. The grading ('none', 'some', 'strong') was intended to allow for both possibilities.

5. If there was strong evidence of prior abuse the relative percentages (tried at home v. never tried) were strong evidence of further abuse 15 per cent v. 8 per cent, some evidence 28 per cent v. 13 per cent, no evidence 58 per cent v. 79 cent.

6. Neither rejection at sweep 1 nor prior abuse are correlated with deterioration if re-abuse and the Goodman score are held constant. In some cases rejection may have been seen by the social workers as re-abuse.

7. A combination of the initial Goodman score, rejection and further abuse accounted for 38 per cent of the variation in the changing scores.

8. For definitions of these measures see Appendix 2.

9. With the exception of age ($p=0.008$) all these variables had very highly significant co-efficients in a multiple regression with childlike attachment as the dependent variable. The same held for the equation predicting change in childlike attachment where only re-abuse ($p=0.006$) did not have a co-efficient significant at $p<0.001$.

10. Both changes showed, as we predicted, negative associations with number of moves. This association, however, disappeared if we took account of the other variables listed above.

11. In a multiple regression the beta for childlike attachment is 0.67 ($p<0.001$) and that for stoicism is 0.24 ($p<0.001$).

12. The correlations remain very highly significant if the initial starting points (Goodman score and relevant attachment score) are taken into account.

13. We tested the prediction with a multiple regression that included initial Goodman score and childlike attachment score as independent variables and change in the Goodman score as the dependent one. The beta for the Goodman score was 0.68 ($p<0.001$) and for childlike attachment score -0.30 ($p<0.001$).

14. This had a positive beta (0.1 ($p=0.12$)) when entered in regression with Goodman score.

15. An alternative explanation could be that both childlike attachment and the Goodman score are approximate measures of some underlying variable 'mental health'. The true measure of this variable would then tend in a sense to lie between the two. If so, on

follow-up both childlike attachment score and Goodman score would tend to move 'towards each other'. Thus in the unlikely event that one child was ranked highest on one measure and lowest on the other he or she would on follow-up tend to have a score near the middle on both. This effect should be apparent if the Goodman score is entered with the childlike attachment score and used to predict change in childlike attachment. In practice, however, no such effect was observed.

16. We created a composite variable – school adjustment – by averaging the ratings of social worker and current adoptive parents or foster carers. Where there was no current carer or where the child was with birth parents, we used the social worker ratings only. We had similar ratings for the children at sweeps 1 and 2 and used these to create an overall measure of prior school adjustment. This correlated 0.42 ($p<0.001$) with our measure of current school adjustment. We had a range of other relevant information from the carers (foster carers, adoptive parents and birth parents). We asked each of these groups whether the child bullied others, was bullied by others, or truanted from school. If they truanted we asked whether the problem was getting better, staying the same or getting worse. These variables were all negatively correlated with school adjustment with correlations ranging from -0.52 (child often fights or bullies other children as rated by adopters) to -0.11 (problems over going to school as rated by birth families). All but one of the correlations based on ratings made by adopters and carers were significant at $p<0.01$ or $p<0.001$. Although the correlations based on ratings made by birth families were similar in size the small numbers involved ($n=14$) meant that none were significant. This pattern provided some evidence for the validity of the school adjustment score.

17. This was included because those who were rated lowest had more scope to improve. Those who had the highest initial ratings had no scope for improvement. Chance variations (e.g. having a carer who was an unusually optimistic or pessimistic rater) will also have tended to favour one group over the other and thus tend to be corrected on follow-up.

18. This was not explained by the fact that the rating was usually made by social workers only, whereas in other placements ratings were an average of the carer and social worker. If anything social workers made slightly more optimistic ratings.

19. On our measures those tried at home did not perform worse educationally in the first two sweeps but did at the third.

20. These data raise three serious methodological problems. First, they are, in some cases, of dubious accuracy. Foster carers can indeed be expected to know if their current foster child is in trouble with the police. However, a foster carer or a social worker who has closed a case may know very little about a young person in independent living. Second, the behaviours are strongly related to age. Very young children do not, for example, get pregnant. Third, we do not know when the behaviour about which we asked took place. A child who was in trouble with the police before moving to a new foster placement but never again would appear similar to one who got into repeated trouble after arrival but never before. Despite these difficulties the data seemed important and we needed to make what sense of them we could.

21. For example, difficult behaviour could lead to removal from home but with less finality than for those removed for other reasons. Or difficult behaviour could make it hard to maintain them in foster care or be motivated by a wish to return home. Or lack of supervision or stress at home could lead to difficult behaviour. In general children who go home may face a variety of problems.

22. The inclusion of disruption in the equation improved the prediction but did not reduce the strength of the association between trial at home and problem behaviour. So the association does not arise because difficult children disrupt and go home as a result.

23. One reason for this was that the analysis was restricted to those still at school at sweep 3 who had been at school at sweep 1. The drop in significance reflects lower numbers as well as smaller co-efficients. In this model the association between trial at home and difficult behaviour was sharply reduced. This reduction suggests that birth parents may affect behaviour directly and also through their effect on school adjustment. For example, by getting children to go to school they may reduce the chance that they associate with difficult teenagers at large in the town.

24. For those in foster care the correlation was 0.41 ($p<0.001$) and for those who had left it was 0.57.

25. If child orientation at sweep 3 replaces child orientation at sweep 1 it is also significant.

26. We have not shown that their mental health deteriorated relative to that of others. We could not test this since we lacked the relevant data for those still at home. However, re-abuse did predict deterioration in mental health and was higher among those returning home.

27. There are two British studies in this list. Sinclair (1971) showed that children in probation hostels who came from 'unsatisfactory homes' were significantly less likely to get into trouble in the hostel than their peers. By contrast they were more likely to do so on return home. Quinton and Rutter (1988) showed that young women leaving the care system and making supportive marriages did 'better' than their peers. Those returning to 'disharmonious' families were less likely to make such good matches, possibly because they fled their homes at the earliest opportunity.

28. This may be reflected in the very positive views which children in our case studies seemed to have of life story work.

Chapter Four

Going Home:
What Makes A Difference?

I thought I was supposed to be leaving when I was 16, because that's the right age, but I got to come home early. I'm glad... I was missing my mum a lot. (Foster child describing return)

A: Yeah. Because when I left Joely, I was sad and happy, but I started crying, because I didn't want to leave Joely.
Q: Yes, that's really hard, isn't it? When you want to be in two places at once.
A: Mmm. And then I went with my mum, and we started visiting Joely. (Foster child describing return)

I kept having arguments and we had this one argument and me mum told me to fuck off and not come back, that were the words she said, 'Don't come, don't bother coming back' so I didn't so she were worried, she'd got coppers out and everything. Anyway I went home next day and coppers were on door. (Foster child describing a failed return)

Introduction

Many of the children in our sample missed their family. Many wanted to return to them. As we have seen in earlier chapters returns were not without risk. Children who went back home were more likely to be re-abused. They also did 'worse' at school and in other ways. The resolution of this dilemma must be a central concern of any fostering policy.

As seen earlier most research on both sides of the Atlantic has not been concerned with this dilemma. Success has been seen as getting the children back home.[1] The major exception to this rule is provided by the Alameida project (Stein, Gambrill and Wiltse 1978). This suggested that purposeful social work based on contracts and a broadly behavioural approach both reduced problems in birth families and enabled return home. Less conclusive British work has also suggested that committed, confident, purposeful social work can have a favourable effect on returns.[2]

Against this background this chapter asks three questions:

- What is the difference between those children who return home and those who do not?

- Among those who return, what is the difference between those who stay and those who do not?

- Among those who remain, what is the difference between those who seem to 'do well' and those who do less well?

Answers to these questions might help define how many and which children might be enabled to return home without undue risk, and also how they could be better supported.

Which children return home?

Three variables dominated whether the children were 'tried at home'. The first of these was the social worker's plans. Children whose social workers in 1998 intended their return were, unsurprisingly, much more likely to do so. The second variable related to return was disruption. Children who had had a disrupted placement before sweep 2 (1999) were much more likely to be tried at home by 2001. The third variable was contact. Children who had weekly contact with at least one relative were much more likely to have been tried at home by 2001 (see Table 4.1).

Over the short term the most important of these variables was the social worker's plans. This was the only variable which needed to be taken into account when predicting return by sweep 2. Over the longer term, however, 'events' play a greater role. We looked separately at children whose return was not planned. In this group disruption was associated with trial at home. Thirty-six per cent of those who had had a disruption by sweep 3 went home as opposed to only 10 per cent of those who had not had one (a significant difference, $p<0.00$). Where a return was planned, disruption had, if anything,

Table 4.1 'Tried at home' by selected variables

		Base number	Tried at home (%)	Chi square
Social worker plans	Yes	54	70	65.02,
return in 1998	No	248	17	df=1, $p<0.001$
Disruption by 1999	Yes	119	43	17.24,
	No	459	24	df=1, $p<0.001$
Weekly contact	Yes	216	38	29.99,
	No	268	16	df=1, $p<0.001$

the opposite effect. Only 63 per cent of those with disrupted placements had gone home as opposed to 81 per cent of the remainder.

It was also true that, over the longer term, contact between home and placement was associated with return even when the social worker's initial plans were taken into account. This suggests that the role of contact is twofold. Over the short term it encourages the social worker to think of return home. Over the longer term it keeps relationships alive and therefore enables return when events disrupt other plans.

In practice it is doubtful if it is contact *per se* rather than the motives behind it that has this effect. Two variables – 'distance from home' and 'prohibition of contact by at least one relative' – are strongly related to frequency of contact. At sweep 1 the mean distance from home of those who did not get weekly visits from at least one relative was 18 miles. This contrasted with seven miles for those getting such visits. Similarly only 37 per cent of those with 'relative prohibited visits' had such frequent contacts as against 47 per cent of those whose visits were uncontrolled. However, despite their apparent impact on visiting frequency, neither prohibition nor distance were related to return home.[3]

Among those who return, which children remain at home?

One hundred and sixty-two children were tried at home at some time over the three years. Some of these had returned quite soon after the first sweep. Just over half (52%) of those at home at sweep 3 were known to be with their families by the time of the first follow-up in 1999. In keeping with this, 52 per cent of those whose families answered our questionnaires were said to have been with their birth families for 22 months or more. By contrast 60 (37%) of the 162 who went home at some stage were no longer there. What differentiated those who left from those who stayed?

Unsurprisingly a key difference was age. The average age in 1998 of those no longer at home in 2001 was nearly 12 years. This contrasted with just over eight years and six months among the remainder.

Surprisingly age was almost the only variable we found which predicted not remaining at home among this group. Girls and young women were somewhat less likely to remain but the difference was not significant. Those who abused substances were less likely to remain. However, this difference disappeared once age was taken into account. Those who had told us in their questionnaires that they missed their home were significantly less likely to stay there if they returned to it. Again, however, this difference disappeared once age was taken into account.

A number of variables were not related to outcome when we might have expected them to be. Children were no more likely to be no longer at home if there was strong evidence at sweep 1 of abuse – nor were they if they had been visited weekly by relatives or if they had a high or low Goodman score. It did not appear to make any difference if the former foster carer kept in touch. Children who had had a disruption by 1999 were slightly more likely not to be at home ($p=0.14$) but again this non-significant difference disappeared if we took account of age. In short we could find nothing which seemed to related to the motivation of child or carer or to the difficulty of the child which seemed to predict this outcome.[4]

One set of variables did seem to have some predictive power. We asked the last foster carers to rate the quality of the environment to which the child was going. Where they were sure that the child was going to a place where he or she would not be loved or would not belong the child was less likely to remain there. These associations failed to hold once we took account of age. We also asked the carers to rate how happy they were about the move on a four-point scale. This did relate significantly to whether a child remained but not after age had been taken into account.

One explanation for this lack of association could be that we either failed to test the right variables or we measured them inaccurately. This could obviously be the case. If it is, however, it is surprising that these variables predicted other outcomes. A rather less comfortable explanation would be that the quality of the placement has rather little to do with whether it lasts. On this account placements at home will only end if problems happen to come to light (and many will not), or the child becomes old enough to vote with her or his feet.

This problem, if it is one, is greatest among those between five and ten in 1998. Eighty-two per cent of those in this age group who were tried at home were still there in 2001. The percentage was rather lower (71%) among those aged four or less. Anxiety about them may have been greater with the result that more were removed on subsequent occasions. The proportion staying at home was lower still (66%) among those aged 11 to 15. It dropped to 23 per cent among those aged 16 or over.

Box 4.1

Abuse and placement breakdown could apparently reflect powerful ambivalent and relationships where children and parent(s) could neither live together nor apart. Two returned home following placement breakdowns and at their wish. As one explained:

> ...they didn't know how I'd react and I were acting right horrible, I wanted to go back with my mum and everything. (Lorna)

Both mothers had worried their children with suicide attempts, and asked for them to be removed. Both undermined the foster placements (Lorna's mum more flagrantly) and wanted their children back. Lorna's mother was now regretting this.

Motivation and outcome

As we have seen, those who returned home seemed to do worse than others. Even contact with families seemed, in certain circumstances or in certain respects, to have a bad effect. As many children want to go home this creates a dilemma: what foster children want may not necessarily benefit them. We hypothesised that the dilemma would be less if motivation influenced outcome. On this hypothesis children who wanted to go home and did so would do better than children who did not. We also thought that children who returned to find a reasonable quality of parenting would do better than others.

In order to have adequate numbers for this analysis we needed a measure of outcome from social workers. Only 25 birth parents answered our questionnaires and this number was too small for any sophisticated analysis. We therefore used social workers' ratings on the 'looking after children' dimension to create a 'social worker well-being score'.

We compared this social worker measure with one taken from questionnaires which had been returned by birth parents (as we included 'home with relatives' as 'return to birth family', some of the 'birth parents' were in fact aunts or grandmothers). Where we had one of these questionnaires we created a second measure: a 'birth parent well-being rating'. This was based on the answers to the following:

- They have been doing well at school or work.
- There are lots of things they enjoy in their spare time.
- They are usually feeling confident.
- There is at least one adult they are close to.
- They have good friends.
- They have learnt to look after themselves.
- They are pleased with the way their life is going.

Each of these questions could be answered 'true' (1), 'mostly true' (2) or 'not true' (3).[5] The correlation between the social worker and birth parent ratings was 0.4 ($p=0.07$). There was therefore some reassurance that they were tapping – albeit inexactly – some underlying dimension of well-being.

We had three relevant measures of motivation:

- whether the child was said by the parent to want to return before he or she did (3), when he or she did (2), not at all (1)
- whether the family was said by the parent to want the child to return before he or she did (3), when he or she did (2), not at all (1)
- the average of the last two ratings as a measure of 'joint motivation'.

Our assumption was that 'wanting an earlier return' would reflect stronger motivation than wanting return at the time it happened. As a check on this we correlated our measures with two other possible measures of motivation both provided in 1998. These were whether the child was said to want to leave the placement and whether the child was visited weekly by at least one relative. The correlations were in the predicted direction although not always significant.

Box 4.2

In the six case studies where the children had returned home parental motivation played a key role. All the parents had clearly wanted the children back, although in two cases the wish was ambivalent, and in two return had not been possible for a time for practical reasons. All the older children were definite they wanted to return. One was too young to express an opinion. His behaviour made it apparent he was unsure. His foster carers described harrowing contact visits:

> It used to be hard to give him back when he was small, because we'd start going down her street, and he'd start screaming, and really crying, and want...he used to have me crying, and I'm holding on to him, and I'm trying to get out of the car, to get him out, and he used to hold on to the car seat, saying, mum, mum, mum. And there's me we'd pull off and leave him, and we'd go and sit in the supermarket, waiting for the supermarket to open, and we'd be sitting there crying in the car park.

The last child, who was quoted at the beginning of the chapter, was ambivalent, wishing both to be with his foster carer and also at home.

- The child's (2001) wish to return was correlated 0.27 with their reported 1998 wish to leave the placement and 0.87 with weekly contact in 1998 ($p<0.001$).[6]

- The family's wish to have the child back was correlated 0.39 with the 1998 wish to leave the placement and 0.29 with 1998 weekly contact.

- The measure of joint motivation (parent wish plus child wish) was correlated 0.41 ($p=0.11$) with 1998 wish to leave the placement and 0.70 ($p=0.002$) with 1998 weekly contact.

The fact that these correlations were in the predicted direction, with measures provided by other people three years earlier, does suggest that they are tapping, albeit imperfectly, what the parties want.

As can be seen from Table 4.2 these 'motivation' variables were, with one exception, significantly related to well-being as assessed by both social workers and birth parents.

Box 4.3

Denise's mother was in no doubt that contact reflected the wish of mother and daughter to be together.

> It broke my heart, the day they came and took her. It's sort of like…you know, it felt like I'd lost her, but it was best for her, and it wasn't as though I couldn't see her, and that. Because over the years, we've always kept up contact, apart from when I was ill, at times, and she didn't see me, but we always kept in touch. I always saw her once or twice a week all the time she was in care.

Denise wanted to be back with her mother. According to the latter she had never understood why she had to be away.

Table 4.2 Measures of well-being correlated with measures of motivation to return

Source of well-being measure	Measures of motivation to return		
	Child's attitude to return	Family's attitude to return	Joint attitude to return
Social worker	0.68***	0.43*	0.64**
Birth family	0.19+	0.56**	0.50**

Notes: Correlations are tau b+=$p<0.1$ * $p<0.05$ ** $p<0.01$ ***$p<0.001$. Numbers vary from 20 to 22.

Other variables and outcome

Quality of parenting could also be an important variable. It was highly correlated (tau b=0.41; $p<0.001$) with the social worker's measure of well-being. Both ratings were, however, made by the same person. So the social worker may have rated well-being high because they thought parenting was good (or vice versa). A rather better test was the correlation between the birth parent rating and the social worker's rating of parenting quality. This was in the predicted direction but low and not significant (tau b=0.19, $p=0.29$).

We also looked at schooling. The parent's rating of how well the child was doing at school was very strongly related to her or his well-being score. As it

Box 4.4

The reasons Denise had been looked after had to do with her mother's bereavement and consequent mental illness and drinking. The situation was now somewhat changed.

> But then I've been slowly getting better. I've had setbacks, and that. And this time last year, she says that she wasn't really happy at the foster carers'. I mean, they were good to her. You know, they were really good, but she just wanted to come home, and then I had to make the decision, and it took a lot to actually decide, you know, the responsibility of looking after her, but in the end, I had to take her feelings into account.

Denise for her part wanted to look after her mother and all agreed that she was anxious about her. Her attachment worries seemed to lead to a condition referred to as 'compulsive caretaking' (Bowlby 1979). On return these problems could be said to lurk but did not dominate. Denise's mother's drinking seemed to be controlled. She had been on a course on dealing with teenagers which she found helpful.

> No, she doesn't really look after me. But the fact that she's here…when she was in care, you see, I was on my own a lot, which I found very, very hard to cope with. The fact that she's here makes my life easier. Because I know she's here. Social services were worried that she'd be an emotional support for me, but I don't think you can actually get away from that anyway. But the fact that she's here makes my life easier, and it makes her happy, although she does tend to try and take the adult role on. That's the thing that you tend to struggle with. She tries to be the parent. I know she only does it because she thinks she's looking after me, but I don't need a parent. But we do tend to argue because she wants to be top person here.

Denise agreed that the return had worked out for the best.

> Yeah. There's been rough times, yeah, but on the whole, I think it's better that I did come here. For mine and mum's sake.

formed part of the score this was not surprising. However, the relationship remained extremely strong when we recalculated the score omitting the rating which referred to school. The well-being score based on the social worker's rating was also associated with the parent's rating of school performance although not significantly so (tau b=0.24, p=0.18).

There seems little doubt that for both social worker and birth parent 'doing well at school' is an important component in 'doing well in general'. Whether a returned foster child who does well at school actually becomes happier and more successful in other areas of their life is more doubtful, although it is in keeping with our data.

The process of return: could more be done to help?

Returns in the case studies varied from the precipitate to the considerably delayed. They illustrated the difficulty – perhaps impossibility – of managing the timing in such a way that it feels right to all concerned. Sudden returns could be experienced by parents as giving insufficient time for them to prepare. Lengthy negotiations over return could provoke anxiety and frustration in the children. Returns, whether or not intended as permanent, could be painful for the foster carers, provoking feelings of betrayal, failure or loss.

According to the birth families the children commonly returned home as they had left it, at short notice.

> Jessica was brought to my house (after a previous visit the day before) at 3am. I didn't hear them knocking. Then at 10am I had a phone call to ask if I would have Jessica back there and then. That's how Jessica came home. I said yes straight away.

This was obviously an extreme case. However out of the 25 respondents only seven said the move had been planned for some time. By contrast eight said it happened at short notice. Even more, ten, said it happened 'suddenly or unexpectedly'. The speed of these events could cause difficulties.

> I think it can be hard for both child and adult when one child moves back home. There are big issues to deal with e.g. trust on the child's part and guilt on the parent's part in some cases – these are feelings that can cause major problems as I have experienced. That is why a detailed and planned move back home and lots of contact and home stays is essential to those issues.

Despite their precipitate nature these moves were, according to the birth families, for the most part welcomed on both sides. Out of the 25 replies, six of the birth families would have liked the move to have taken place earlier, 16 when it did and only three did not want the child back at all. The children were said to be even keener on return. Sixteen were reported as wanting to come back earlier. Six were said to want to come back at the time. Only one was said not to want to come back at all. Two families did not answer the question. This impression that the children wanted to be at home fits with our case studies and other evidence. Foster carers reported that over 80 per cent of those at home with their own families wanted to be there. The analogous figure for social workers was 90 per cent.[7]

Voluntary or not the return home is not usually an easy process. The amount of adjustment involved on both sides was considerable. Usually the child had to get used to a new situation. Half had to get used to a new school, a third to a new family member, and just under two-thirds to new houses and new bedrooms. Three-quarters had to get used to one or more of these changes.

Box 4.5

Implicitly or explicitly return highlights the issue of explanation. If the child can return now whose fault was it that they left in the first place? The child's removal may not be the only event to be explained. In the case studies removal was commonly linked to suicide attempts, mental illness, separations and accusations of abuse. Cathy, for example, had been taken into the care system for apparently having sex with a lodger at the age of 12. Her mother discussed the consequences of this in Cathy's presence:

> And that's what broke the marriage up. But my husband knew that
> it wasn't going to work anyway, but when she was took off me, that
> was it. It did break up the marriage. And I was on tablets. And I tried
> to drown myself, and all. That's how it was.

One question at issue is who is to blame. Parents in the case studies variously blamed another spouse, themselves, social services and the child. The children seemed to be reluctant to blame anyone with the possible exception of social services or the police. Their accounts were, as it were, of a series of events followed by a statement 'and then I lived with X for a while'.

A: Because I went there, because something happened when I was 13. My mum had this lad to stay, and he nearly had sex with me.

Q: Oh dear.

A: And I got took off my mum and dad, and my mum and dad split up because of that, and I was in care from the age of 13 until I was 16. (Daughter of mother quoted above)

The children were, however, returning to families where it was important to participants that 'the official' family explanation of events was accepted.

Asked what was 'difficult or easy' about the process only 6 of the 25 birth families returning a questionnaire stated without qualification that 'everything was OK' or – more commonly – left the question blank. The difficulties raised by the others included jealousy of other siblings, managing travel to school, getting used to have the child around, the child's mood swings, and the need to arrange a new house.

For the birth family also the arrival posed potential problems. Around a quarter reported that the return had led to difficulties over work, three-quarters that it had led to at least some degree of family tension, more than half that it had led to financial problems, a quarter that it led to a shortage of room, and six out of ten that it had led to other worries. Only a fortunate three reported none of these sources of stress. Clearly 25 replies are not a reliable basis for predicting percentages among foster children returning home as a whole. On these figures, however, even a much larger sample is not going to identify many trouble-free returns.

Box 4.6

Return home, like leaving it, raised attachment issues. Two of the children showed marked distress at leaving their foster carers. Two showed marked childlike attachment towards their birth parents – one stuck so close to her mother she was nicknamed 'Klingon'. Two showed no obvious difficulties which were brought to our attention, although one of these experienced the breakdown of a placement with his mother and transfer to his father which was what he wanted.

The initial honeymoon period did not necessarily last. The two children who had stuck close to their parents suddenly began to join the teenage culture, stay out late at night, and refuse to do any chores. At this point some parents experienced a belated empathy with the foster carers.

> I found as she was hitting her teens, she was sort of like rebelling against them. And since she's come home, she's rebelled against me! [laughs] You know, at that time, I suppose I thought they were a bit too hard on her, at times.

Help provided

In relation to social work help the families faced, albeit to a more acute degree, the same dilemma we will find among adoptive families. They wanted help but they did not want the intrusion and potential judgements that came with it. One mother, for example, voiced her difficulty in matching the money her child had in foster care.

> I also think parents should be helped more money wise especially when people are unemployed and can't afford to get him things and take him out. I also think I should have someone to talk to about things but then again I feel I can't trust them. They gave me no help and advice about money when my son came to live with me. I…don't understand everything so I have had to just manage.

Some asked for help but others 'kept their head down' and got on with their lives.

> [Danny] wants it to be just myself and his brother and no more social services. They have asked for the care order to be removed and we've both agreed to it. He has been allocated a young people's person (I don't know who yet) and he wasn't pleased at all. I think he's a bit fed up with being passed from pillar to post and just wants to enjoy the rest of his life with his family and no one else. I totally agree with [him] in this matter. It's time he settled down properly to enjoy what's left of his childhood.

This ambivalence over accepting help was matched with an ambivalence in providing it. Social workers wanted to help. However they, and more particularly their managers, were acutely aware of the other demands on their time. Overall it is likely that fewer than half the children living with their birth family had a current social worker.[8]

Undoubtedly some parents felt 'fobbed off':

> If social services helped me or anyone in authority helped I would be all right. A lot of people get grants when they have children go live with them from social services, but not me. Face does not fit. Never had much help from social services since my ex-husband started hitting my eldest girl. Always took his side anyway. I was always reporting them for things what was happening and what was done or not done when [child] was in care. Got nothing in my new home, cannot get any help anywhere.

As implied above the families wanted practical help with money and accommodation. Overall six out of ten said that more help over money would have made the move easier and a third would have liked help with housing. Six out of ten wanted 'more support' from social services. No doubt this included advocacy or direct help with material things. However, they might also want a chance to talk things over on their own or a 'mediator' who could enable different sides to communicate.

Box 4.7

Only one of the six case study children who returned home was receiving active social work help. One case which was seen by the interviewer, a qualified and experienced social worker, as needing help and willing to receive it was closed because the child moved areas and was seen as low priority. Others were closed because it was felt that everything that could be done had been done and the child was probably old enough to look after her/himself. It is easy to criticise this situation. In practice the ambivalence of the families was such that it was not clear what hard-pressed social workers could do.

> And when she left care we tried to get [specialised agency] involved again, you know, to sort of keep the placement stable and then we'd write and let them know when we were coming and we'd turn up and they wouldn't be there and we'd make other appointments and we turned up and they wouldn't be there and in the end we just wrote and said 'well, you know, we'll sort of leave you to it' and then…about a year later [pause] this year mum put in a complaint that we'd not supported her. (Social worker)

Q: …what happened when you came out, did you do, have you seen anybody since or anything from Social Services?

A: No, no.

Q: No?

A: No, don't want to. (Young person from same case)

In contrast to the above, one young person, however, was clearly getting significant help from a counsellor at school which she discussed with the interviewer.

> It's just a relief to get it all out. It's like, every week, everything… I write everything down for her, and then I'll go in, and we'll talk about it. I've actually been seeing her for about a year and a half.

Her mother confirmed the value of this arrangement. She said that she and her daughter found it difficult to talk and that it was good that her daughter had this outside outlet.

With communication, support and encouragement between partners and social worker whom we trusted, very much worked well instead of being on one side. Also his teacher too. Therefore regular meetings at home between parents, social worker and teacher helped a lot in a relaxed room.

Another, however, experienced no such teamwork but rather felt demeaned and intimidated:

I would have been a lot easier if the social services hadn't been always expecting me to make a complete mess of things, so I'd be what they always believed me to be. The world's worst mother. Everything I planned I get them always throwing my past in my face. Without this it would have made me and my son bond quicker instead of making me afraid to touch or even cuddle my son for many months without being asked why I'd done it, or being watched constantly like my home was a prison.

Birth families returning their questionnaire may have had more active social work than others. A third of these families said they got a lot of support from their worker over the move. A further 44 per cent said they got 'some support'. About half also said they got at least some support from foster carers at this time. A third stated that this was 'a lot'. In addition a third said that they had a lot of help from their families. Around four in ten stated they had no help from their family at all.

The extent of support from services obviously reduced over time. Only a fifth said they were currently getting 'a lot' of help from social workers. In addition seven of the families said they were getting other 'specialist' help. Only one said that this contact with other professionals was 'a lot of help'. Only three said they were getting a lot of help from foster carers. A quarter said they had a lot of help from family and a fifth that they did so from friends.[9] Birth families are generally more troubled than foster families. They seem to receive less support for dealing with equally difficult children.

Does the process of arrival or help received relate to outcomes?

We expected that the outcomes of return would be related to among other things three groups of variables:

- continuity – the extent of change involved in return

- problems – the number of problems the family experienced as a result

- help – the extent of support received.

We explored these hypotheses without finding any evidence in favour of any of them.

Contact with foster carers

It was apparent from the case studies that contact between birth families and foster parents could be – although it often was not – very significant. We had various measures of this contact. These were:

- how often the foster carer had contact with the child (from foster carer questionnaire)

- the number of different kinds of help contact involved (foster carer questionnaire)

- whether birth parent said carer gave support at the beginning (a lot, some, none)

- whether birth parent said carer gave support now (a lot, some, none).

These measures were not correlated with our outcomes. Why the conflict of evidence between our statistics and the gut feel we get from the case studies? One reason may be the quality of our measures. Thus although one of the young people did go back to the carers for Christmas this contact was not a strong indicator of the importance of the relationship. A further reason may be that basic quality of the child's experience was as our measures suggested determined by the quality of parenting, the experience of school and the motivation of all concerned. Given these basic building blocks foster carers could, in our view, both enhance the quality of the child's and its family's experience and enable dangerous situations to survive. They were, however, unlikely to exercise a very major influence on outcome.

Box 4.8

In two of our six 'return' cases there was no contact between foster carer and child. In another the child went back once for Christmas and there were occasional encounters in the street or supermarkets. In three the contact was frequent and significant. The parents in these latter cases saw the carers not as competitors but as experienced, practical people who did not look down on them and shared with them a concern for their child's welfare. In two of them the foster carers took on the role of extended family. In one case this took the form of providing holidays as it were with a favourite aunt. In another the foster carers played a continuing and crucial role, managing crises from the trival – when transport for school did not turn up – to the serious as when the child was dangerously ill and his mother was wanting to discharge him from hospital. The same mother described her experience of support from the foster carers:

> It's like an extra sister. Yeah? So he's, like, got an extra mum and a dad. We get on all right. Just like a member of the extended family. Every time we go round their house, I always feel like I'm welcome…it gives me a break. Also, being autistic, he's also hyper-active, so by the time he's in bed on a night, I feel about an hundred!…it's nice just to have a lie-in, for once!…I mean, it's nice for him to have a father figure, and to always be there, without me actually having to go out and find one, because I've just got rid of one, and I thought, to put it bluntly, I don't want another one! So it's nice for him to have a bloke there especially when it's the toilet training, training him to stand up and have a wee. At least Terry's there on hand to show him that boys do it standing up.

Conclusion

In the short term children return home because this is what is planned. Over the longer term they go back because of events and the powerful, if sometimes ambivalent, ties between children and their parents. The returns themselves are often problematic. Much probably depends on whether the situation which led to removal has been in any way resolved. Sometimes, but not always, there have been important changes. If so the case studies did not suggest that they occurred through the agency of social services. The basic determinants of outcome seemed to be the quality of parenting the children received on return, school and the motivation of parent and child. Systematic help from social services was rarely given, and hardly ever intensive. We failed to find any form of help that statistically affected outcome.

Having failed to get statistical evidence of what works we can make no firm suggestions as to how matters should be improved. Instead we rely on suggestions made by our interviewees. These, however, were at least compatible with what we have found. Four suggestions can be made.

First, foster carers might more often be used as in our last case example – i.e. to provide support for both mother and child and occasional respite care. The mothers in these cases may need mothering as well as the children. 'Short break' residential care (as suggested by one of the children in the case studies), specialised foster care, or even successors to the former settlement houses might be used for teenagers in the same way. It is hoped that the effect would be to make the situation less desperate for both parent(s) and child. The arrangement might also offer a safety net at times of crisis, and provide the child with some ordinary, enjoyable experiences.

Second, children within these difficult, ambivalent situations need to have access to adults whom they trust and whom they can talk on a regular basis. The counsellor at the school provided a lifeline to one of the children in our case studies. An education social worker had done so earlier to another. Former foster carers would probably provide a listening ear to two others. An important feature of these arrangements was they seemed to have rather little to do with formal qualifications and to be available to children in the context of their ordinary lives.

Third, there should be experiments in making training available to parents in how to deal with teenagers. The one parent who had been on such a course found it helpful. There is American evidence that an effective approach is to train parents and foster carers in the same methods (Chamberlain 1998b).

Box 4.9

The return children in the case studies talked in a meaningful way to a wide variety of people. Qualifications were not a passport to being an acceptable confidante.

A: ...they put me into art therapy and then she went so it were just this psychiatrist...and, ooh no, I couldn't, I couldn't speak to her. Everything I said to her were like, fucking this and fucking that, and it were just mad.

Q: Cos that's how you were feeling or just you couldn't get on with her?

A: I couldn't get on with her and it were way I were feeling an' all.

Fourth, and contrary to the views of earlier researchers, it might be helpful if social services were less wary of care orders. A number of the placements in the case studies had been undermined by parents who, for example, authorised their children to stay out way beyond the time the foster carer thought appropriate. Similarly, some social workers felt that accommodated children should not go home. In these cases they sometimes resorted to subterfuges, pretending to parents that they had more power than they really had. A care order might clarify some of these situations. It need not presumably mean that the child should not go home. It would, however, encourage clarity over what would have to change if return were to take place.[10]

Box 4.10

> Well, I think we try and avoid this sort of [voluntary] arrangement if possible, do you know what I mean, because we don't have any real parental responsibility for the children and…do you know what I mean, mum could have come at any time and taken her home really [pause] but on the other hand doesn't support it. I mean I, at the end of the day it doesn't make a lot of difference, but if she's got her mother's consent to be out till midnight it makes it very difficult doesn't it, because we, we don't know where she is, she's run away and we have to get the police involved but mum does know where she is and is giving permission…but we obviously wouldn't agree to her being out at those times of nights with the people that she's with, you know. (Social worker discussing an accommodated child)

What this chapter does do is reinforce the dilemmas outlined in the last two. Some parents and children desperately want to get back together. Arguably this reflects their unassuaged care-giving and attachment needs. Advocates of permanence think in these circumstances re-unification should happen. Arguably they have failed to take sufficiently seriously the dangers involved. Resources, experiment and determined effort by practitioners are needed if this dilemma is to be reduced or resolved.

Summary of Chapters 3 and 4

1. Children who went home generally wanted to be there and their families wanted to have them. Nevertheless they did worse than others in a number of respects and seemed to receive little effective external support.

2. There is scope for reviewing the philosophies surrounding return home. It is not necessarily the touchstone for improved parenting or family relationships.

3. There is also scope for increasing the support given to those who do return, paying particular attention to schooling, parent preparation, practical support for parent, mediation between parent and provision of independent support for the child. In some cases foster carers could play a key role.

Notes

1. Results have been mixed. Some, but not all, American 're-unification' experiments suggest that intensive efforts accelerate return, even if in the longer term they have little effect on the overall proportion of 'returnees' (Fraser *et al.* 1996; Sherman, Newman and Shyne 1973; Walton *et al.* 1993). For a review see Little and Schuerman (1995).

2. This was the predominant predictor of lasting return in Bullock and his colleagues' study (1993). Unfortunately it is easier to be confident, committed and purposeful when the case is going well, all concerned want the same thing, there are not major risks and so on.

3. Evidence from earlier studies suggests that teenagers in particular often 'engineer' their returns home with social services taking a relatively passive role (Farmer and Parker 1991; Vernon and Fruin 1986).

4. Farmer and Parker (1991) found that children who had at least one failed return home were much more likely not to remain there if returned. This result is intrinsically plausible but we failed to confirm it. Indeed frequent returns were positively but not significantly related to remaining at home if we allowed for age.

5. The reliability (alpha) of the social worker well-being score was 0.92, that of the birth parent welfare score 0.85. For clarity we have reversed the scoring of the latter so that a high score indicates high well-being.

6. These are non-parametric correlations.

7. There is contradictory evidence. Eighteen of the children had answered a questionnaire in 1998 when only eight of them said they wanted to go to their families. However, children seemed to change their mind over this question. Thirty-three answered a questionnaire then and later when in foster care in 2001. Those who said they wanted to go to families or relatives in 1998 were no more likely than others to say this in 2001.

8. This crude estimate is based on the proportion of questionnaires returned by a current social worker (49%) as opposed to previous social worker (33%), team leader or with other person with knowledge of the child. We assume that current social workers would if anything be more likely to return a questionnaire. For comparison the proportions of current social workers returning questionnaires for children in residential care (89%), new foster carer (89%) or index carer (75%) were much higher. Birth families returning questionnaires were slightly more likely to have a current social worker reporting on them.

9. These percentages are much lower than for our original sample of foster carers for whom we asked the same questions. Sixty-three per cent of them report 'a lot' of help from their family, 35 per cent a lot from friends (birth parents 24%), 15 per cent a lot from neighbours (birth parents 0%), 36 per cent said they had a lot of support from the child's social worker and 55 per cent a lot from the family placement worker. The only similar percentages were for 'other relatives' (24% in both cases).

10. Against this it might be argued that in practice the courts cannot really be used to enforce such orders, that once children reach 16 or so they will flout them anyway, and that it might be counterproductive to use them. Perhaps the basic premise is that there should be clarity about what each side expects of the other and that social workers should be quite clear about what they want if the child is to return – one of the basic assumptions of the Alameida project (Stein *et al.* 1978).

Chapter Five

Adoption: Who is Adopted and How Do They Do?

She started calling me mum after about six months. And I was advised that I shouldn't let her, which I found quite difficult, and I couldn't bring myself to say to her, you know, 'you can't call me mum', so I used to add – 'I'm your foster mummy', and go about it like that, but she didn't – she used to just call me mum, and she carried on calling me mum. In fact she drove me nuts, because she would say 'mum, mum, mum, mum' 24 hours a day, for what seemed like months on end, because she just liked the sound of it. (Foster carer who went on to adopt)

Introduction

The wish to return more children home was one core plank in the 'permanence movement'. The wish to get more adopted was another. In the 1970s a variety of reasons – the increase in abortion, the lowered stigma of illegitimacy, demographic change – led to a drop in the numbers of newborn babies available for adoption. These 'market pressures' combined with the push for permanency and the discovery of 'drift' in foster care to both create and legitimate the practice of adopting older and 'special needs' children.

Adoption offers these children important advantages. It can provide some form of security for life. Nevertheless adopters and adoptees take an emotional risk. An adoption breakdown may be extremely painful for both sides. Moreover it is now apparent that the results of these late adoptions are not as good as were once claimed. Their breakdown rates are sizeable (47% among children aged 10–12 in one study; Thoburn et al. 2000). The children's behaviour is often difficult and despite devoted parenting their emotional problems may prove resistant to change (e.g. Rushton, Treseder and Quinton 1996; Rutter *et al.* 1998).

So it is important to compare adoption and fostering, to determine if possible their relative risks and disadvantages, and to understand what may contribute to the various outcomes. The present study can make a contribution to this task, albeit one limited by the relatively brief period of follow-up.

The potential contribution of the study to the body of work on adoption lies mainly in its origins as a study of foster care. Apart from the pioneering work of Lowe and his colleagues (2002) there is little British work on the reasons why some children are adopted while others enter long-term fostering, on the consequences of the lost attachment to foster carers as children become adopted,[1] or on the degree to which adopted children 'improve' on the psychological status they had as foster children.

Against this background we will examine:

- why some children were adopted when others were not
- how far children, carers and social workers want adoption for these others
- why some were adopted by their own foster carers and others by strangers
- how adopted children fare compared with similar children not adopted
- whether stranger adoptions do 'better' or 'worse' than foster carer ones.

The exploration of these questions should cast light on the degree to which adoption is a viable alternative to return home or long-term fostering – a way out of the dilemma discussed in the previous chapters.

Background and outcome variables

Ninety (16%) of our 596 children were adopted. Seventy-four of their parents (82%) responded to our questionnaires. The response rate was particularly good among those who had adopted a child they had previously fostered. Twenty out of 21 (95%) of these responded. Nevertheless, we also achieved an unusually good response (78%) from 'stranger adoptions'.[2]

Our main outcome variables were:

- stoicism score
- childlike attachment score
- Goodman score
- family integration score
- family exclusion score
- educational ratings.

These measures are described in Appendix 2.

As will be seen adopted children are generally adopted when very young. Before the age of three we did not have our usual measures of psychological status. This has made it difficult for us to allow for the child's 'initial state' when comparing, for example, the outcomes for children adopted by their index carers with those adopted by others.

Our background variables all came from sweep 1. They comprised:

- age
- sex
- initial psychological status scores where available.

We had variables measuring the 'difficulty' of children under three. As they did not relate to our outcomes we have not included them.

Why were these children adopted when others were not?

Adoption is reserved for young children. Forty-four per cent of those we knew to be adopted were less than two when we first met them. Ninety-one per cent were less than six years old. Children who were six or over when they first entered our sample were very rarely adopted. In analysing the reasons for adoption or otherwise we need to look at these different groups separately.

Children aged less than two at sweep 1

Adoption and birth family were essentially the only two options for this age group. The first thought of social services was to ensure a child remained at home or return them quickly. In some situations, however, this was impossible. The social services then invariably thought of adoption. Overall three-quarters (37) of the 50 children in our sample aged less than two were adopted. Ten were with their birth families at sweep 3.[3] Of the remaining three one was lost to the sample but was known to have gone home in 1998. And two were withdrawn from the study by the local authority.

Those who were adopted were almost invariably considered to be unsafe with their birth families. Twenty-one of the 23 adopted children on whom we had social work questionnaires at sweep 3 were said by their social workers to be in this situation.

Those who subsequently went home were (at the time of sweep 1) also the focus of anxiety.[4] Children in whose cases there was strong evidence of abuse were somewhat more likely to return home (6 out of 14) than when there was some evidence (1 out of 8) or no evidence (1 out of 11). The explanation for this is unclear. Some where there was no evidence may have been removed at birth or have had parents who asked that the child be adopted. In other cases social workers, in keeping with the spirit of the 1989 Children Act, may have been trying to give birth families every chance.

Box 5.1

The case studies suggested that the choice between adoption and return home was influenced by a variety of factors. The most obvious were the clarity of the evidence of abuse, and the degree to which mother or family contested the adoption. Other factors – the willingness of the birth family to work with social services, changes in the situation such as father moving out, and the particular attitudes of the social worker and manager immediately concerned – seemed to play a part in particular cases by encouraging efforts at rehabilitation. It was these latter factors which probably explained why some families would lose a child at birth or shortly after while efforts were made to keep other babies with the same family.

Children aged over two but less than five at first sweep
We had information on 76 children aged between two and four at sweep 1. By sweep 3 we had lost track of a small number (4%) of this group. The placements of the remainder divided into three – birth family (21%), foster care (35%) and adoption (39%). As with the younger group there is a question of why they do not go home. There is also the additional question of why those who do not go home are not adopted.

Our case studies suggested unsurprisingly that children did not go home because the homes were not seen as safe for them. The statistical data supported this. The social workers at sweep 3 suggested that in three-quarters (72%) of the 51 cases on which they commented the child could not go home

Box 5.2

Our case studies also suggested reasons why these children were not adopted. Some of the children were placed with relatives, were described as very disabled or had carers with whom they had bonded but for whom the fostering allowance was a key consideration. The families with whom the child was placed might want the extra back-up which the social services were seen as providing both financially and in terms of dealing with the birth family. These exceptions were understandable. In other cases, however, there did not appear to be a clear-cut rationale against adoption. For example, other children had been removed for adoption from the same family, sometimes at birth, but this particular child was not. In these cases it seemed that some measures had been put in place which were felt to make the situation tolerable (for example, a male partner had moved out) and as time went on there was an acceptance of the status quo.

The case study child who was adopted in this age group had a mild impairment. Her foster carers were approved as her adopters because they had shown they could deal with her special needs. There was, however, another reason – the child's attachment to them. As the social worker explained:

> Sarah and Toby were very much of the opinion that they'd adopted two children, they just wanted to foster, and they said that Sonia adopted them, really. [laughs] Attached herself to them, so I think once they'd got the decision that Sonia was going to go up for adoption, I think Sonia attached herself to them so much that they just thought, that's it, you know.

because it was unsafe. They also suggested a variety of other reasons. These included the opposition of the courts, the child's reluctance, the bonding between the child and foster carers, the reluctance of the family to have the child back, the lack of any effective family and a miscellaneous 'other category'. These judgements almost invariably coincided with the belief that the home was unsafe. However, in 14 per cent of the 51 cases there was no suggestion of a lack of safety and the other reasons seem to have tipped the balance.

The statistical data pointed – more strongly than the case studies – to the importance of early decisions on whether to maintain a family link. None of the ten children placed with relatives at sweep 1 were adopted (a highly significant difference). Seven children were placed with their birth families after sweep 1 but were nevertheless no longer there on follow-up. None of these were adopted. Overall almost exactly half of those in foster placements at sweep 3 had either had a birth family option tried or were maintaining a family base through a relative placement. None of those whose social workers had pursued such family options were adopted.[5]

These decisions over adoption may have influenced and been influenced by patterns of family contact at sweep 1. Among those for whom we had the relevant information we knew that 85 per cent of 13 children who were at home at sweep 3 had weekly contact with a relative at sweep 1. The same was true for 64 per cent of the 25 in foster care at sweep 3 but only 17 per cent of those adopted at sweep 3. Around half those without weekly contact and subsequently adopted had a restriction on contact with at least one relative.

The remaining foster children were significantly more disturbed than the adopted children on our childlike attachment score ($p=0.026$, Mann-Whitney U) and the Goodman score ($p=0.016$, Mann-Whitney U). Within the age group they tended to be older ($p=0.11$) and were rather more likely to be disabled ($p=0.08$ on one measure). These differences are in the same direction as those reported by Selwyn and her colleagues in their analysis of differences between those adopted and those not in a sample who had experienced a best interests decision (Selwyn *et al.* 2003).

In summary social services' efforts to maintain family links pursued a 'birth family option' through relative placement or trial at home. The 'family option' seems to have resulted in return in about a fifth of cases and may have pre-empted adoption in up to half the remainder. In other cases they may have been influenced in favour of adoption by lack of contact between family and child, although the decision to pursue adoption may itself have resulted in efforts to reduce contact. In contrast to the situation among those aged less than two the difficulty of the child probably had an impact on whether or not he or she was adopted.

Children aged six and over at sweep 1

Adoption was very rare among those aged six or over at sweep 1. Only 2 per cent of them were adopted by sweep 3. Only one of these children was aged over eight. Numbers were really too small for statistical analysis. In this age group, age was the only factor identified as distinguishing between those adopted and those not.

The 'market for adoption'

We did not consider that adoption was an option for those who were in independent living or with their families. However, we wanted to know whether those who were currently fostered might have been or might still be adopted. We assumed that this would only occur if the child, the foster carer or the social worker wanted it. We therefore asked for their preferences. As all those aged one or under at sweep 1 were adopted or with birth families the questions were not relevant to them.

Views on adoption when children aged two to five at sweep 1

We had questionnaires from carers of 21 of the 27 children in this age group who were known to be fostered at sweep 3. Five carers, a surprising proportion (26%) of this admittedly small number, said that they would like to adopt the child. One (5%) wanted the child adopted by someone else. By contrast they thought that only two (10%) of these children wanted to be adopted by them and one by someone else.

We asked the foster carers if any of a number of conditions would make it more likely they would adopt children in this age group. One in five (19%) said that more post-adoption support from social services would have 'very much' influenced this. A further one in seven (14%) said that it might have done so. Other relevant factors which they said would have definitely made a difference were agreement of social services (33%), help with legal process (24%), a speedier court process (19%), stopping contact with birth parents (5%) and financial help to adopt (29% definitely, 14% possibly). Nearly half (48%) of those fostering children in this age group said that one or more of these steps would have 'very much' influenced the likelihood of their adopting.

We had only 17 questionnaires from social workers for this group of 27. They wanted two to be adopted by their current carers and one to be adopted by someone else. They felt that three children wanted to be adopted by their current carer (two) or their previous one (n=1).

We had 14 questionnaires from children in this age group (now aged five to eight). None of them said they wanted to be adopted by their carer, although all but one wanted to stay until they were at least 18 and most of them for longer than this. Even from this small group it was apparent that although a carer might be willing to adopt, the child might not wish to be adopted.

Box 5.3

Natasha was fostered with now subsequent adopters at the age of five following repeated failures at rehabilitation. After initial wariness she bonded strongly with the foster mother following a severe illness when the foster mother had stayed with her in hospital. Social services wanted her to be adopted by relatives who were willing to do this.

> Natasha had got so fond of us, thought of us as her family, and wanted to stay. And it was like, we didn't need another daughter – it was like – [laughs] – we already had four. But we'd obviously grown to love this child, and she wanted to stay with us, and we wanted her, so it was the same on both sides, but it wasn't something we'd set out to do. And we were made to feel that it's a no-go area, really. 'This child was put to you for fostering, not for adoption.'

The foster carers got a solicitor and spent savings they could ill afford. The case went to the high court but was dropped through the decision of the director. The other potential adopters stayed in touch with the child and the new parents and were regarded as family friends.

Views when children aged six or over at sweep 1

Is there is a 'market' for adopting older children which might be tapped by a radical change of policy? We asked the foster carers, social workers and children whether they favoured adoption for the fostered children in this age group. The form of the questions differed. We asked carers and social workers if they favoured adoption by the carer, others or no adoption at all. We only asked the children if they wanted to be adopted by their carer or stay with the carer for varying lengths of time which we specified. The potential number of replies to each of these questionnaires was 178. Overall:

- 9 per cent of 126 foster carers replying wanted adoption for the child

- 14 per cent of the 103 social workers replying wanted this

- 9 per cent of the 98 children replying wanted to be adopted by their current carer.

In the case of the children a desire for adoption seemed to be the product of long stay. At the time of sweep 1 those wanting to be adopted had already spent an average of 45 months with their carers (as opposed to 28 for the sample as a whole). None of them had left their index carer in the meanwhile. On average, therefore, this small group had spent around seven years in the placement by sweep 3. It seems natural that they should want to 'regularise' their situation.

All the foster carers favouring adoption wanted to adopt the child themselves. Most of the social workers favouring adoption also suggested this option (11% v. 3%).

At first sight these figures suggest that if the wishes of the parties were followed around 10 per cent of this sample would be adopted, almost all of them by their current carer. This, however, assumes that wishes coincide. Children who want adoption are not always matched with carers wanting to adopt. Nor are carers who want to adopt always matched with willing children.[6] Assuming both to be necessary this would clearly reduce numbers of adoptions – probably by around a half. Numbers are too small to make any precise estimate.

This discrepancy could, arguably, be reduced by policy steps. We looked at the seven cases where the foster carer did not think the child should be adopted and this despite their belief or the child's own statement that this was what the child wanted. In four of the seven they stated that some change would have made a definite difference to their wish to adopt. The steps mentioned were prohibition of contact with birth parents (two), the agreement of social services (one), and greater financial (one) and other support (one) after the adoption. One also said that the agreement of the birth parents would have made a big difference.

We looked at another small group where the foster carer was willing to adopt and either the child, the social worker or the foster carer said the child also wanted adoption. In these cases we also had information from the social worker on the reasons the child had not been adopted. The reasons seemed to be much the same as those brought forward in other cases. The child was too old (n=1), too difficult (n=1), had been tried before for adoption (n=1), was too settled in the foster placement (n=1), did not want adoption (n=1) or had birth parents who would not agree to it.

So the upshot of this enquiry is that:

- there is a small perceived market for adopting older foster children
- it is unlikely to exceed 10 per cent of the population (limit of carers and children interested)

- it is most likely to be tapped through foster carer adoptions
- it would require attention to the factors that inhibit carer adoptions
- other difficulties would also require close attention on a case-by-case basis.

To state there is a market is not of course to imply that it should be tapped. We return to this question at the end.

Comparing children adopted by carers and those adopted by others

We compared children adopted by their carers with those adopted by others. We found a number of significant differences.

Briefly – and as judged from information at sweep 1 – those adopted by their carers were on average one year older ($p=0.11$), more likely to be described as disabled ($p=0.001$), more likely to score highly on our measure of 'learning, behaviour, communication' problems ($p=0.001$), and our measure of 'being a difficult baby' ($p=0.004$), and more likely to have child-oriented carers ($p=0.025$) who scored low on our rejection score ($p=0.027$). They were somewhat less likely to come from an ethnic minority although the numbers were too small to reach significance. All but one of the 21 for whom we had the information were with couple carers. This was a higher percentage (95%) than that for children adopted by others (83%) but again the numbers were too small for significance.

In general therefore carer adoption does not appear to be routinely considered for all children. Rather it seems to be used for children who might otherwise be difficult to place – i.e. those who are disabled and less 'attractive' as babies. If time passes with no outside adoption placement and their carers are child-oriented and attached to them carer adoption may occur.

Outcomes of adoption and fostering compared

Adoption is commonly thought to be more 'permanent' and hence better for a child than fostering. Is this really so? And if it is, does it make any difference whether the child is moved between placements or stays with the original carer either adopted or fostered?

These are complicated questions. We began by considering whether at sweep 3 there were any differences in 'outcomes' between the four groups (fostered by index carer, adopted by index carer, fostered by other, adopted by other). *We made these comparisons for children aged eight or less at sweep 1.* Beyond this age virtually no one is adopted.

Briefly there were significant differences between the groups on almost all our major outcomes of interest: childlike attachment score ($p<0.001$), stoicism score ($p<0.001$), Goodman score ($p<0.001$), exclusion from the family ($p<0.001$), school involvement rating ($p=0.006$), educational progress rating ($p=0.039$), total school performance rating ($p=0.009$), school problem composite rating ($p<0.001$). The only exception to this pattern of significant differences was that the family inclusion score did not differ significantly between the four groups ($p=0.084$).

On all but the school ratings there was a clear pattern. The 'best' scores were for those adopted by index carers, the next 'best' for other adopters and the worst for those fostered by someone other than the original carer. In the case of the school ratings many of the differences were less pronounced. However, it was clear that children fostered other than by their index carer were doing 'worse'. In addition both fostered groups had more school problems than either of the adopted ones.

By themselves these results mean little. As we have seen, children who are adopted tend to be younger and in some ways less difficult than those fostered. So it is not surprising that their outcomes are apparently better. Before deciding whether these differences are due to their placements we need to take into account what they were like in the first place.

Our approach to this was the same for all our variables. Where possible we first created a change score – for example, by subtracting a score at sweep 3 from a similar score at sweep 1. The extent of change obviously depends to some extent on the initial score (some scores can only 'improve', for example) so we needed to take the initial score into account. We also needed to take account of age since this is the variable which most obviously distinguishes those adopted and those not. Our overall 'model' examined whether the facts of being adopted and of having a changed placement (whether to adopters or carers) since 1998 had an impact on change. The model allowed for age and initial score on the variable of interest.

The results can be summarised as follows:

- Improvement in childlike attachment was better when the child was adopted ($p=0.031$) and the child had not changed placement ($p=0.048$).

- Improvement in 'stoicism' was better when child was adopted ($p=0.001$) but the effect of placement change was not significant ($p=0.18$).

- Improvement in the Goodman score was not significantly related to adoption ($p=0.11$) or placement change ($p=0.53$).

- Improvements in the inclusion and the exclusion scores were not significantly related to adoption or placement change.

- Improvement in our school performance rating was not greater when the child was adopted or had not changed places.

The last result requires a qualification in a way the others do not. There was an interaction. Change of placement was apparently 'worse' for the child when he or she remained in foster care. By contrast it was apparently slightly 'better' for the child when he or she was adopted. The reason for this is unclear.[7]

Why do these changes occur? We predicted that those children who would show more positive changes would:

- be younger

- not have had a placement move

- be adopted

- have more child-oriented foster carers

- have fewer foster or adoptive siblings.[8]

For reasons already explained we included a high initial score on the variable concerned in all our models.

Three of these variables turned out to account together for nearly two-thirds of the change in our 'stoicism' score:

- The greater a child's age the less the positive change ($p=0.014$).

- The greater the number of children in the house the less the positive change ($p=0.006$).

- The worse the initial score the greater the degree of positive change ($p<0.001$).

The reason that adoption does not appear in this model is that it is strongly associated with both age and number of children in the household. On average adoptive households contained one (strictly speaking 1.1) child fewer than foster homes at sweep 3. Even in this age group where all were aged less than eight they were on average almost exactly three years younger. If the number of children in the household is omitted from the model, adoption enters it replacing age and associated with change at a high level of significance ($p < 0.001$).

Box 5.4

The difference between adoption and long-term fostering is partly symbolic. Foster carers are not parents while adoptive carers are. One child in our case studies was too young to appreciate this difference. The others clearly were not. The word 'mum' was very important. Two sisters insisted that the two women who adopted them should be called mummy Carey and mummy Pamela – not 'Carey' and 'Pamela' as suggested. The other two children both went through a phase of using the word 'mummy' on all possible occasions. Photographs could be another important symbol.

Q: After Natasha was adopted, did that change her view of being here, at all? How did you handle that, once it was all over?

A: Nothing changed, except she was a part of the family, because she had that stability. And she had me going out spending a fortune on that photograph!

Q: What, this one here?

A: Yes. There was one up there that just had the four girls, and myself and Simon, and before she was adopted she used to stand up there, and have me take photographs of her by the side of the picture, so that she could be in the picture.

In short, foster children of this age are most likely to come out of their shell if they are adopted. Part of the explanation for this probably has to do with the fact that adopted children are younger and younger children are more likely to change in this way. In addition adopted children typically do not have to compete for attention with so many other children as their peers in foster care.

Our analysis did not greatly help us to improve our predictions in relation to changes in childlike attachment, school attainment or family exclusion. However, it did bring out the interesting fact that age is associated with positive change in the 'childlike attachment' score but no change or negative change on the stoicism score. Older children find it increasingly easy to curb their 'childlike attachment' behaviour but increasingly difficult to be open about their emotions.

Conclusion

Children who were described as difficult or had learning and behavioural difficulties were, after allowing for age, less likely to be adopted. So too in the two to five age group were those who had weekly contact with a relative. However, in this sample the main determinant of whether a child is or is not adopted is his or her age.[9] If children are to be adopted this process basically has to be begun before they are six. That said, there are a small number of older children who have stayed a long time with the same carer and who would like to be adopted by them. In some but not all cases their carers would also like to adopt them. Encouragement of these adoptions – through, for example, continuing allowances and support – would have a small but noticeable affect on the number of children looked after (cf. recommendation in the Parker review, 1999).

The findings bring out the crucial nature of the decisions that are taken early in a child's care career. Social workers commonly tried to maintain family links through what used to be called trial at home or through placement with relatives. Where this happened subsequent to inclusion in our sample the child was, as far as our information went, never adopted.[10] This finding does not mean that trial at home should not be attempted. It does, however, emphasise the crucial nature of the decision that is being taken and the need for a clear-sighted assessment of the issues involved.

In general our findings were mildly favourable to adoption. Adopted children were 'doing better' on most of our outcome variables. In part this may have been because they were easier to start with. However, adoption seemed to have a genuine impact on the variable we have called 'childlike attachment'. It also seemed to have a positive one on our 'stoicism' variable. In this respect, however, it may well have been other variables – particularly the smaller average number of other children in adopting families – that had the good effect.

Carer adoptions tended to do rather 'better' than adoptions by strangers – a finding that replicates American research (Sellick and Thoburn 1996), although it may not hold when the children become older (Selwyn *et al.* 2003). As we have seen carer adoption is a plausible way of increasing the numbers adopted. Already they seem to be used for children who would otherwise be difficult to adopt.

Overall the findings reinforce the importance of two aspects of 'permanence'. First, moves between carers (the opposite of 'objective permanence') seemed to have a negative impact.[11] Second, it does seem that the 'symbols of family life' are important to the children. Adoption differs from foster care most obviously in its meaning – on a day-to-day basis it looks much the same. It is perhaps this difference in meaning which appeared to give it some better outcomes than foster care. This interpretation would fit with the importance some children attached to calling their carer 'mum' and the significance for some of family photographs.

In conclusion most fostered children do not want to be adopted. There is, however, probably scope for modestly increasing the number of adoptions, partly by encouraging carer adoptions. This could well be of benefit to the children themselves.

Notes

1. Thoburn and her colleagues (2000) give this as one of the three main 'challenges' of adoption. (The others are lack of a genetic link with family and the traumas that have often preceded adoption.) Thomas and her colleagues (1999) have explored the views of adopted children on this severe loss.

2. Given the high response rate we did not expect to find any significant differences between respondents and non-respondents and we found none. The term 'stranger adoptions' is usually used to mean adoptions by non-relatives. For convenience we use it for adoption by people other than foster carer.

3. Children of this age who return home typically spend a short time in the care system. Compared with those who stay longer they are thus less likely to be found in a 'cross-sectional' sample such as ours. In theory a foster home that took two children could fill one place with a particular child who stayed for a year. The other place could be filled with 52 different children, each of whom stayed for one week only. At any one time 50 per cent of the children in the home would be long stay. However, the proportion of long-stay children entering the home over the year would be 1/53.

4. We had only 27 questionnaires completed by social workers on children in this age group at sweep 1. However, the seven who were seen as entering because of 'an emergency in the community' provided five of those not subsequently adopted, whereas the remaining 20 provided only three.

5. Concerns about the effects of the emphasis on rehabilitation on the process and likelihood of adoption have recently been raised by Selwyn and her colleagues (2003) and by Ward and hers (forthcoming). The point is not that rehabilitation should not be tried with young children but rather that it is a risky business with implications for the availability of alternative plans, realistic support in the community, and the strict monitoring of progress (see also Sinclair 2005).

6. Tau b, an appropriate measure of association, is 0.47 which, while very highly significant, is far from being as high as it could be.

7. We explored the possibility that the moves occur for different reasons. Children can move within foster care for negative reasons e.g. because they may be considered 'difficult'. By contrast they move to adoption for positive ones. So it could be that our finding

reflects the reason for the move rather than the result of it. In practice we found little evidence for this hypothesis. The effect remained when we omitted children known to have had a disruption and those with any evidence of learning difficulties. An alternative hypothesis is that moves do have bad effects on education (e.g. because of changes of school) but that this is concealed by the educational support provided by 'stranger adoptions'. Carer adoptive parents by contrast may show no greater enthusiasm for education than other carers.

8. This hypothesis was based on work by Quinton *et al.* (1998) and Rushton *et al.* (2001).

9. The key comparative study is by Lowe and his colleagues (2002). They compared those children with plans for adoption with children with plans for long-term fostering. Like us they found that age was the key factor but that emotional difficulties and contact with parents probably also played a part in decisions over whether a child should be fostered or adopted. We did not find, as they did, that gender and abuse were related to the decision.

10. A number of children had been tried at home prior to inclusion in the sample but were nevertheless adopted. Trial at home therefore does not prevent adoption. It is, however, a fair inference that it delays the time when adoption is considered and makes adoption less likely.

11. It is possible that deterioration antedated and brought about the move rather than vice versa. Given the ages of the children this seems unlikely.

Chapter Six

Adoption: What Makes A Difference?

Yes, we did go to court – we went to the High Court, up in London, but to be honest with you, it was so horrendous that I can't remember – we seemed to be going backwards and forwards to court – and we had to hire a solicitor, which cost us a lot of money. (Former foster carer who adopted)

There is such a long…there seems to be so much delay, you know… And these are children's lives that are being postponed. (Adoptive parent)

I can't imagine life without them. I can't remember…and we've sat and talked about this, Simon and I have – do you know – the sad thing is we had 13 years where we spent our time trying for children. If we'd have known then what was going to happen, we could have enjoyed that 13 years, and done all sorts of things, instead of going through the IVF, and all sorts of grotty things like that, but I can't remember what our life was like before. I can't remember how we did things before. It's really funny! We must have had all this time before children! (Adoptive parent)

Introduction

As we have seen, the outcomes of adoption were comparatively, and for the moment at least,[1] good. Despite this, it is important that the process of adoption receives as much support as possible. This is partly because it is, as our case studies made clear, difficult. It is also true that delays and frustrations may put off some potential adopters and lead others to drop an application. For these reasons, it is vital that the adoption process is well supported. There is already a body of relevant UK research on this issue. Some important recent studies have been funded by the Department of Health and summarised in the Parker review (1999).

This chapter is intended as a contribution to this literature. It deals only with the children who were adopted. It aims to describe the process from the point of view of the parents. Where possible it relates differences in process to differences in outcomes. In most cases we found no differences of this kind. We only mention them when we did. Many of our findings are similar to those of others and we make relevant comparisons at the end.

Waits and delays

Adoptive parents have to face four waits. First, they have to apply, go through the selection process and be approved by a panel. Second, they have to be matched with a child who is to be placed with them. Third, they have to wait until the child is placed. Fourth, they have to wait until the placement is made legally final. As will be seen, our sample expressed considerable dissatisfaction with the length of time all this took. One couple said the process took five years.

We only asked in detail about two of the potential delays – that from approval to identification of a child and that from identification to placement.

On average adopters waited around seven months from the time they were approved as adopters to being matched with a child in our sample. The range, however, was quite considerable with some adopters waiting no time at all as the child was already with them while one waited for three years.

> We cannot believe that with so many children waiting for adoption it took three years to find us suitable children. Although we were considered for some child-minding this time, it seemed we were ruled out quite quickly but we were not informed one way or the other and our papers then seemed to slumber in the offices of the relevant social workers and (since original files were always used) this meant our papers could not be circulated to other social services departments. Also some of the social workers we met were very reluctant to answer our questions regarding the children they represented. However, when we eventually were linked to two children we ultimately adopted, both our social worker and theirs were helpful. The treatment we had received up to that point must make many couples lose interest in the whole process.

Most adopters waited for a much shorter time than this. Three-quarters (72%) waited for less than seven months. There was a tendency for adopters who had waited for over six months to have rather more disturbed children but the differences were not significant. The period from identification to the arrival of the child was shorter – on average 2.45 months, although in one case ten months – and quite unrelated to any of our measures.

We asked the parents whether the time was too long, too short or about right. Two-thirds of those replying felt that it took too long. Only one parent thought it was too short (in this case the time from approval to placement was only three months). On average those who thought the time too long had waited ten months from approval to the child's arrival. Those who thought the time about right waited only six – a difference in the predicted direction but not actually significant.

> My daughter was placed with me in 1998. I applied to adopt her in 1999. I am still [2001] in the courts going through this process. Her social worker went off long-term sick. [The] social services did not feel it was a priority to get her schedule two report completed. I was told this when I phoned after being advised that the courts had already made two requests for this report. Once the allocated social worker returned it took another six months for a report requested on her birth parents to be completed. Her birth parents, having initially agreed to the adoption, then decided to actively contest the adoption. It then took longer for the Guardian to complete her report.

Support over the adoption process

The adopters reported that most of those closely involved with the adoption process were helpful to them. Eighty-six per cent thought this was true of their own social workers, 75 per cent that it was true of the children's social workers and 61 per cent that it was true of the foster carers. In 20 per cent of the cases they had no contact with the foster carers and in 70 per cent of the cases they had no contact with the birth family (in the remaining cases the birth families were more likely to be seen as helpful [12%] than unhelpful [5%]). The only sizeable volume of complaint related to the children's social workers who were seen as unhelpful on the whole by 18 per cent of the adopters.

Few of the adopters thought the process was managed badly by the agency (5%) or very badly (11%). Many (41%) thought there were good and bad points but even more thought it was managed well (16%) or very well

(27%). In general the main negative comments were about delay and about the factors thought to contribute to this – lack of liaison between departments, delay in completing forms, social worker sickness, a lack of diligence on the part of social workers, a lack of concern with the child and an excessive desire to propitiate birth families.

Other comments dealt with lack of information. Positive comments were at least as frequent and covered similar ground but in a much shorter fashion:

> All the agencies and carers liaised well with each other and were practical when it came to making arrangements, never losing sight that 'the child' was their primary consideration.

> Own social worker was very supportive and very thorough. Our child's social worker was also the same and was very concerned and interested for the child's well-being. We have nothing but praise for them both.

There seemed to be diverse opinions over whether or not foster carers were hindered from adopting. One of those commenting thought they were.

> I think in general the decisions made by social workers' managers are not in the best interest of the child e.g. too much concern for birth family and not enough for child. Even after how long child placed and settled social worker managers are very anti-foster carers adopting – it usually only happens when social workers think nowhere else will be found because of birth family problems (health – mental/history of sex offence).

Another who was not adopting a fostered child had a very different experience:

> I had been fostering for seven years and had been assessed and supported by the same worker throughout and therefore the assessment process went smoothly as she knew our family and our capabilities. A child had been identified at the time we were approved and introductions were arranged very quickly.

Box 6.1

Adoptive parents in the case studies reported contrasting experiences with foster carers. One parent had adopted three children. Her experience with the child in our sample was good.

> We were only meant to be there an hour and a half, and we ended up staying there forever – we were spending the night! They fed

and watered us, and…and she was really nice and open, and everything about Katherine, we knew. And it was all very relaxed with Veronica.

She contrasted this with what happened with the siblings.

Unfortunately it wasn't the same with the other ones. We were never welcome in their house, and at the end, it was very difficult. They'd…she'd never…when we went there, she'd never not had Julie on her lap. The last day, when we went to pick them up, Julie was sat on the floor, and she was pushing her away, and saying, 'no, you're not my baby any more, you're not my baby.' So Julie was upset…

The problems of the handover were exacerbated by the collection of a large crowd of relatives to witness the event and then by lack of detailed knowledge about the children:

…when we actually took them home, it was awful…and we didn't know anything about them, really, so…it was only when we got them here, and I was trying feed Julie, and Andrew said, 'she doesn't eat that', so I said, 'well, what does she eat, then?' He said, 'Barbara mixes it with water', so I couldn't really understand what they were talking about, and we went shopping, and he pointed to the [unclear] packet food, and he said, 'that's what she eats'. And she was two and a half, nearly three, then. So she'd…that was what she was eating, and I didn't know she didn't sleep in a bed. As far as they told me, she had her own bed, but she didn't, she had a cot, so when she came back here, the first night of being in a bed, she was hysterical.

Settling in

Only one parent said they had no expectations of how difficult the settling in process would be. Of the remainder a quarter (26%) said that it was more difficult and a quarter that it was less difficult than expected. Just under a half (46%) said that it was much as expected.

Unsurprisingly children with high childlike attachment scores had carers who found the process of settling in more difficult ($r=0.42$, $p<.001$) as did children with high total Goodman scores ($r=0.35$, $p=0.006$). More surprisingly difficulty was not associated with the number of children in the home, whether the child had siblings or whether the siblings were also adopted.

In general the adoptive parents said that the child was as they had been led to expect. Differences were either that the child's difficulties had been misinterpreted – for example, that behavioural difficulties had been misinterpreted as learning ones – or that difficulties had been underplayed. Occasionally the parents complained that the description was more negative than the child justified or that they were told about the history not the child. Sometimes the result was that the child flourished despite an apparently gloomy prognosis:

> When Stephen came he was quite a distressed child with quite marked behavioural problems and a degree of developmental delay. We were told his language was slightly behind. Now he is a very bright, able child.

At other times the parents undoubtedly felt they had been misled:

> We did not appreciate that her hearing and language skills were as underdeveloped as they were or that her behavioural difficulties were as acute.

Overall a quarter of the parents said they had been misled to some extent and a further 8 per cent that they had been misled. This measure was correlated with our measure of family exclusion ($r=0.43$, $p<.001$).

Support once the child had been adopted

Support, as the adoptive parents perceived it, came mostly from relatives and friends. Two-thirds stated that they received 'a lot of support' from family members and four out of ten that they did so from friends. No more than one in nine said that they received as much from neighbours (9%), social workers (9%), adoption workers (11%) or other professionals (4%).

We asked what support they got which was particularly helpful or unhelpful. One reply picked up a number of themes which occurred elsewhere:

> Friends babysitting. Coming on days out. Visits to family where cooking done for us. Our social worker. Helpful post groups in technical process of adoption matters to some extent. Visits by child's social worker – lovely girl but did nothing – very worrying as they work in [sic] for hours. Very unstructured – didn't know what they were looking for. She went off work ill for a while and then came back and told us to ignore the team leader and trust our own judgement – which was the best advice we ever got. No problems with child's problems when placed.

This reply is typical in a number of ways. Many replies picked out the importance of family and friends and the pleasantness of the social workers or adoption workers concerned. However, they also noted that they wanted support from these workers at the times they wanted it and to be of a kind they wanted. The fact that parents felt they could call when needed was appreciated. Some also objected to the lack of apparent structure and purpose in some social work interviews.

Box 6.2

In the case studies attachment issues were as pervasive in adoption as elsewhere. One mother found the initial enthusiasm and clinging unnerving.

> ...you assume you're going to bond instantly. You know, it's like a baby, really, and you don't, and it does take a while, and it takes a while to get used to them, and the other side of it is actually, from friends who've also done it, is that the children are far more affectionate, and will throw everything into it, and tell you they love you a hundred times a day from day one, and actually, that's quite difficult, because you know, you've built yourself up for, 'what if they don't like us?', and they're claiming undying love, and actually you haven't really got to know them, and don't even know if you like them, let alone love them. (Adoptive parent)

This enthusiasm could also be combined with caution and uneasiness away from home.

> She was very bubbly, but had a real nervous giggle, but then there was the down side. She just tried to please everybody. She wasn't particularly keen on women, and she gave me a wide berth. Took to my husband, and went to sit on his lap, but she was quite emotional...she was quite secure while she was here at home, but as soon as we went out, even if it was just for a walk, or anything, she would just curl up, just go within herself. (Foster carer who went on to adopt)

Children were rivalrous of each other, feeling perhaps that if one child was loved they themselves would miss out.

> There was quite a lot of rivalry between Julie and Katherine in the beginning. Mainly from Julie. Julie was quite good at getting in between whoever...if she thought she was not getting the attention, she'd get in between...she'd get in between me and Simon, and get in between me and whoever had...whatever child I was talking to at the time, and she was quite good at that, and also she was making herself sick on a regular basis. (Adoptive parent)

Frequent unrequested visits from social workers or health visitors could be experienced as undermining. One commented:

> Health visitors/school nurses don't have the experience of adopted children and don't accept that parents should be left to ask for help if it is needed rather than spot balling a child because they are adopted and with some emotional delays.

Others were grateful for availability without intrusion:

> Level of social worker input was about right. Would have liked life book a bit earlier, not a major issue given age of child. Helpful to know we can telephone adoption agency at any time if needed.

Practical advice on how to handle difficult behaviour was appreciated when it was asked for as was the prompt delivery of life story books and a sense that social workers were professionals whose activities had a rationale. Absence of these things was also criticised.

> I have received the best advice/support from playgroup/nursery teachers and also from friends who have children. Also our social worker has been very supportive and had taken time to assess our daughter's behavioural difficulties and recommend coping techniques.

> Pre-adoption – too frequent visits by his social worker – visits lasted hours with no structure – not told what they wanted. However have had to drag life story book [out of them]… No practical help e.g. with his behaviour or [assessment of] his delayed learning and development. In fact this was angrily denied as any comment taken as a criticism of care provided pre-arrival here. Most help from friends – babysitting, helping on days out, etc.

Other kinds of help were variously appraised. Some parents found groups for adopters helpful as showing they were not alone, some that there could have been more encouragement for groups to continue and some feeling that groups were used by 'moaners' and they did not want to attend them. Other workers, individuals or provisions singled out for praise or blame included schools, educational psychologists, special neighbours, adoption allowances (or lack of them), foster carers (praised for friendly support or criticised for possessiveness) and information (or lack of it).

The perceived level of support was related to the number of foster, adopted or natural children the adoptive parent had living with them. The greater the number of children (particularly adopted or natural children) the less the level of support from any source (family $p=0.001$, friends $p=0.009$, neighbours $p=0.082$, social workers $p=0.097$, adoption workers $p=0.004$, or other professionals $p=0.019$). Arguably parents with other children are either seen as experienced and offered less support or feel experienced and ask for less of it. There is evidence, to some extent in this report, but more strongly in Quinton and his colleagues' study, that the presence of other unrelated children makes it more difficult for children to settle (Quinton *et al.* 1998).[2] If so, the trend for such families to receive less support is unfortunate.

Subjectively the level of support received is undoubtedly important to parents. Whether it affects the adopted children is less clear. The parents of children with high childlike attachment scores or high Goodman scores perceived significantly less support from 'other professionals'. This, however, does not necessarily mean that the level of support was affecting Goodman score. Other professionals are presumably more likely to be involved when the child is difficult. It is unlikely, if not impossible, that support from them is making the child difficult.

The same parents perceived significantly less support from family and friends. The direction of cause and effect is more difficult to determine in this case. It could be that difficult children alienate family, that the persistence of difficulties raises expectation of family support and makes offers of support appear less adequate, or that the lack of support itself makes the parent handle the child less well. One way of handling these uncertainties is to examine those cases where we had childlike attachment and total Goodman scores from the foster carers prior to the adoption. High difficulty on both scores was positively related to lack of support from family but not significantly so. However, if we took previous level of difficulty into account a high level of family support was positively related to positive change on both the total Goodman score ($p=0.004$) and the childlike attachment score ($p=0.023$).

This analysis is still not conclusive. First, the number of cases is very small (18 for childlike attachment and 15 for the total difficulties) and conclusions are therefore vulnerable to the effects of exceptional cases. Second, even if the association is genuine the direction of cause and effect is unclear. It could be explained on the grounds that it is the persistence of (say) childlike attachment difficulties which causes families to withdraw support rather than vice versa. Support from families may well lessen the likelihood of difficulties but also be reduced by difficulties.

Box 6.3

The parents in the case studies reinforced the qualitative comments in questionnaires. They testified to the importance of a wide range of support from friends and relatives, of discussion with other adopters (not necessarily in groups), and of the occasional helpful input from professionals, such as psychologists. Social workers were seen as helpful before the adoption (although some of the procedures were seen as rigid and bizarre) but after adoption were rarely seen. There was also the difficulty of speaking honestly to professionals who had power and were in a position to pass judgement.

> I think there is a big feeling of not wanting to fail. And that anything you say will be seen as failure. Or that if you…you know, that sometimes you can say something about a partner, or brother, or whoever, and that's fine, but for somebody else to say it, it's not OK, so you know, there were times that we felt like saying, 'oh, we can't stand it, we've got to give them back', but we'd never dream of saying that to a social worker, even if we'd had a really awful time, in case it was taken the wrong way, and actually they thought we meant it. (Adoptive parent)

Overall nearly a quarter of the parents (23%) expressed themselves very satisfied with the support they received from all sources. Nearly six out of ten (55%) said they were satisfied. Fourteen per cent said they were dissatisfied and hardly anyone that they were very dissatisfied (3%) or not in need of support at all (5%). Ignoring the latter group parents tended to be more satisfied when the total Goodman score at sweep 3 was low ($r=0.27$, $p=0.032$) and (where the score could be computed) there was more positive change on the total Goodman score ($r=0.55$, $p=0.028$). So parents who had weathered the storm may well have been grateful for support in difficult times or seen it as actually contributing to change.

Contact with birth families

Exactly half the families said that there was some form of contact with birth families. There was no significant difference in this respect between stranger and foster carer adoptions. Eighty-three per cent of the parents where there was some form of contact were satisfied with the situation over it. So too were 89 per cent of those where there was no contact.

Among those where there was some contact the relatives involved were, in order of frequency, mothers (57%), siblings (51%), grandparents (30%), fathers (14%) and other members of the family (8%). The low level of contact with the last two groups is perhaps worth further investigation. Some of the potential benefits of contact might be available through aunts or cousins and the father's as well as the mother's side of the family.

We asked whether contact was face to face, by telephone, by letter or by 'postbox'. Overall 12 out of the 37 had postbox contact only. Ten of these 12 involved contact with birth mothers (including in two cases birth fathers). The remaining two had contact with a sibling in one case and a grandparent in another. Contact was invariably 'once or twice a year'.

At the other extreme 19 adopted children had face-to-face contact. Seven of these cases also involved postbox contact and we were not able to distinguish which members of the family were involved in which kind of contact. Thirteen of the 19 cases involved no more than contact once or twice a year. In two cases, however, face-to-face contact was monthly and in four it was more frequent than that. Four of these cases seemed to involve contact with the mother and two contact with grandparents.

In the remaining six cases where there was contact this involved letters, telephone or a combination of the two. Three of the six had contact with siblings, one with a father, one with a mother and one with a grandparent.

It would not perhaps be expected that this level of contact would have a detectable effect on the psychological status of the children. We ourselves were certainly not able to find any. As we have seen, most of the adoptive parents found the level of contact comfortable to themselves. Consistently with this most did not comment when given the opportunity to do so. Those that did comment picked up themes similar to those identified by foster carers. Some commented on the unreliability of some birth parents and its impact on the children:

> Contact is hit and miss on birth parents' side and children seem nonplussed when they do not receive a card/letter.

> Because of the good bonding between child and birth mum we supported 'open adoption'. We would have been happy to have face-to-face contact three or four times a year. Birth mum stopped contact before the adoption and went months not ringing them, then would ring several times a week. Child became confused. Now we have twice weekly letterbox contact and a few calls.

Box 6.4

Adoptive parents generally demanded reasonable behaviour. Being adopted was not an excuse. Nevertheless they tried to distinguish 'ordinary naughtiness' from disturbed behaviour. There were two additional problems. First, difficult behaviour was naturally effective at attracting attention and anxious concern that the children may have wanted. Second, some behaviour (for example, refusal to go to school) may have been partly prompted by insecurity and a fear of rejection. Somehow the carers had to ensure that the behaviour stopped without increasing the fear of rejection that might lie behind it. Generally they found that difficult behaviour did reduce as the children became more settled and learnt what was expected. Some carers and parents also reported intuitive but successful responses.

> ...[she] had a wolf, imaginary, that lived in this house, and if anything was done to Melanie, it was the wolf, and I asked the psychiatrist for help with this, and he told me it was the wolf within the child, and I said...[tape cuts out] ...wait any longer, because this wolf was pushing Melanie down the stairs, and pinching her all over, so I said to Ellie one morning, 'I've had enough of this wolf living in my house – we're going to get rid of him today, we're going to open the door, and we're going to shoo him out into the street, and we're going to shut the door quickly, and he's not coming back any more.' And we did that...[tape cuts out] ...it was as simple as that, and yet, you know, the psychiatrist didn't unravel it that way. (Foster carer)

> ...she asked me what I was doing, and I said, 'I'm cooking my dinner', and she said, 'I'm hungry', and I said, 'well, I'm really sorry, but I've not cooked you anything.' And she looked at me strangely, and I said, 'well, you don't eat it, so I'm not going to cook for you any more', and I didn't... She was just sat there, and she said, 'but I'm hungry', and I said, 'OK, you can have something', and I put her a bit on the table...and it was like I had taken her power away, she then didn't have me over a barrel. I wasn't saying, 'oh, darling, you've got to eat, you've got to eat'...now – she eats for her country! [laughs] (Adoptive parent)

So they combined empathy with inclusion rather than rejection and control, as it were cuddling the child while restraining them (an approach that also worked well on occasion).

Others noted the need to distinguish between the impacts of different members of the family (contact with siblings and grandparents seemed less threatening):

> I think it is in the child's interest to see his Nana and for this reason she comes about every five weeks at my request. However, I am seriously considering stopping birth mother contact as she always upsets our son and he doesn't like contact with her.

Box 6.5

In the case studies contact with birth families was not problematic for the adoptive parents. Where it was, it was terminated. Two families had friendly contact with relatives of the child but not the parents. The two others had effectively no contact at all. Few difficulties were reported. One commented on an inappropriate letter from the children's father beginning 'Hi sexy girls'. Another found that relatives tended to remember the child as younger than he or she was and respond to them accordingly. There was also a difficulty that relatives could inform children of events which they did not remember and which were upsetting for them. One adoptive family changed their telephone number to avoid troublesome telephone calls from a grandmother.

> And on a selfish side, if ever we need to know anything, we've still got contact through them, so that, you know, if anything medical ever came up, we'd still get answers. And it's never been a problem. If they'd been the sort of people that had interfered, or, you know, caused trouble, or whatever, I think we would have stopped it, but they never have. They've always been really good. (Adoptive parent on contact with relatives)

Additional points related to the difficulty of arranging contact with siblings, the wish of a small number of adoptive parents to meet the birth parents, and the perception of the adoptive parents that many of the children were too young to be much concerned about contact.

Contact with foster carers

The literature on social work contains frequent reference to the importance of family ties to children who are looked after by other people. Much less is made of the potential impact of ties with foster carers. Nevertheless in many cases a child will have spent more time with particular foster carers than in their own family. Their relationships with these carers are real and potentially important. For these reasons we asked the adoptive parents about them.

Twenty of the adoptive parents answering our questionnaires were themselves the former foster carers. The remainder generally, but by no means universally, had a favourable view of fostering. Over half (57%) agreed that the child had got a lot out of fostering and 81 per cent that the carers gave them useful information. Nevertheless nearly a fifth felt that the child had not benefited much from fostering, a fifth did not know, and a sixth stated that the carers had given no useful information.

We asked the parents if the children had contact with the foster carers. In two cases the adoption was too recent for any pattern of contact to be established. Half the remainder never saw their former foster carers. To judge from the comments in questionnaires the reasons were various. Some adoptive parents saw contact as potentially disruptive:

> Contact ceased from the time that our daughter was placed with us, although I write to the foster carers regularly. I think any other arrangement would have led to confusion and disruption.

Others felt that the child was too young for contact with former foster carers to be relevant:

> The child was with foster carers as a baby (nought to nine months) so continuing contact not relevant.

Others, while not necessarily opposed to contact *per se*, felt that with the particular foster carers involved it would not be appropriate:

> Her former foster mum was a bit possessive – keep on writing letters and sending presents at the very beginning of the adoption stage. Fortunately, our social worker has stopped all these.

In other cases there were practical problems of distance, the child did not appear to want contact, or the foster carers themselves were reluctant to continue it:

Box 6.6

Two of our case studies involved carers who had begun by fostering the child. In one of the other cases the parent had a good relationship with the previous foster carer of one of the children, but very little with the one who had fostered the other two. The main reason was the difference in the way the children reacted to their former carers.

> And that's...you know, it's never, 'oh, we're going to see Katherine's foster carer'. It's, 'we're going to see Veronica', and that's how they look at it, and it's...you know, Katherine knows she used to live with Veronica, but in her mind, that's how everybody carries on.

> Yeah. Whereas Andrew never wanted to go back and see them [carers]. We did say – we actually got to, well, just round the corner, and he was hysterical, 'I don't want to go, I don't want to go – please don't take me in there'... He doesn't want them to have a picture of him, and he's always said this, right from the beginning: 'I don't want to see them.'

In the other case the foster carer had been quite clear she could not keep the girls for financial reasons but they had been with her for two years and bonded with her. She described a traumatic parting:

> Melanie screamed and cried and went like that with her hands, 'mummy, mummy', and I had to walk out, and it was awful, and Ellie ran behind us, and said 'when are we going to see you again' [tape cuts out] and I had to say, 'I don't know' [tape cuts out] but that was really traumatic, because, you know, I could hear that child screaming, 'mummy, mummy!' in my ears.

Understandably the adoptive parents followed a more usual pattern, tailoring off contact while maintaining good relations.

> The couple that fostered the child were not, I consider, very good foster parents and showed no great interest in keeping in touch. I have been sending a Christmas card with a brief note.

Nearly four out of ten (38%) of the 'stranger adopters' saw the carers 'once or twice a year'. Commonly this seemed a 'level' that was achieved as the child settled in the adoptive family, felt secure and 'moved on'. Contact was then continued at a low level because it was pleasant, the foster carers remained interested and it was thought to give more meaning to the 'life story book':

> Initially the child had contact with the foster carers, mainly through me inviting them to our house. Three years on, however, this has dropped off as the child has such a full life and has 'moved on' and doesn't request any contact now.

Some adoptive parents kept the level of contact low because it was seen as being upsetting for the child:

> We see the foster carers on an informal/unplanned basis which does not threaten child as he still feels uncomfortable and ill at ease that he might have to go back to his foster carers. They keep in touch with birthday and Christmas cards.

In the remaining 12 per cent of stranger adoptions contact was more frequent – monthly (4%) or more often still (8%). Unsurprisingly in the cases where contact was frequent the carers were seen to have made the initial contacts easy and to have benefited the child. These continuing contacts were invariably pleasant, if not necessarily seen as particularly significant:

> The child's foster carers are now family friends and we visit on a regular basis, but we do not live in each other's pockets.

In a small number of cases, however, the foster carers seemed to play more significant roles:

> The foster carers were brilliant and have become family friends and Auntie and Uncle to all my children. We see them at least once a week. My daughter is aware that she used to live with them and loves to hear about what she used to do there.

A small number of children (12%) were said to miss their foster carers. We had expected associations between this perception and the age of the child at sweep 1 and the length of time they had then spent in this placement. We did not find them. However, children who missed their former foster carers were significantly more disturbed.[3] This association need not necessarily be a causal one. Nevertheless some parents felt that the lack of contact was upsetting for their children:

> The foster carers became impatient with our child's need to talk to them occasionally for about a year (reducing over time). Our child was very disappointed not to receive a present from her foster carers only four months after she had left. (This needn't have had much monetary value – it was seen as a withdrawal of love.)

One parent perhaps implied that children reacted to the rupture of previous placements by a stoical withdrawal from emotional investment:

> Child had many foster carers and one adoption placement that broke down. He does not appear to miss anyone.

In keeping with this quotation the less the adopted children saw of their former foster carers the higher their stoicism score ($r=0.39$, $p=0.015$). This finding could have many explanations.[4] It is, however, possible that the association is one of cause and effect. Some European countries use residential care for very young children prior to adoption. The reason is that they think it harmful to allow the child to form attachments and then break them. The issue of whether children should at least be reassured by occasional visits of their former carers' continuing concern is therefore an important one.

One parent clearly thought that at least some contact was beneficial:

> This was a critical part of his settling with us. We too benefited. He was over two when he was placed with us and he was afforded and still is afforded what we see as the essential assurance that his foster family still love him. We could see it was hard for them but they could see it was in his best interests. If you are in a position to influence policy, please promote continued contact for at least several months – children need to know that they are still loved by the families they love. We believe it makes it easier for them to make the transition.

One parent who had adopted a number of children commented:

> We have a good relationship with foster mum, but not with our other foster carers of other adopted children – which is a shame – contact is very useful.

In the absence of further evidence this may well be the most balanced position. Clearly many children do settle well in adoptive placements without any contact with their former carers. A small number benefit because the carers become family friends. This depends on location and a high degree of compatibility between the families. There seems no reason to discourage it but it can hardly become the basis for policy. Many children may be best served by a tailing off of contact which acts as a reassurance until they 'move on'. In promoting this it should, however, be realised that contact can be very difficult and distressing for any or all of the three parties involved. It should probably not be 'forced' or continued when it is apparently doing harm.

Conclusion

The process of adoption is not an easy one for the new parents. It involves delay, frustration, a process of being assessed and judged, a continued anxiety that they may not get what they want, and the shock of being suddenly responsible for a new and often frightened or difficult human being. These difficulties may be compounded by a lack, as they see it, of accurate information about the child, difficulties in asking for support for fear of being found wanting, and, on occasion, difficult handovers from foster carers.

Despite these problems we found few associations with our outcome measures. They were not, for example, affected by greater or less delay. More importantly, and despite the drawbacks of the process, the vast majority of adoptive parents clearly found the effort worthwhile.

The issues listed above are familiar in the literature. All are found within the Parker review (1999). There are a number of points where our work either strengthens or adds to their conclusions.

First, there is the importance of external support from friends. As the Parker review comments this was valued by adopters. Difficulties were associated with lower levels of informal support, a conclusion also reached by Parker. Perhaps friends and family were frightened off by troublesome children. However, we had some evidence that informal support may help adopters reduce attachment difficulties in the children. This suggests that the strength of support networks should form a key element in the assessment of adopters.

Second, our findings on social work support were very similar to those reported by Parker. These included the generally high levels of appreciation of social workers, the difficulty in asking for social work support, the evidence that it and other professional support was concentrated on the most difficult children, and the lack of evidence that it did any good. Two conclusions might be drawn from this. First, it may not be wise to assume that adopters should go to social services for support over the psychological and emotional problems of their children. They might find it easier to go elsewhere and ways should be found of making this easy. Second, it is not clear that any particular group of professionals has the answer to these problems. Since the need is apparent, there is a danger of supplying support which does no good. Further research and development in this area would seem to be necessary.

Third, we confirmed the evidence on the potentially problematic but in practice probably benign effects of contact with parents. Parker concluded among other things that a high proportion of children had some form of contact; that contact was not legally forced on adoptive parents who did not want it, although some parents might feel that adoption was conditional on contact; that the level and nature of contact was extremely varied – far too varied for any simple assessment of its effects; that it was important to distinguish between contact with different family members; that contact raised a large number of potentially difficult problems and issues; but that in practice contact seemed to do little damage and some good. All of this would be borne out in our study. The crucial point seemed to be that the level of contact was typically low and that if it was thought to threaten the placement the adoptive parents seemed able to stop it. Evidence from elsewhere in our study suggests that contact could be highly damaging. The caution with which the issue seems to be being approached therefore seems appropriate.

Fourth, our evidence would support Parker's views on the potential importance of contact with foster carers and the reasons why this does not always take place. Thomas and her colleagues (1999) found that many children wanted contact with former foster carers. Perhaps the main conclusion of the chapter is that contact with former foster carers is at least as important as contact with birth parents. The children had often spent longer with these carers than with their own parents. They had bonded with them and missed them. Children who had less contact with their former foster carers showed more symptoms of stoicism. This raises again the issue of handling such difficulties and of the role of gradually tapered foster carer contact in assuaging them.

For the rest the chapter gives evidence of much good practice and of the scope for more.

Summary of Chapters 5 and 6

1. Adopted children do 'better' on a number of criteria than those who go to other destinations. Carer adoptions may do particularly well, at least in the short run.

2. The scope for increasing adoption is limited by age and the views of carers, social workers and children. Nevertheless greater decisiveness when young children are first fostered, a more positive attitude to carer adoptions and attention to the barriers to adoption would probably increase the number of adoptions to a limited extent.

3.   There is also scope for improving the process of adoption through attention to the suggestions of adoptive parents, the process of handover by foster carers and subsequent contact with foster carers.

Notes

1.   There is evidence that breakdowns are more likely among late adoptions, particularly teenagers (Fratter *et al.* 1991; Thoburn *et al.* 2000), and even early adoptions may face difficulties in the teenage years. None of our adoptees was adopted in their teens and only one had reached over the age of 11.

2.   Unlike other researchers we did not find that the presence of birth children made placements more likely to fail (Sinclair, Wilson and Gibbs 2004). Rushton and his colleagues similarly failed to replicate these earlier findings (Rushton *et al.* 2001). The reasons for the contradictory findings in this area are still obscure.

3.   There were three possible values for 'misses carers': 'yes' (1), 'don't know' (2), 'no' (3). Overall 'Anova' with the Goodman score as dependent variable is significant ($p=0.028$). The mean square can be divided to show a significant linear trend ($p=0.008$) and also deviation from linearity ($p=0.05$).

4.   Possible explanations of the effects of visiting on stoicism include the following. Visiting could reduce 'stoicism'. The less stoical children might miss their carers, ask for visits and get them. Less stoical children might be more attractive to their carers who would therefore seek contact. Carers who were more loving or child-oriented might produce less stoical children and be more likely to visit them. We tried to test some of these hypotheses by holding steady: 'child misses carers', Goodman score (proxy for attractiveness) (sweep 3), carers saying they were fond of child (sweep 1) and the child orientation score (sweep 1). Correlations with sweep 3 variables held constant were significant; those with sweep 2 variables held constant were of similar size but of lower significance because of smaller numbers. If, for example, child difficulty had been responsible both for a low level of visiting and for lack of change in stoicism, holding the relevant variable steady should have reduced the association between change and visiting. So as far as we could test, the effect of visiting seemed to be a real one.

Chapter Seven

Foster Care: Can It Offer 'Permanence'?

Yeah. I mean, I always knew I couldn't go home, but I didn't kind of think that I'd be in care this long. But I also didn't think I'd be back with my mum. That's kind of strange. (Foster child)

Introduction

As we have seen, adoption provides a satisfactory placement from foster care. It is, however, in effect, if not in law, only available for the very young. Other possible placements are provided by a return to the birth family, residential care, and independent living. In this study social workers and foster carers tend to regard all of these with grave suspicion. This lack of 'satisfactory exits' faces foster care with a dilemma. It is not conceived as a method of treatment – something which will enable a child to change so that he or she can better survive the rigours of what awaits them. On the other hand it does not appear to provide a long-term alternative way of life.

The question is what kind of permanence does foster care provide? Some studies assume that long-stay fostering is essentially similar to adoption. Its breakdown rates are similar (Fratter *et al.* 1991; Thoburn *et al.* 2000). It may be experienced as offering permanence and it is this subjective feeling that is important (Lahti 1982). It may even be that if foster children can be per-suaded and supported to stay on in foster care after 18 they will do as well. However, there remains the question of whether these possibilities are realised; of how far foster care is in effect a temporary refuge, a port in a storm rather than a family for life (Thoburn *et al.* 2000). This is the issue with which the next two chapters are concerned.

In this chapter we consider the role of foster care itself. We ask the following questions:

- How far and for whom does foster care provide 'objective permanence'?
- How far does it provide 'subjective permanence' (a sense of belonging)?
- Is there scope for increasing these different kinds of permanence (e.g. through residence orders or enabling children to stay beyond 18)?

Method

In the main we use the methods and measures introduced in earlier chapters. We do, however, make much greater use of the questionnaires returned by the children. We had 126 of these questionnaires, a response rate of 54 per cent.

The key determinant of response rate was local authority. In one authority we had a 75 per cent response rate from 55 potential respondents. In another authority only 26 per cent of a potential 46 respondents replied. The 'low return' authority decided to deliver the questionnaires through the social workers while the others delivered theirs through the foster carers and this probably accounted for its unusually low response rate.

A second major difference (and difficulty with using postal questionnaires) between those responding relates to 'learning and behavioural difficulties'. The response rate among those with no such difficulties was 62 per cent. Among those whose difficulties were 'mild' it was 64 per cent. Among those whose difficulties were severe it was 33 per cent. In addition, the latter group will often have required help to complete their questionnaires so that their responses are also more suspect than those of others.

In other respects those responding and those not responding did not differ much. Compared with non-respondents, respondents were on average as old, as likely to be female, as disturbed (on the Goodman score), as likely to come from a minority ethnic group, and as likely to have experienced a disruption. The only differences we could find were that they were likely to have:

- lower childlike attachment scores at sweep 1 ($p=0.039$) but not at sweep 3

- lower stoicism scores at sweep 1 (p=0.008) but not at sweep 3
- more child-oriented carers at sweep 1 (p=0.052) but not at sweep 3.

These variables were not strongly related to the way those who did return their questionnaires answered the questions. Those with low childlike attachment scores at sweep 1 were significantly less likely to say that they had a choice over their placement or that they met their foster carer before arrival. In other ways their responses did not differ. The only difference in the replies of those with low stoicism scores at sweep 3 and others was that they were less likely to say they had changed schools.

We could find no difference between the replies in either the highest or lowest response rate authorities and those in the others. The presence of learning difficulties seemed to make children less likely to acknowledge that they missed their parents. Their replies were otherwise similar to the rest.

In general, therefore, the reliability and validity of the replies does not seem to be affected by response rate bias to a significant extent.

How far did foster care provide 'objective' permanence?

In a cross-section of foster children those who have stayed for a long time in the same placement are in a minority. In 1998 only 18 per cent of our sample were in one that had lasted for longer than three years. As we have seen, in 2001 a quarter (24%) of the sample were fostered by the foster carer they had had in 1998. An additional 4 per cent were adopted by the same carer. Around three-quarters of the sample had therefore had a change of placement in the last three years.

As we saw in Chapter 2, the main determinant of 'not staying put' was age. Only 8 out of 106 children aged less than four were still with their index carer. This movement reflects the determination to get these children back with their birth parents or adopted. At the other end of the age range children were equally unlikely to stay with their foster carers when they were aged 15 or over. Only 13 out of 134 aged 15 or over in 1998 were, as far as we could ascertain, still with their foster carers in 2001.

It follows that if foster care offers 'objective permanence' it does so only to a limited extent. In our sample it really offered it only to those aged between 4 and 14 in 1998. Within this restricted group a rather more impressive 38 per cent were still with their index carer while 24 per cent were with a new one. A further 6 per cent had achieved 'objective permanence' with an adoptive parent.[1] These figures, however, need to be further sub-divided by age.

Box 7.1

Mary was two when she came into the sample and five at sweep 3. She could be described as having 'permanent fostering', differing from others who were adopted only in the extent of her impairments. These were severe. She could not walk, was for a long time thought to be totally blind and had only one word, 'mummy'. Her behavioural symptoms – banging her head and poking her eyes – were severe and distressing. Her mother was 14 at the time of her birth and a short-break placement at seven months rapidly led to a long-term one. The foster carer described the process from her side, 'I got the bug, and I just loved her, you know, she's just great...' This initial bonding led to a request to adopt. However:

> ...my link worker actually said to me, 'Don't do that – long-term foster her, because she's going to need so much stuff, you'd be better off to long-term foster her.' (Mary's foster carer)

This made no difference to the carer or others' view of the situation or to future plans:

> I don't think of her any other way than as my daughter. And I mean most people call me mum – I mean, doctors call me mum...all right, we foster her until she's 18, 19, and then what?...she's staying here, basically. I mean, they're not going to take her away from us and put her into a residential home, or whatever – when she gets bigger, she's going to be hard work – she'll be heavy. I do realise that, and that I'll have to change dirty nappies when she's 20...it makes no difference...

The carer was very happy with both the school ('It's such a small school that it seems that every teacher knows every child') and the relationship with the birth family:

> I always...let mum know that she's gone to hospital, things like that... But no, she hasn't seen her for about 18 months. I think they're just getting on with their own lives, really...they [extended family] can come any time they like. Just phone up and make sure I'm going to be in...they all come round, yeah...they're a really lovely family, you know. It's just one of those things, isn't it?

And so the carer got on with the business of caring, delighting in her foster daughter and her steps forward. 'You know, personality, she's lovely, she's just starting to sit up by herself. Which is wonderful.'

In general, foster care was providing 'objective permanence' for a sizeable number (40%) of those aged five to ten at sweep 1. Time in placement was a strong predictor. Only a fifth of those in placement for less than a year were still with their index carer at sweep 3. This proportion rose steadily (45% for one to two years, 60% for two to three years, 80% for three years plus).

The proportion staying on with their index carer was similar (37%) among those aged 11 to 14. This group, however, had on average had longer placements when we first picked them up at sweep 1. If we allowed for this fact a difference became apparent. Forty rather than 60 per cent of those who had been in placement for two to three years at sweep 1 were still with the index carer at sweep 3. The same was true for 60 rather than 80 per cent of those in placement for three years. These lower proportions among the older group reflect the influence of fostering breakdowns, a topic to which we now turn.

Disruption and the chance of 'objective permanence' in foster care

Over the course of three years 29 per cent of the children had, on our defini-tion, experienced a fostering disruption.[2] The majority of those with other foster carers (53%) or in residential care (87%) had experienced a disruption at some point since 1998.

Those aged less than five in 1998 were unlikely to suffer a disruption. Less than 8 per cent did so. Disruptions were more frequent (23%) among those aged five to ten in 1998. Here they did tend to be concentrated among those who had spent less time in placement. A quarter of those in placement for less than two years disrupted. Only one in seven (14 per cent) of those there for two years or more in 1998 did so.

Disruptions were more frequent still (48%) among those aged 11 to 15 in 1998. Out of 92 children who had spent less than two years in placement 49 (53%) disrupted. So too, however, did 40 per cent of those who had spent two years or more.

Over the age of 16 disruptions can be headed off. The breakdown of a relationship between a foster family and a child need no longer be defined as a disruption. Instead the parting can be defined as a move to independent living. For this or other reasons the frequency of breakdown among this group fell to 31 per cent. Again, however, it was more common among those who had stayed less time. Thirty-nine per cent of those who had spent less than two years in the placement experienced a breakdown. This was true of only 23 per cent of those who had spent two years or more.

These results suggest two conclusions. First, the risk of placement break-down does reduce with length of stay. Amalgamating the differences between those who had stayed for less and more than two years after allowing for age does yield a significant difference ($p=0.01$).[3] Second, the period when most children are at secondary school is associated with a substantial risk of break-down even among those children who have been a long time in placement. These conclusions could be tested in more elaborate analysis. In our last book (Sinclair, Wilson and Gibbs 2004) we predicted disruption over 14 months. The greater length of follow-up allowed us to test this model over three years.

As already explained our model was essentially that a child's adjustment to a placement depends first on her or himself, second on how he or she gets on at school, third on the characteristics of the foster carer, fourth on how he or she and the foster family get on – something that is not entirely predictable from the other factors – and fifth on the birth family. To be more specific children who score high on measures of disturbance and who do not want to be in the placement will tend to disrupt. So too will children who are not happy at school and are not helped there. Children whose carers are not child-oriented and do not get on with them will also do badly. Finally, the relationship with the birth family is important. Where there is strong evidence that the child has been abused, unrestricted contact with birth families predicts breakdown.

We restricted our tests of this model to children who were five or over at sweep 1. We also added a variable 'in same placement for two years or more in 1998'. Table 7.1 gives a model predicting breakdown for all this group. As can be seen this suggests that placement breakdowns are more likely if children have been placed for less than two years, have high childlike attach-ment scores, are not happy at school and have foster carers with relatively poor parenting skills. Age was not significant in this model. This, however, reflects the fact that among those aged 11 or over, older teenagers were rather less likely to have breakdowns than younger ones. If, however, age is entered into the analysis simply as 'under 11' or '11 or over', it becomes a highly signifi-cant predictor.

Other variables can be substituted for those in the table. The Goodman score can be substituted for the childlike attachment and be equally signifi-cant. The rejection or the foster carer child orientation score can also be sub-stituted for the parenting one. Whatever the substitution, the results suggest that the broad areas of 'time in placement', 'personality', 'school', 'being aged 11 or over' and 'foster home' are key to the outcome.

Box 7.2

In the case studies the contrast between 'permanent' and less permanent fostering was most apparent among those who were teenagers at sweep 3. The features which marked out a permanent case at this age were the same as those characteristics of Mary at five: the commitment of their foster carers, a child settled at a school with which the foster carer was happy, a long-term future which was seen as involving the family and relationships with the birth family that involved acceptance on both sides.

Leroy came to the index placement around the age of nine following a placement breakdown, and a history of rejection and cold unstimulating care. On arrival Leroy stole from family members and was very difficult. Four years later he was a changed person (a fact confirmed by his Goodman score which improved dramatically). Factors that contributed to this seemed to be: the commitment and firmness of the carers with whom he was now moving to Scotland, his own decision to commit to the placement, his ability to reach a *modus vivendi* with his mother and relatives – he was not vulnerable to them and made his own decisions about when he saw them – and initial 'statementing' at school where the provision of an adult to go with him enabled him to take time out from class when he needed it. He was now acting as a full member of the family, contributing his DIY skills and seen as capable of going to university. (At present he had ambitions in the police.)

Robert's placement had just broken down after five years. Relationships with his birth family remained unresolved – he could not understand why his mother did not visit and was neglected on contact with his father. According to the foster carers he was very jealous of another foster child who arrived around the time of his own move to secondary school where he got in 'with the wrong crowd' and his behaviour brought him into conflict with the carers. He engineered the breakdown by making allegations, suddenly asked to come back but found the carers had had all they could take. His social worker felt he now committed to no one: 'I think he has very little trust in people. He has no trust in his friends…emotionally, I think…something in him has died.' So the childlike attachment which had been apparent on arrival and perhaps in the jealousy of the new foster child was replaced by a compulsive self-reliance.

An interesting feature of these analyses is that contact with an educational psychologist predicts the absence of breakdown over the first 14 months but not in the longer term. This may suggest that our original finding that such

Table 7.1 Predictors of three-year fostering disruption rate

Variables in 1998	B	S.E.	Wald	df	Sig.	Exp(B)
Placed 2+ years	-0.727	0.289	6.316	1	0.012	0.483
Childlike attachment	0.217	0.059	13.752	1	0.000	1.243
Happy at school	-0.916	0.229	16.023	1	0.000	0.400
Parenting skills	-0.563	0.254	4.912	1	0.027	0.569
Constant	2.902	1.226	5.607	1	0.018	18.215

Note: Exp(B) is the value by which the odds of the event change when the independent variable increases by 1 unit.
Key: B = Regression coefficient Beta; S.E. = Standard error of B; Wald = Wald Statistic

contact was predictive was a chance one. It was, however, consistently and highly significant in a variety of analyses. An alternative explanation is that educational psychology may have an effect but that this is relatively short term.

Table 7.2 presents the same set of variables but for the restricted number of cases where the social worker had said that there was strong evidence of abuse. As predicted, cases in which there was unrestricted contact were more likely to break down after holding these other variables constant.[4]

Table 7.2 Predictors of three-year fostering disruption rate: strong evidence of prior abuse

Variables in 1998	B	S.E	Wald	df	Sig.	Exp(B)
Placed 2+ years	-1.414	0.418	11.449	1	0.001	0.243
Childlike attachment	0.133	0.084	2.533	1	0.111	1.142
Happy at school	-0.953	0.324	8.635	1	0.003	0.386
Parenting skills	-0.524	0.358	2.148	1	0.143	0.592
Contact unrestricted	0.855	0.436	3.839	1	0.050	2.352
Constant	3.135	2.076	2.279	1	0.131	22.979

Note: Exp(B) is the value by which the odds of the event change when the independent variable increases by 1 unit.
Key: B = Regression coefficient Beta; S.E. = Standard error of B; Wald = Wald Statistic

The message of these analyses is therefore the same as that of the case studies. The key to maintaining placements is skilled committed fostering, a low level of childlike attachment on the part of the child, a school where the child is happy, and prior continuity of placement. A *laissez-faire* approach to contact with previously abusive parents may threaten placements, even given these otherwise good conditions.

Disruption and the chance of further family placement

Objective permanence, as we defined it in the introduction, requires a family placement. As we have seen a number of children were placed with birth parents following disruptions. Disruption therefore does not necessarily prevent family placement. As seen below, it was nevertheless strongly related to kind of placement at sweep 3. Its importance in this respect, however, varied with age.

Among those aged less than five in 1998 disruption did not seem to influence the type of subsequent placement. Three (23%) of the 13 children in this age group who were with new foster carers had experienced disruptions. Arguably the disruption had influenced where they were now. In addition to these three, seven more children had placements that disrupted. Their destinations seemed to be decided on other grounds.

Among those aged between five and ten disruption was related to having placements within the care system. All the small number (seven) in residential care had disrupted. So too had 43 per cent of those with a new carer. These two forms of placement accounted for 18 per cent of the children who had not disrupted but 66 per cent of those who had.

Among those aged 11 to 15 fostering disruption appeared to be a major reason for placement destination. Sixty-nine per cent of those with a new foster carer had experienced one. So too had 85 per cent of those in residential care, 86 per cent of those with their families and 54 per cent of those in independent living. Disruption at this age is more likely than at an earlier one. It is also more likely to prompt a re-evaluation. Children of younger ages may return to their birth families because this is what is planned or wanted. Teenagers may return because their social worker has run out of other places to put them. Similar reasons may prompt the use of residential care or, for older children, independent living.

Among those aged 16 or over the role of disruption in determining placement reduced. In this age group the majority (71%) were in independent living. Their disruption rate (38%) differed little from the overall rate for those in this age group.

Overall, disruption has a mixed effect on 'objective permanence'. It enables children who have not settled in foster care to return to their birth families. It makes more likely the impermanence which characterises placement in residential care. It brings forward the time at which rootless teenagers have to cope on their own.

The extent of subjective permanence in foster care

By all accounts the children fostered in 2001 showed an impressive degree of commitment to their foster placement. Asked how far the foster child felt part of the family 84 per cent of the carers said 'a great deal'. Similarly, 80 per cent were said to trust the carer 'a great deal' and 86 per cent to be quite sure that the carer cared for them.

The children themselves demonstrated a similar degree of commitment, although the degree again depended on whether they were with index or other carers. Their answers to open-ended questions showed that they thought of their foster family as a family. As we will see again in the next chapter the meaning they gave to this and their attitudes to it were coloured by a number of factors.

Those with their index foster carers (54 respondents) were predictably the most enthusiastic. Fifty-five per cent stated they wanted to stay with their foster carers until they were over 18 or 'forever'. A further 16 per cent of this group wanted to be adopted by their carers. Very nearly three-quarters of this group (71%) were therefore seeing their foster family as their long-term family base. The remainder were more equivocal saying they were not sure how long they wanted to stay (9%), or that it was only for a year or two (9%) or until they were 18 (12%). Ninety-one per cent of them wanted to see a lot of their carers when they left and none did not want to see them at all.

Those with new carers (38 respondents) were more cautious. None wanted to be adopted by their carer. Only a third (31%) wanted to stay beyond 18 or 'forever'. One in eight (13%) wanted to stay no more than a few months at most and a further 5 per cent no more than two years. Eight per cent were still unsure. The most common answer (42%) was 'until I am 18'. Two-thirds of the children would have liked to see a lot of their carers after that but more than a quarter (28%) wanted to see their carers no more than 'a bit'. Two were quite clear they would not want to see their carers at all after leaving.

We explored the factors which predicted the difference between those who, according to their carers, were committed to their placements in 2001 and those who were not. Unsurprisingly, those with new foster carers appeared, in the carers' accounts, somewhat less committed. In 2001 they scored significantly lower on the family inclusion score ($p<0.01$), but did not differ significantly on the exclusion score. In 1998 they had scored significantly higher on the family exclusion score.[5]

Box 7.3

Holly's foster care experience illustrates the uneasy compromise that long-term foster care can sometimes be. It had drifted on without commitment and threatened by an ambivalent relationship with her mother with which it had not been possible to deal. Holly felt she should have left home earlier.

> It's OK, but originally I was meant to be here for a short-term, but I mean, it's like four or five years, now, so I think – well, really, I don't really know the difference between short-term and long-term, because I'm meant to be here for short-term, and it just goes on to long-term. (Holly)

> I don't really see them [birth family], so...I don't tend to think about them...that much... Just try not to think about them too much, but when it does come, I deal with it.

Q: ...But there's nobody else outside here that you talk to about it?

A: Not really. (Holly)

> That's my theory: she'll push friends away from her by her comments. Quite nasty, too – it's almost as though 'you can't get close to me, because I don't want you hurting me', and I don't know whether that's true or not, because I'm not a psychologist, but it certainly seems that way. (Holly's carers)

> Holly and mum's relationship is a very funny relationship – mum is, 'you're my darling, you're the best child in the world, I really love you, come and sit on my lap, I'll give you a cuddle', and then six months later, it's 'I wish I'd drowned you at birth, you're the most horrible person I've ever come across', and this and that... (Holly's carers)

Q: Was there anything that could have been done better?

A: Basically just got me out when things started to go wrong, instead of letting them drag on.

Q: Away from your birth family?

A: Yeah... (Holly)

As can be seen from Boxes 7.3 and 7.4, the case studies suggest that attachment behaviour was associated with a lack of family inclusion and with exclusion. Children who were anxiously attached aroused feelings of claustrophobia in their carers who sometimes responded by trying to limit their invasions. By contrast children who were compulsively detached retreated to their rooms and stayed on the outside of the family circle. The associations reported in the footnote support the idea that these kinds of interactions, based as they are around attachment, may be quite widespread.

Box 7.4

Of the three case study foster children not on residence orders or previously described, one had recently had a placement breakdown and two were not fully committed to their current placement. Like many of those who returned to their birth families they had strongly ambivalent relationships with their own families. Their behaviour, their carers' accounts, and, in two cases, their interviews with us showed a persistent yearning for mothers who were inconsistent and at times rejecting. Their parents made at best only fitful efforts to get them back but were nevertheless unwilling for the placements to succeed. As this interview illustrates there was a dilemma.

Q: So how do you enjoy that time with your mum?

A: I can't really – I jump up and down – but [people] told me a long time ago that I should not be friends with my mum because of what she did...

Q: But you're upset when you come back here are you...?

A: I usually cry in my bedroom but they can hear me crying my eyes out so I come downstairs.

Q: Do you feel part of Melanie's family?

A: No because I like my own family... [Would you have liked anyone to adopt you?] I dare anyone to adopt me...

Q: So that's a definite no no to adoption?

A: No no no no.

Within the home their behaviour varied between a wary uncommunicative stoicism and openly jealous demands. This behaviour made it difficult for their foster carers to commit to them. Jealous hostility to new partners could disrupt the carers' relationships and made it too difficult to formally or informally adopt the child into the family. Small thefts could make it difficult to trust them.

The sense that they did not truly belong could be exacerbated by the fact that others did (for example, another foster child might be adopted), by the uncertainty that sometimes seemed to surround the placements which drifted into being long-term, by the acknowledgement that it would stop at 18 and by the bureaucratic requirements of foster care life. Whatever foster care was for these children it was not family life. So they had no family in which to be.

Do residence orders provide a greater sense of permanence?

We were aware that just over 4 per cent of the sample were on residence orders. These orders were very much more likely to be made when the carer was a relative. At sweep 1 just over 4 per cent of the sample were known to us to be with relative carers. These carers were looking after 28 per cent of the children whom we knew to be on residence orders by sweep 3. This was true of only 3 per cent of the remainder ($p<0.001$). None of the children fostered by relatives at sweep 1 went on to be adopted by 2001. So it is likely that in some cases residence orders are used as a kind of 'relative adoption'. This would be in keeping with Hunt's recent (2002) review which suggested that placements with relatives, while in many ways no more or less successful than other foster placements, did last longer.

Apart from the involvement of relatives, four things seemed to distinguish those on residence orders from the remainder of the sample. First, they were more likely to have at least weekly contact with a relative living outside their foster family ($p=0.045$).[6] Second, the carer at sweep 1 was more likely to have a high child orientation score. Third, the child was more likely to have been abused prior to being looked after.[7] Fourth, the child was more likely to be fostered with her or his sibling.[8]

These findings suggest that residence orders are in a sense a solution to a dilemma. The existence of abuse makes it difficult to return the child to his or her home. The existence of a bond with home either through frequent contact or through a relative placement makes an adoption unlikely. In this situation the existence of a child-oriented carer seems to offer an opportunity for long-term fostering regularised and perhaps made less expensive by a residence order.

Residence orders apparently offer greater security than fostering. Social workers considered that 82 per cent of the residence orders on which they reported offered long-term security. The comparable figure for other placements was 62 per cent.

There were other predictable contrasts between those on residence orders and those fostered. They were less likely to have experienced a disruption since 1998 (9% v. 53%), or a change of placement (14% v. 39%), and more likely to want to use the carer's home as a family base (82% v. 53%).[9]

Children on residence orders had significantly lower family exclusion and stoicism scores (but not childlike attachment and inclusion scores). These differences were not necessarily the effect of having a residence order. Children may have been placed on a residence order because they were well settled or settled well because they were on an order. Only in relation to the stoicism score did we find evidence of improvement beyond what might have been predicted from our data in 1998 and here the difference fell just short of significance ($p=0.12$).

A further difference related to expectations. Sixty-two per cent of the carers with a residence order expected the child to stay with them beyond the age of 18, 24 per cent were unsure about this and only 14 per cent were quite sure they would not. By contrast only 40 per cent of children looked after by foster carers were expected to stay beyond age 18, 32 per cent might stay on and 29 per cent definitely would not. Despite the small numbers the differences in these trends is significant. Whatever happens in practice, children on residence orders are more likely to be seen as likely to stay as long as they wish.

Residence orders have the further advantage that they 'normalise' the placement. The former foster carers can take the decisions that most parents naturally take. As we have seen they may also have the advantage that they encourage a longer-term view of the placement. On the negative side they may decrease the financial recompense for fostering and the social work support available.

Box 7.5

The case studies of those on residence orders suggested that they were not adopted at an early age because of initial efforts at rehabilitation. When it became clear the child could not go home, ideas of adoption (if any) were dropped because of opposition by a birth parent or because it was thought important to keep siblings together. When it was clear that the placement with the carer was long term and stable a residence order was suggested. Carers might want it because it gave them certain rights and because they did not want interference from social services. They did not want adoption because of the financial implications or because the child did not want to redefine themselves in this way (e.g. by changing their name). In these circumstances a residence order might be suggested as a 'half-way house' between adoption and fostering. The 'downside', if any, was the lack of back-up (e.g. in dealing with birth families) and sometimes a reduced level of financial support:

> Well, so far, we haven't done [gone for adoption order], now, because we'd just lose more money, but it doesn't seem any different than a residence order, really, because we've got no social services, or anything, and you haven't got to change your surname, which I don't want to do... It [residence order] all sounded really good, because we'd get rid of [social worker], we'd still get the money, we'd get to keep our computer, we'd get to do away with social services, and everything, and basically they took all that back. It probably would have been better getting adopted!...it seemed like no point, really – it was just the same as being fostered, but it just had a different name to it, and everything...it's just basically that I lost the money! (Foster child)

To an outsider three of the four case studies had the appearance of 'quasi-adoptions', albeit in one case an adoption which was threatened by the efforts of the birth family. In this case a relative carer was glad of the continuing support of social services, since without them she did not feel that the situation could be contained. The final case involved a confident, experienced carer who valued the residence order because of the rights it gave her. She was proud of her former foster child, highly committed to him, and adept at involving him in all family activities. At the same time she continued to involve the mother in looking after him on an occasional basis.

Box 7.6

Future expectations differed between foster children and those on residence orders. The contrast was, perhaps, most evident in two outwardly similar teenage children, both with experience of highly ambivalent mothers, and both apparently having decided that their birth families now had nothing to offer them. One, currently on a residence order had, as it were, freedom to play with ideas about her future, conscious that she had a family to fall back on:

Q: What sort of age are you thinking of moving in to have a flat, then?

A: About 21.

Q: 21, yeah.

A: Well, when I'm 15, mum and dad are going to start giving me about £20 a month, or something so I can afford a car, and when I do that, I'll start a job that pays well. I don't really know if I'll enjoy it, but I'll carry on doing drama, singing, and dancing, and then I'll move to London, because you get more famous people coming from London, really...when I'm 21, and then till I'm 25, and then if I don't get famous, I'll come back home.

Q: Come back to live round here, or come back to live at home?

A: I don't know, really. It all depends what I can afford.

The other child in foster care was matter of fact about her future. She made no reference to ongoing support from her foster carers:

Q: And how long do you expect yourself to be staying here?

A: For the next three years.

Q: And how old would you be then?

A: 18.

Q: Have you any thought about what's likely to happen to you after that?

A: I'm going to get assessed, and then hopefully move out into a flat, or a sort of bedsit.

Would anything make it more likely that foster children stay after 18?

> Well, my care order is until I'm 18, so I can stay here till I'm 18, but I don't know whether I can stay here longer than that. I don't know whether I will do. I might even move before I'm 18, I don't know yet. It depends how things go.

A key difference between foster and ordinary children is that the former are very unlikely to stay with their carers after 18. On our definition this makes their placements less permanent. For this reason we asked the foster carers if anything would make it more likely that the children would stay beyond 18. Some left the question blank or said that the issue was too remote:

> We think this is a difficult question to answer. Too far in the future for one thing.

Others said that nothing would influence them. Their reasons for this varied. Some said they in any case treated the child as their own. Others wrote that it was up to the young person, who wanted to move out. Others felt that the decision was down to them and they had decided against allowing the young person to stay.

Despite this, very nearly a third both answered the question and suggested steps that would help. Some felt that social services generally expected the young people to move on at 18 but that this was not necessarily geared to the needs of the child:

> Social services prefer young people to move out by 18 years of age. There has to be some very special reasons to stay beyond 18. We have requested for this young person to stay on.

By implication what was needed was a relaxation of this expectation – the assumption as one carer put it that things should 'take their natural course'. One who seemed to take this view wrote that her foster child would not be staying. Nevertheless, she implied that other cases could be influenced by a more relaxed attitude:

> No. He is looking forward to independent living. However, I've had one come back at 22 and is now living with us temporarily until he gets on his feet again. It's very important to still be involved and social services should not have a cut off point, bringing up children is an ongoing thing. Some of the biggest difficulties are post 18 years.

Most of the other suggestions revolved around financial help, further education, and 'support'. One carer who was determined her foster children should stay with her if they wanted to was nevertheless concerned about the cost:

> I would be worried about the financial side but no matter what, my two girls can stay as long as they want.

Another was similarly happy for the foster child to stay. Nevertheless he commented:

> He is welcome to stay after 18, until independent living with or without financial help. With financial help we will obviously be able to provide more.

Others wrote simply that continuing allowances were either required or would help. Funding for education or training was seen as particularly crucial, although it was also acknowledged that this was something which social services did provide:

> Help support foster carer and child, i.e., I want John to go to higher education.

A small number mentioned that their foster child had learning impairments and wanted continuing support with these. Others wanted practical support, in one case 'an extension' to their house.

As some of the above quotations make clear, support was not seen simply as something that would benefit the carer. Rather it was necessary for child and for carer. In one case the lack of long-term support seemed to influence the carer's decision:

> I had a foster son who stayed till he was 20, as a lodger, but when he wanted to leave, he had nowhere to go to, if a foster child goes at 18, he gets a room in a hostel and then a bedsit or flat, so in the long [run] I'm not helping them by letting them stay, and quite a few I've had all come back to see me and I help them when I can.

One carer thought that what was needed was that social services:

> ...understand that chronological age is not always the mental age of the young people. They are mostly unable at 18–19 to go into independent living. They always turn to carers for financial/personal help rather than social workers. Can be very stressful as they still see themselves as having same rights as when they were fostered.

Requests for further support are, perhaps, the natural answer to this problem. When the issue actually arises, further support may make a difference to the situation. However, some carers may find further support (other perhaps than financial support) unnecessary or intrusive. That said, the carer comments do raise the issue of whether the assumption that young people should move at 18 is too easily made.

Conclusion

The extent to which foster care offers permanent placements is limited. Only those who were between the ages of 4 and 14 at our first survey had any substantial chance of being there on follow-up. Younger children were indeed likely to stay on for lengthy periods of time. Nevertheless, they had to negotiate the hurdle of their teenage years. Four in ten of those who were aged 11 to 14 and had spent two years in placement at our first survey in 1998 had nevertheless experienced a disruption by our follow-up in 2001.

Despite these limitations most of the foster children in our sample were seen by their carers as settled in their placement. Most of those still with their index carer wanted to use the foster home as their family base, being adopted by their carers or staying on beyond 18. The case studies showed that these settled cases included some where there was strong mutual commitment between child and carer. However, there were also foster children in the case studies who had been a long time in their placements but were at best ambivalently committed to them. For various reasons they could not return home. They did not want to be adopted. An unfulfilled yearning for home or a wariness of human relationships left them with no settled place to be.

It was thus only a minority, probably between one in six and one in seven of our original sample, who had achieved permanence in foster care in the sense that they were still with their original carers and they wanted to use the foster home as a base. This minority, however, is vulnerable to disruption and subject like others to the expectation that they move at 18. It is apparent from the case studies that foster care can offer permanence. It is apparent from the statistics that it rarely does.

There would seem to be two broad approaches to providing greater permanence in foster care. First, it is important to reduce the incidence of breakdowns in foster care. This is easier said than done. Both the statistical data and the case studies suggest that what is required are the abilities to:

- handle disturbed attachment behaviour on the part of the foster child which can otherwise alienate the carer and lead to a vicious circle of mutual rejection

- minimise interference with the placement from birth parents who cannot easily tolerate their child being either with them or away from them

- enable the child to come to a *modus vivendi* with their parents so that they are not torn in their own minds between yearning and rejection

- enable the child to adjust to school and enjoy her/himself there.

These abilities probably depend first on the qualities of the foster carer. Child-oriented carers do better in these respects. They require skilful social workers able to intervene to prevent the escalation of negative 'spirals of inter-action' between carer and child and willing to act authoritatively and proactively over contact. (Prohibiting a family member contact is associated with a lower risk of breakdown when there is strong evidence of prior abuse.) They require the co-operation of school and perhaps an educational psychol-ogist. In the last study we showed that contact with an educational psycholo-gist was associated with a reduced risk of breakdown over 14 months.

There may be additional contributions from counselling and life story work. It was quite clear from the case studies that some counsellors were pro-viding a lifeline to their clients. Others (including social workers) broke the ice and allowed the child to talk about difficulties which as a result they later found it easier to talk over with their foster carers. Life story work was the one form of intervention for which no one seemed to have a bad word (one child described it as 'well decent'). We have no statistical data on the effects of these interventions. However, absence of evidence is not evidence of absence. It would be wise to assume for the moment that they are important.

Given these conditions the case studies suggest that difficult children can come to feel secure in foster care and that this in turn allows them to come to terms with their situations. Psychologically at least they can then 'move on' and settle down.

The second task is to change the assumptions surrounding foster care. It is not clear whether the greater use of residence orders or equivalent would promote this or simply recognise situations where assumptions had already changed. It would probably reduce the support available to the carers. This would require caution as lack of support is one of the reasons adduced for carer reluctance to keep children after the age of 18. Perhaps what is required is a range of provisions – a determination as it were to have the best of all worlds on as many occasions as possible. So adoption need not be without financial and social work support. There seems no reason why foster care should not have some of the 'normality' which is the prized element in residence orders without losing the security of backing from social services. Why is it that it apparently takes a social worker to authorise a 'sleep-over' or a school trip? Much, perhaps, could be done by practice rather than by legislation (indeed practice on 'sleep-overs' does seem to have changed). Before exploring such themes, however, it might be wise to attend to the views of the children themselves. This is the task of the next chapter.

Notes

1. Of the remainder, 18 per cent were with their birth families (24% had returned there at some stage). Others were in residential care (7%), independent living (3%) or in some way lost to follow-up (3%).

2. We counted a placement as disrupted if any of our sources – foster carer, social worker or family placement social worker – said that it had disrupted between sweep 1 and sweep 3.

3. The difference would no doubt be more pronounced if it was possible to allow for period at risk. Those in placement for two years or more are generally expected to stay there. They are therefore potentially at risk of a breakdown for the full period of follow-up. Those placed for shorter periods may often have plans involving adoption or return home that reduce this period at risk and therefore the likelihood of breakdown.

4. The association remains marginally significant if the non-significant variables are dropped from the equation (p=0.053).

5. We related our three measures of 'subjective permanence' to each other. The results suggested that they might be measuring related but different things. Those who wished to use the foster home as a base (i.e. to be adopted by the carer or stay beyond 18) had significantly lower family exclusion scores (p=0.008). They did not differ on the family inclusion scores. High family exclusion scores went with low family inclusion scores although not very strongly so (r=-0.17, p<0.05). A high family exclusion score was predicted by high childlike attachment at either sweep 1 or sweep 3. Behaviour which suggests an apparent wish to be close is according to the foster carers associated with a feeling of exclusion. A high family inclusion score was best predicted by a combination of a low stoicism score at either sweep 1 (p=0.003) or sweep 3 (p<0.001) and having a child-oriented carer at sweep 3 (p<0.001). The wish to use the foster home as a base was predicted by a low stoicism score at sweep 3 (p=0.052) or at sweep 1 (p=0.055).

6. This finding was partly influenced by the greater involvement of relatives in this form of caring. However, the frequency of contact was also slightly greater when the carer was a stranger.

7. Where there was no evidence of abuse no child was on a residence order. Where there was some evidence of abuse the proportion was 2 per cent. Where there was strong evidence the proportion was 9 per cent (chi square for trend=8.03, df=1, p=0.005).

8. Thirteen per cent of those on residence orders at sweep 3 were fostered with a sibling at sweep 1. The comparable proportion among those fostered at sweep 3 was only 6 per cent.

9. The significance of these differences was 0.11, 0.02, 0.11 (all Fisher exact tests, two tailed). Given that these are consistent predicted differences it is probably safe to take them as real.

Chapter Eight

Foster Care:
Does It Feel Like A Family?

I mean, some people say, 'Yeah, but that sort of thing goes on in all families', and I'm like, 'well, how am I supposed to know that?' I mean, I've been in care ten years, and it's just like not a normal family, do you know what I mean? It's not like, mum, dad, kids – it's foster mum and dad, and foster kids. It's not normal at all. (Young person in case study)

Yeah. I mean, it'll never feel like your proper home, because you know it ain't, but when you've been in care for as long as I have, you get used to it… (Young person in case study)

It's not a foster home, it's my home. (Child replying to questionnaire)

Introduction

Foster care presents children with a rather ambiguous offer. It provides family care but only for a limited time. The skills it demands are in many ways those needed by parents. Yet carers are increasingly denied the title *foster parents*. It can generate strong relationships between carers and children but they are almost inevitably cut short. All this raises the question of how far foster care should be seen as family care. In this chapter we pursue this issue through the questionnaires returned by the foster children. This is relevant to the issue of how far foster care can offer permanence. It may also cast some light on how the system would look if it were designed by the children themselves.

We ask six questions. From the point of view of the children:

- Is foster care real family care?
- What should the roles of birth and foster family be?
- Can you belong to your birth and your foster family?
- How do social workers affect relationships with foster and birth families?
- What about a foster family helps or hinders a sense of belonging?
- What about the care system helps or hinders a sense of belonging?

Is foster care real 'family care'?

We asked the children to complete a sentence which began 'Fostering is...' A minority were factual or cautious in their replies. So fostering was described as 'when you have been taken away from your parent for a certain reason or you have none', 'for children who can't be with their parents', 'important to lots of children', 'not bad', 'OK', 'okay much of the time', 'OK but can be hard at times', 'different', 'not bad', 'much of a muchness', 'alright', 'a clever project in a way'. Others emphasised the variability of fostering, something which could be at the beginning 'scary' but become good, which might be good in itself but bad because of the need for it, and which definitely depended on which foster carers were involved. So fostering was seen as 'sometimes good sometimes terrible' or as 'horrible and good at the same time'.

Much more commonly the children were clear and definite in their views of fostering. A small minority were dismissive describing fostering as 'bad', 'weird', 'rubbish', 'boring' or 'crap' or commenting that 'I don't particularly like it and can't wait to leave'.

Much more commonly they were positive, with their replies reading like a thesaurus of synonyms for good. So fostering was variously described as 'great', 'cool', 'exciting', 'ace', 'fine', 'brilliant', 'wicked', 'a life saver', 'lovely', 'very good', 'good', 'the best thing that happened to me', 'very nice to me', 'nice', 'helpful', 'fun and happy' and 'fun and nice'. Others, regardless of grammar, finished our sentence with another, for example, 'I love being here', 'I love them to bits' or 'Everybody loves me here'. Others coined aphorisms such as 'Fostering is love', 'Fostering is another mum', 'Fostering is when someone looks after me forever', 'Feel safe. Feel warm'.

Behind these evaluations of fostering lay the question of how far and if so in what way the current foster family should be regarded as 'a real family'. Again all possibilities were represented. Some were definite:

They are my family.

Others were less certain. Very commonly they said that it was 'like a family', or 'like a proper family', comments that seemed to stop short of a full endorsement. As one put it:

Although it feels like my family there's always that part of me that knows they're not.

Another commented on the latent insecurity of this position:

I want to stay here for ever. I don't feel I belong here.

And if there were no other sources of support the child's position could be difficult indeed. As one put it simply:

I feel all alone.

Others by contrast did not look for full family support from their foster family:

I sometimes feel a little restricted. I love my foster family but would like to go home some time in the future.

Whether they liked foster care or not the longing for home or for members of it was commonly seen as the bad thing about foster care.

What should the relationship between foster and birth family be?

We asked the children to write down their two main wishes for their future. In the main their replies focused on jobs (good ones or particular ones), money (enough), the family they hoped to have, their wish to be a good parent, school (good grades or to go to university). Some also mentioned sport and particular material goods such as PlayStations. Others had more immediate, less realistic, or more idiosyncratic wishes – to see their mum on Monday, to play football for Manchester United, to have a Ferrari, to swim with dolphins and to have their belly button pierced.

In general, what was striking was the 'ordinariness' of these desires. In one respect, however, their replies differed from what might have been expected from children living at home. One or both of their wishes commonly focused on reinforcing or changing their own relationship with foster carers and birth family. There were four logical possibilities and all were represented.

The first possibility was that they should return to their birth families. Usually the parent preferred was their mother. So children wrote that they wished to 'go back to mum and dad' or 'to live with my mum'. However, other relatives were also mentioned. So children variously wanted to live with their 'dad', 'family', 'dad and brother' and 'uncle'.

A second possibility was that they should return to their birth families with the explicit proviso that they should stay in touch with their foster carers usually identified by their first names: 'To move back in with my mum but still see my foster family.'

A third possibility was to stay with their foster family but see more of their birth family or particular members of it. One child, for example, wanted:

> To be a happy and an amazingly good person. Also I do not want to move. To be able to see my family.

Both the motives for and extent of this desired contact varied. Some contact was for reassurance. So children might wish for 'my mum, dad and brothers to be happy in the future' or for their 'nan and grandad not to die'. Some might be to satisfy longings and ruminations that had no grounding in actual contact: 'to find my real dad'. Some wishes seemed to be acknowledged by the child as unreal:

> I wish I could see my mum on Monday.

> I wish I could fly.

Commonly, as discussed later, the wish was for more contact with siblings and hence perhaps a greater sense of being part of a real family. Most common was the desire for more contact with the child's mother so that:

> I can see more of my mum when I want wherever I am.

Others emphasised their need to stay where they were over and above any contact with their birth family. So they variously emphasised their wish to be adopted, to stay with their foster carers and for their parents to let them get on with their new lives:

Hopefully I will be adopted by my foster parents of nine years.

To stay with my foster mum and dad for always.

For my real mum to let me live a normal life with my family here in my foster family.

Can you belong to your foster and birth families?

I feel happy in this family. I feel happy without my real family.

Foster care is...OK, but I would sooner be at home.

Fitting into this foster family is...awkward...because...they're not my family.

Fitting into this foster family is...rubbish...because...I have my own family.

As the quotations we have just given make clear, the children had varying perceptions of the implications of being a foster child with a birth family of their own. These perceptions are further complicated by the fact that 'family' can denote a wide collection of individuals to each of whom a child may have a strong and different reaction.

The need to differentiate between family members was illustrated by the issue of contact. The children's wishes for contact were often for contact with specific members of the family. So they variously missed their grandmother, mother or father or wished:

To see my two little sisters that I only see once a year if lucky.

See my mum's two new babies.

Stay with my brothers forever.

Nevertheless, a longing for contact was not universal. As we have noted above some foster children did not want to go back to the past. Reminders could be painful and contacts could be undesired. A 'bad thing' about one foster placement was that:

...my real grandma and grandad live up the street and don't talk to me.

As the case studies showed, the dilemmas around family were highlighted by the question of what to call a foster mother and father. This issue could be fraught:

Q: I mean, have you always called them mum and dad, or is that something you started to do?

A: I didn't when I was little, because my mum told me not to. My mum goes 'don't call them that, they're not your mum and dad', but then Sally told me to call them mummy and daddy Potter when my mum wasn't around, so I called them that when my mum wasn't around, and then when my mum was there, it was Linda and Nigel, and so I think they got confused as well! [laughs]

The case studies illustrated the way in which the child's loyalties interacted with discipline. Some parents on contact tried to undermine the foster carer's discipline (e.g. by enabling the child to have a belly button pierced). Equally some children felt their foster carers did not have the same right as their own parents to discipline them:

I think she just turned round and said to her, 'you can't tell me what to do – you're not my mum', and all that. I think it stemmed from there, really. (Birth mother discussing child)

Other children saw their move from their family as 'necessary'. They did not necessarily welcome it. Some reacted by seeing their placement as something of which they had to make the best, since by comparison it was at least better than the alternative:

...it's a lot better than my real parents.

Foster care is...better than the streets.

Others were grateful for what they saw as a life-saving move:

The best thing that could have happened at the time. It has only changed my life for the better.

...if I didn't have it I wouldn't be here (i.e. alive).

All this group of children seemed to feel that they needed to be away from their family for their safety:

Foster care is great, it's what I needed and wanted. I had a right to live in a safe environment and that was provided. But I had to put myself there first because I wasn't listened to.

When my mum is drunk I know being with my foster family, I'm safe.

How do social workers affect relationships with birth family?

The different perceptions of family provided social workers with a minefield through which they clearly had to pick their way with care. A number in the children's eyes failed to do so.

We asked them if the social workers had done anything they liked and anything they did not like. Not all the replies related to contact with families – nevertheless contact and the related issue of whether the child will live with relatives are clearly crucial to the child's perception of their social worker. Some were praised for enabling contact:

> They still let me go and stay with my mum and see my nan and grandad, auntie, uncle and nephew.

> Met with my dad (even though it turned out bad).

Others were criticised for seeking to enable contact:

> The social worker I have at the moment won't leave me to get on with the family I am with. She keeps offering to arrange meetings with my own family.

> Made it look like my birth mum has control over whether she sees me.

There were particular criticisms of social workers for forming alliances with members of the family the child did not like or failing to control contact. So bad things allegedly done by social workers included:

> Let my grandad still see me at weekends.

> There are a lot of things negative that they have done. One social worker befriended my step-dad and did not listen to what I wanted. This resulted in me writing a complaint and getting a new social worker.

Relations between family members clearly involve very strong feelings of guilt, loss, love, fear and anger. It may be easiest for those involved to blame the hurt on social workers:

> Bad things done by social workers. This stupid B*t*h! Did her best to make sure we wouldn't get contact with our younger sisters... She...switch my words round turning our family against each other.

Box 8.1

Q: I mean, what would you do if you were a social worker working with children?

A: I'd quit.

Q: You'd quit?

A: Yeah.

Q: It wouldn't appeal to you as a job?

A: Not really. I wouldn't really want to help kids, children.

Q: No?

A: No – if I did something wrong, then I'd go home feeling really guilty that I had messed them about.

Q: A lot of responsibility?

A: Yeah. I'd like a job that at the end of the day, you can...like a hair-dresser, or something – you can make a mess of it, and then just dye their hair a different colour, or something.

Particular skill may therefore have been needed by social workers who had enabled a *modus vivendi* – an arrangement where the child lived with one family while retaining an easy relationship with another and which enabled one child to say:

> What I like about foster care [is] that I feel like I have two families.

As we have seen some foster children were grateful for their removal from home. Others criticised the fact that they had been left too long at home and their distress had not been heard. Despite this some criticised the workers for the original decision that they should not live at home:

> Because they have moved me from my mum.

> Taken me and my two brothers away from our mum. Taken my half sister away from my mum.

The children had various requirements of social workers, not all of which involved their birth families.[1] Nevertheless, a key requirement was that social workers should see the situation over their family in the same way as they themselves did.

What about a foster family helps or hinders the sense of belonging?

> Fitting into this foster family is…important…because…you have to live there.

> Foster care is…sometimes good and OK, other times horrible, depending where you are.

As we have seen, a key factor in whether a child felt a sense of belonging in foster care was the way he or she located their foster family in relation to their birth family. Some saw an opposition and gave their loyalty to one family or the other; some felt they could have two families; a small minority felt they belonged nowhere.

Against this background there were nevertheless other factors which influenced the child's sense of belonging. Some of these had to do with the nature of the care system. We deal with these later in the chapter. Other factors have to do with interactions in the foster family – whether the child feels accepted and fairly treated, the guidance and love provided by foster carers, disputes over discipline and independence, the composition of the family, the material things provided. We consider these immediately below.

Acceptance and equal treatment in the foster family

Equal treatment was very important to foster children. They were quick to note if the carers' children went on holiday with them but they did not. They brooded on slights and injustices, real or imagined, and on occasions they had been blamed for sins they did not commit:

> Feeling I can't be myself because of the foster carer's own child. They come first and a constant line is said 'Blood is thicker than water'!

More commonly they commented on the absence of unfairness:

> Fitting into this foster family is…really great…because…they treat me like their own family.

> Fitting into this foster family is…easy…because…I am not treated different.

This fairness and welcome made the children feel that they belonged, that they had, at least for the time being, a substitute family:

> Fitting into this foster family is…as good as being in my own family…because…I get the same.

> I'm accepted as part of the family and this is my home, and I've been encouraged to feel this.

Foster carers taking on parental roles

There are various common expectations of parents – they should love you, be there for you, and bring you up to be a reasonable member of society. Foster carers were seen as taking on parental roles in relation to advice, and by providing love:

> They love and guide me in the right way.

As we will see later parental advice from foster carers was by no means universally appreciated. Nevertheless, some children saw it as something carers should provide:

> They treat me like their own child. They give me advice on things.

> Fitting into this foster family is…good…because…they help you with problems as well.

> Foster care is…brilliant. They kept me out of trouble with the police and advised me on a lot of things.

Love, and the looking after that went with it, was not a universal requirement or expectation. One child paradoxically commented that being loved and treated as the baby of the family was a bad thing about foster care. However, there was no doubt that for many children what they saw as love was very important. As such it went integrally with being part of a family, along with birthday parties, pets and good food.[2]

> Fitting into this foster family is…good…because…they really look after me.

> They really love me. I like working with my dad. I have a big brother and sister.

Love and appreciation could grow in return:

Fitting into this foster family is…I love where I am…because…they're like my real family. I love them with all my heart.

These people are really nice. I love everyone here even the animals.

Disputes over discipline and independence

Guidance, as we have seen, was well regarded in our questionnaires. Guidance, however, shades into discipline. Here there was much more ambivalence and opposition. Some indeed accepted that discipline was part of family life. It was accepted provided it was seen as fair:

I am treated like any other of their children. I have to be told off for things I have done wrong just like any other child would.

Others, however, objected to rules and what they saw as 'strictness'. Some children saw the worst things about foster care as the battles of everyday life:[3]

I have to tidy my room.

Cleaning my teeth.

Getting up early for school.

Others objected to the way discipline was exercised. They did not like being shouted at or, as they saw it, humiliated:

They shout at me all the time and send me upstairs.

Being told not to talk stupid when I'm not…

I have to come in too early. I'm sick of being shouted at.

Others objected to lack of choice and negotiation over what the rules were:

I have too little say on my social hours.

I think that people 16 plus should be able to make their own decisions about issues concerning times to come home in the evening etc. More independence.

Having the freedom to voice your own opinion on what goes on in your care home without placement breakdown. Recognition from carers that their young person has had a different way of coping with situations and they should be respected for that.

As the foster children grew older, conflicts over rules could, it seemed, become defined as conflicts over identity. Some of these conflicts could focus on the badges of teenage culture. So foster children might object because:

> ...[social worker] stopped me from doing things such as having a mobile phone.

> Because she tells me what clothes to wear and what shoes to buy.

> I can't do things like get body piercings or go to sleepovers and is very strict.

These strictures were balanced by other children's appreciation of the relaxed nature of foster care. This could be seen as:

> Good because I have time and space to myself and there is not many rules.

> They are really laid back. I'm allowed a lot of freedom.

Others, however, felt that they were gradually outgrowing foster care. As we will see later, some foster children define their departure from their foster family as a positive move to independence. Others anticipated that this would be so:

> I'm happy here but can't wait until I have a flat.

> I like it here but would like to go when I am older.

Composition of foster family

The issue of who was in their foster family and how they got on with them was naturally of key importance to the foster children. How they got on varied:

> Fitting into this foster family is...very, very, easy...because...the family is very easy to fit into.

> Fitting into this foster family is...most of the time fun...because...I get on with the people and sometimes not.

> Fitting into this foster family is...quite hard sometimes...because...sometimes we just don't agree.

A key factor was obviously the carers themselves. So some children noted that:

> Foster care is...OK because there are people around my age and my foster carers are kind as well.

Foster care is…a good and a bad thing [depending on who the carer is].

Apart from carers the worst things about foster care included:

My brother.

Sharing a bedroom with my sister.

My foster sister. She's a thief and a liar.

A fairly new girl who came to live here. She keeps butting in and being nosy.

Box 8.2

The case studies made the obvious point that it was not just the number of children that mattered; it also mattered how old they were, how they behaved and how the foster carers divided their time between them:

Q: Right – so you lived in quite a few different foster homes, then?

A: Yeah.

Q: Can you remember how many? Was it two more, or…?

A: Erm, I stayed with someone for a week. There was one that had lots of other children, but they were all like my age, so that was different, because we all just played together, but the other one, they were all older, they were all like eight or nine, and I was like four, so that was different.

Q: So that was harder, because you kind of sensed that they didn't always have time for…they had more time for their own children than they did…?

A: Yeah – none of them played with me, or anything – I was just sat by myself!

Q: Aw. Right – so it makes a difference having children your own age to play with, as well?

A: Yeah… I was happy when she had a baby, because I always like little babies, but when they talk, when they'd learned to talk, I just…wanted them to go… [we had these two foster children]. Michael was really mardy if he didn't get his own way, and mum and dad focused a lot on him, but Arran, she got jealous of Michael, so it was just… I just went with my dad, really – my mum didn't really have any time for me, so I just stayed with my dad.

These comments might suggest that children did not want to share their foster home with siblings or other foster children. In practice, however, there was great variety. Some did indeed want to be on their own:

> Fitting into this foster family is…easy…because…there is only the parent and me.

Others, however, liked the bustle and variety of a large home:

> There is lots to do and it is a big family so there's always someone around so you don't get bored.

> Fitting into this foster family is…good…because…I have got two foster brothers.

Others valued the presence of siblings or the fact that they were placed with relatives:

> Fitting into this foster family is…easy…because…I am with my two sisters.

> I am with my brother and we love it here.

> I live with my blood family. (Good thing.)

Some children seemed particularly pleased because they were in a house where there were babies:

> Fitting into this foster family is…okay…because…lots of grandchildren to play with.

> I like my family and my sister (foster) and the babies in the house.

Material things

> Fitting into this foster family is…brilliant…because…Pamela does nice puddings.

A number of children commented on material things as either the best or (less commonly) worst things about foster care. Their importance was tied up with issues that have already come up – sharing, identity, love, independence and 'having fun'.

The most commonly mentioned material provision was 'having a room of one's own'. So the best thing about foster care could be that:

> I get my own room, I am very happy where I am.

Conversely the worst thing could be:

> I share a bedroom.

Bedrooms could be important to a child's identity as the case studies illustrated:

> Q: Does it [bedroom] feel like your own, or does it still feel like your sister's?
>
> A: It feels like Naomi's, because when she was in here…this isn't her bed: I've had my own bed, but that, that, that CD player's hers, that wardrobe's hers, that's hers, the curtains are hers, the wallpaper's hers, the lampshade's hers. Those two pictures are hers – I've never been able to reach them to get them down!

Material provisions could also signal that the child was no longer different from other children:

> I get pocket money, I get to go angling and I get treated like another of their children.

Or that they were grown up:

> …get treated like a young adult. I get clean clothes and pocket money.

Or that they were allowed to have fun:

> There are activities to my interest that I am treated to like ballet, dancing, singing, drama.

> Eating chocolate, comics, Fox Kids, someone to play with.

Activities like everything else related to and were interpreted in the light of attachments. One teenager explained her good relationship with her foster 'dad' on the ground that they had a lot in common:

> Yeah. And when I was in year five, I wanted to do drama, and he paid for me to do that, and everything, and he took me every week, and he's really supportive, really…

Others emphasised that they were loved – 'I get lots of love and playstation games' – and that in general they could take part in the good things of the consumer society. So the good things about foster care could be:

The computer, going on holiday.

Lots of holidays, big house.

Get well fed, take on own a lot on holidays abroad.

Good food, my own bedroom, my own TV and video.

In these things the contrast with their own family may well have been sharp.

What about the care system helps or hinders a sense of belonging?

Foster care has much in common with ordinary family life. It differs from it most sharply in its limited duration and in its necessary connection with another family which also has rights in the child. These fundamental issues recur throughout this book. However, there are other factors that tend to make foster care something other than family care. We consider these below.

Child's prior history

Children arrive with their families with a history. Some have just experienced a breakdown in fostering. They may regret the loss of the previous placement, resent the move, and miss the previous foster family:

I was annoyed because I kept moving from one place to another.

Fitting into this foster family is…hard…because…everything is strange and social workers dump you and leave you.

Fitting into this foster family is…hard…because…I was moved and I was just getting to know my last one.

They may have faced a forced removal from a family home. One found fitting in:

Hard at first, but I was upset because my mum couldn't look after me any more. But now I am happy and settled.

They may feel that they have too little time to adjust. One found the experience:

Rushed and I was not given a choice because social services had nowhere to put me and they didn't want me to go where I was happy.

They find a family whose rules and customs are certainly unfamiliar and may well be different from those of the last family with whom they lived:

> Fitting into this foster family is…hard…because…you don't know people that well.

> Fitting into this foster family is…very hard…because…they have different ways of living, their religion is not always the same and you are usually just dumped there and for a long time never see anyone i.e. social worker.

Understandably they commonly find the experience upsetting and, a frequently used word, 'scary'. So they described the experience or themselves as:

> Sad, nervous, lonely.

> Hard because I had to get to know people again and make new friends.

> Frightened because I had not been in foster care before.

A number of children said that the process was made easier because they already knew somebody in the placement:

> Fitting into this foster family is…quite easy…because…I got to know them before I moved there.

This useful knowledge can occur in various ways. Sometimes the child goes with a sibling. One found the move:

> Upsetting because I didn't know anyone, but I came with my sister so I felt OK.

Some had contact with the carer in other settings. One found moving into foster care:

> Exciting because I know Monica from school who used to teach me how to cook at the infants' school.

Others appeared to have had contact because of a previous placement, their own or a sibling's, or because they had had placements with the carer for short breaks or day care:

> Fitting into this foster family is…OK, because I fitted in well. I knew the foster carers before I came here with my sister living here.

> Fitting into this foster family is…been OK…because…I came for day care.

> Fitting into this foster family is…very easy…because…I have been to them before.

Others were fostered with relatives:

> Fitting into this foster family is…easy…because…they are my nan and granddad.

> Fitting into this foster family is…fine…because…I am with part of my family.

Irrespective of the initial process the children have to learn to fit in:

> …coming here was a nightmare because I didn't know what was going on. I didn't know the family, but now I get on with them like a house on fire.

> Fitting into this foster family is…hard at first but got easy…because…you do not know their way and what they do but it gets really easy…

A number of children said that the length of time they had been in the placement or the fact that they had been there since a baby and did not 'know any different' made 'fitting in' no longer a problem:

> Fitting into this foster family is…easy…because…I've lived here for nine years.

> Fitting into this foster family is…easy…because…I was 15 months old.

> Fitting into this foster family is…the only home I know…because…I was here since I was 18 months.

Being subject to legal and bureaucratic arrangements

> I feel different from every other child.

> I am part of the family. I don't see myself in care.

> Try to make foster children's lives as normal as possible.

Many of the children's complaints had to do with the legal and bureaucratic arrangements within which their experience of family took place. It was this framework which enabled the frequent moves to which they objected, which allowed social workers to influence which family members they saw and which defined the families with whom they were allowed to live. The fact that their carers were paid raised for the children issues – more evident in the last study than the present one – of whether they cared for love or for money. Whereas the moral ties of family life are expected to persist for life, the financial and legal arrangements which underpin foster care mostly stop at 18. In these ways the official context of foster care defines its nature and hence the kind of complaint which the children level at it.

In practice the framework enables good things in the children's eyes as well as bad. As we have seen many were grateful that they were at least safe and many were attached to their carers. Nevertheless, there were two aspects of foster care which were particularly closely tied to bureaucratic requirements and for which none had a good word. These were the restrictions which were placed on foster children in relation to certain normal activities and the widely held belief that foster care was stigmatised and not seen as 'normal'.

The restrictions to which there was most objection seemed to be so-called 'sleep-overs'. Similar issues arose over 'dangerous activities', and school trips, activities which most children are able to undertake without reference to a social worker. A number of the children's recommendations focused on getting rid of these restrictions:

> I would like to stay with friends overnight without people having police checks. It should be OK if my mum and [foster carer] said so.

> I believe that my foster parents should be able to sign a form for me, like permission to go on a trip without going through my social worker.

> I'm not allowed to do dangerous activities, e.g. jet skiing, with my foster family.

Box 8.3

...they can't go and stay at friends', unless they've had a check, and things like that. I can understand why all that's in place, you know, but it singles her out. She always felt singled out. (Child's birth mother)

I didn't used to like that at all, when I was in foster care – I was different to everyone else. Being here with my mum, it was all right. (Child)

A number of children seemed to feel that any contact with a social worker was stigmatising. So they recommended:

No – no social worker. It makes me feel not normal – no offence.

One wished for the future:

To be happy and have nothing to do with social workers.

Others emphasised the normalcy of foster care – a quality they implicitly acknowledged others might doubt:

Foster care is…just like having a normal mum and dad.

Foster care is…isn't like everyone thinks.

Foster care is…not as bad as people who have never been in care think.

Perhaps for this reason those fostered with relatives could be at pains to point out that this was not really fostering at all:

Foster care is…I'm not fostered. (Relative fostering)

Conclusion

This chapter has relied almost exclusively on comments from the children's questionnaires. Many of these emphasise the children's diversity. Over the crucial issue of their relationship with their birth family the respondents have very different views. Some want to go home and have no more to do with the care system. Some want to go home and see their carers a lot. Some want to stay where they are and see their family or particular members of it more. Some want to be adopted by their carers or at the least stay in their placement and get on with their own lives. Corresponding to these broad divisions some see foster care as essentially family care, some see it as a safe and satisfactory alternative to a bleak life, and some see it as a threat to their family bonds. Social workers are largely accepted or rejected according to their success in responding to and negotiating these varying requirements.

Views on what makes good foster care seem to be less varied. There is diversity on whether they want to be the only child in a placement or would value other children and if so whether they would be children of a similar age, babies and so on. However, there is little disagreement that carers should care for you, perhaps even love you, treat you fairly and as a member of the family, listen to you, do things with you, offer advice, and, perhaps, although there is less agreement here, provide rules and control. At older ages at least they should relax the rules, negotiate, and listen to the teenager's side of the story. These basic provisions should be supported by adequate material goods, a room of your own, holidays, activities and encouragement of your interests.

In the children's eyes arrangements outside the foster family should also be adapted to make it less out of the ordinary. It helps if the child knows the family before arrival, comes with a sibling or knows somebody there. Relative placements, while not always ideal, certainly have this advantage. Rules which single the child out in relation to their friends are widely resented. Most parents do not have a family police-checked before they let their child spend the night there. Most do not have to ask a social worker before they can agree to a child going on a school trip. Foster children do not see why they should be made conspicuous by having to go through these time-consuming hoops.

So if foster care were designed by the children it would meet these requirements. This would not, of itself, resolve the agonising dilemmas of their relationship with their birth families. It might, however, provide a safe space in which they themselves could come to terms with these dilemmas and in time, psychologically, move on.

Summary of Chapters 7 and 8

1. In this sample children in foster care were safer and seemed to do better than would have been the case at home. Nevertheless breakdowns, particularly among teenage placements, the pull of home and the expectation of moves at 18 mean that few children both stay for a lengthy period in the same foster home and experience it as a 'permanent base'.

2. A combination of skilful practice, changed expectations about moves at 18 and 'the normalisation' of foster care should, it is hoped, make it more secure and 'permanent' for more foster children.

3. This in turn might enable children to re-evaluate their relationship with their birth families and achieve a relationship with which both sides are more at ease.

Notes

1. In essence social workers are praised for getting children good foster homes, for moving them if unhappy, for listening to them and seeing, if not necessarily agreeing with, their point of view, spending time with the child at McDonald's and similar places, for getting grants for holidays, singing lessons or other key expenses, for moral support in difficult times and perhaps above all for enabling contact when this is what is wanted. They are criticised for failing to do these things, for interfering in what is not their business, for separating child and family, for continually moving the child, for failing to listen to the child's point of view or giving him or her a say in decisions, for not keeping the child informed, not finishing what they promise and being unreliable about appointments and generally inefficient. A tolerant comment on them was that they were nice but rather disorganised. The saddest comment in this section criticised not social workers but social services. 'Yes social services have taken my social worker off me after eight years with me. It has hurt me very much. He has been a great friend to me.'

2. On the latter, however, there were differing views. Two children said the worst thing about foster care was having to eat vegetables. Cats were variously criticised for being bad for black clothing, dangerous to one child's fish and 'generally annoying'.

3. It was not always clear how fundamental these objections were. One child, for example, objected to not getting 'my own way'. This rather blunt way of putting it seemed to undercut the moral position that was apparently being taken. Perhaps it was written with tongue in cheek. Similarly a child may accept the need to get up for school but still not like doing it. As one child philosophically put it, 'There are things that annoy me but they are just normal everyday things that would happen wherever I was living.'

Chapter Nine

Leaving Foster Care

A: Yeah. I mean, because I'm getting older, I want my independence, as well, and I just…when you know that you can move out, you want to, do you know what I mean?

Q: Right.

A: But you don't, as well, because you don't get everything that you get when you're living with someone. If you get what I mean.

Introduction

As we have seen, around one in five of our sample had achieved, in a sense, adult status. Either they had reached the age of 18 or although younger than this they were already living independently rather than with their families or carers or in some form of residential care. This group of young adults are commonly called 'care leavers'. A raft of studies (Biehal *et al.* 1992, 1995; Broad 1998; Stein and Carey 1986) have been concerned with their difficulties and support.[1] These studies have helped to put care leavers on the policy map. Recent legislation (Leaving Care Act 2000) has been designed to improve provision for them.

The previous research has emphasised the transitions faced by care leavers – leaving home, dealing with the job market, further education or parenthood, finding a partner. Typically they confront these changes at a much earlier age than other young people and accomplish them over a much shorter period. Their success in managing these accelerated and compressed transitions has been shown to relate to their previous lives in the care system. Poor educational performance and disrupted care careers have both been shown to predict how well they do.

Our own data on leaving care revealed a paradox. Just under half the children who answered our questionnaires said that they wanted to go on living with their foster carers beyond the age of 18. Only around one in ten actually did so. Why then did they move? Did they choose to do so? Or was it a matter of the assumption that young people of this age move on? These questions are central to our concern with providing 'permanence'.

This chapter is concerned with these issues and particularly with:

- the routes to adult status – the reasons for which young people leave the care system early, leave for independent living around 18 or remain after 18 with their birth families or foster carers

- evaluations of these moves – what the young people, their carers and social workers think of them

- the possibilities for improving the quality of the moves – for example, by delaying them.

Much of this has been surveyed before, most recently by Biehal and her colleagues (1992, 1995). In revisiting this territory we make comparisons where we can. We also try to exploit the advantages of our prospective methodology.

Although the term 'independent living' implies that the young people were on their own, we will in fact be considering two overlapping groups: those who had moved into independent living, including some aged less than 18; and those who were over 18, including a small group who remained with their foster family or returned to their own.

Method

The chapter draws mainly on three sources of data: 83 questionnaires from the young persons' last foster carers (72% response rate), 62 from social workers (53% response rate), and 49 from the young people themselves (42% response rate, 47% of those mailed a questionnaire). Overall we had at least one questionnaire on 104 of our 116 who were living independently.

For each source of data we compared those responding to non-respondents in terms of age, sex, total Goodman score at first contact, whether first placement disrupted and other variables we thought might influence response. The only difference we found concerned the young people. Those replying were more likely to have foster carers who said they had been involved in providing some form of support after the young person left. This bias reflected the fact that we had contacted many of the young people through their former foster carers. It may mean that on average our respondents were more favourable to their carers than a true sample would have been. However, we also contacted the young people through social workers and aftercare teams. The respondents certainly included some young people who were very negative about fostering.

There are a number of methodological problems in analysing these data. The 'facts' we wish to explore are often elusive. For example, we want to know whether the young person 'wanted' to leave care when they did. As we will see, the young people were sometimes ambivalent about this and would be hard put to say whether they wanted to leave or not. Moreover, the moves took place in the past and some social workers responding may not have had direct experience of the events on which they commented. In addition the samples are sometimes small (49 in the case of the replies from the young people).

For these reasons we would be cautious about putting too much weight on any particular finding. Nevertheless, the findings from all three sources of evidence seem to support each other. This consistency gives us more confidence in the conclusions we reach.

The reasons for independent living

Leaving early

The main difference between those who were in independent living and those who were not was obviously age. Two-thirds of those aged 15 at first contact (and thus 18 or over at sweep 3) were living on their own. By contrast only 13 per cent of those aged 13 or 14 when first contacted (and thus 16 or 17 when we followed them up) were living independently and not in some kind of hostel.

The first question of interest is why this younger group of care leavers were living independently when their peers were not.

The most striking feature of the young (16 to 17) age group in independent living was that they had had difficulty in settling. Six of the nine on whom we had the relevant information had had a placement disruption by follow-up in 1999. All but one had had either a disruption or the failure of a family placement by the time we followed them up in 2001. The difference in disruption rates between this group and their peers was not quite significant ($p=0.067$, Fisher exact test). Nevertheless, the figures suggest that independent living for this group is used for difficult young people who do not find it easy to live in foster care or at home.[2]

John had had a large number of foster placements when his last long-term one broke down. According to his social worker:

> He'd been in foster care for quite a while, and wanted to return…but [the managers decided] that it would be setting him up to fail if we set up another placement for him…we were trying to find somewhere for him to live permanently, and it was proving to be a little difficult, because they're thin on the ground, foster carers.

Older young people

We had information on the probable location of 120 out of 135 children in the older (over 18) age ranges. Eighty-nine (74%) of these 120 were believed to be living with a partner, on their own or with friends. Thirteen (10%) were with their families and 17 (14%) were still with foster carers or adoptive parents.[3] In addition there were two at 'other location' and 13 whose addresses could not be found.

The fact that three-quarters of these young people were, in the ordinary sense of the word, living independently suggests that this is the expected solution. Why nevertheless do some stay with their foster families or return to their birth families?

The 17 young people aged over 18 in 2001 and living with their foster families differed significantly from the others in three ways. They were:

- on average younger ($p=0.020$)
- more likely to have said on one of their questionnaires that they would like to stay with their foster carers till they were over 18 or 'for ever'
- more likely to be on our widest definition 'disabled' (63% v. 18%).

So this outcome is probably influenced by choice and by either the greater objective difficulties facing disabled children[4] or a greater acceptance that it is 'legitimate' for them to stay on with their foster carers. In general the factors that predict placement breakdown (high Goodman score, unhappiness at school, high childlike attachment, relatively short time in placement at sweep 1, no relative forbidden contact) are all negatively associated with staying on. Lack of numbers, however, means that the association is not significant. As these young people are younger, albeit over 18, than the others it is likely that few of them remain for a long time with their carers.[5]

Box 9.1

Ken had a learning impairment and had been fostered for five years with the same carers. The assumption had been that he would stay on with his foster carers. His carers explained:

> we tried for a long time, so we went down that route for a whole year, being sorted out, and in the end they wanted this IQ test and he had a bit over the level where they would do adult fostering.

So the upshot was that he moved down the road and the future was still uncertain.

Older young people with their birth families

An obvious difference between the young adults with their birth families and the remainder was that they were more likely to have returned home by the time we followed them up in 1999. This, however, was not a complete explanation since 10 of the 16 known to have gone home at that date were no longer with their families at the second follow-up.

Surprisingly those still with their families were no more likely than others to have told us in a questionnaire that they wanted to go home on leaving foster care. They were, however, significantly more likely to have been seen by their foster carers as not committed to foster care (6 out of 12 were seen in this way as against 6 out of 82 who had returned home but were no longer there (Fisher exact test, $p=0.026$)). Home perhaps had been less of a positive choice

Box 9.2

Tara had considered returning to her father before going to independent living. She explained:

> I was going to get a house to live in with my dad but then I had a second thought... I'm thinking no, if I do this, this is going to be big. If I live with my dad, it's not going to blow over. I'm still going to get it chucked in my face whatever happens with my mum and dad, and I'll still get the blame for it.

A less confident young woman under pressure from a foster placement breakdown might well have taken a different decision. This would have meant a less than positive choice for returning to a birth family.

than a response to the young people's dislike of foster care. In keeping with this suggestion, only 3 of the 12 who had gone home at some date but were now living away from it were seen by their foster carers as returning through a planned process.

Moves from foster care

The young people's experience

The care leavers who replied to our questionnaire took on average a reasonably optimistic view of the move from foster care. Asked what they had wanted to happen at the time, around a quarter said they would have liked to stay with their foster carers. Over half wanted to live on their own or with a partner or friend of their own age.

We grouped these respondents into three main groups. The distinctions were based on whether in their view they had wanted to move, had had no choice about the move, or had left because of a quarrel between themselves and the carers.

The first group (positives) consisted of 19 cases who took a positive view of the move. They did not emphasise, as others did, the bad points of carers or fostering. Instead they were generally full of praise for their carers although one or two had found the lack of independence irksome. However, they felt that it was time to move on and generally saw themselves as moving for positive reasons – for a job, to go to college or university, to look after a child, or just to enjoy 'independence':

I wanted to move on to university and I was 19 years old as well.

I was happy because I was going to move in with my boyfriend and get ready to have my baby.

I had a couple of bad foster homes but when I found Jane and Mike all changed. I knew they were the ones for me. I was treated as one of their own... I wanted to get out on my own. I couldn't live with Jane and Mike for ever.

They described themselves as happy about the move, albeit in some cases a happiness tinged with sadness at leaving their carers or anxiety about how they would cope. Nevertheless, they felt ready for the move and did not feel that they were being forced out (see Table 9.1).

Table 9.1 Young people's views about leaving foster care

Outcome wished for by young person	n
Stay and be adopted by foster carers	3
Go to other adopters	–
Not to be adopted but to stay with foster carer(s)	8
Go to residential care	–
Go to live with a parent(s) or other relatives	4
Live with a partner or other friends your age	6
Live with older people that you knew	–
Live on your own	23
Live with adoptive parent(s)	–
Go somewhere else:	2

Source: Questionnaire to young people at sweep 3 (n=46).

> I felt I was ready to start a life for myself independently. Sooner or later I was going to leave foster care anyway, so why not when I felt ready (I was 17 years 11 months)?

> …happy [about] being independent – not happy [because I was] sad to leave home, anxious about new environment.

> I was happy about moving from foster care but I would also have been happy to stay in foster care but with my situation it was best to get my own place. My foster carer did let me and my son stay there till I found somewhere to live. She wasn't kicking me out though, it was my own choice.

This element of choice distinguished them from our second group of ten cases who did not feel ready and did not feel that they had a choice. This group varied in their descriptions of foster care, some valuing it and some not. Their emphasis, however, was on the fact that they had been forced out, an event which they variously attributed to their foster carers, social services or a combination of the two:

> I moved back with my dad after being with my foster parent four and a half years because she wanted more foster kids in as she would get more

money… I was unhappy at the way my foster parent could throw me out (and we were friends).

I was 18 and social services no longer had an obligation to support or help me.

People thought I was ready to move [respondent did not].

Unsurprisingly these young adults did not like the way they were moved. In this respect their reactions varied from the mixed to the very negative. Like the first group they valued the prospect of freedom. At the same time they variously felt that they were not ready for the move, that things moved too fast or that they were suddenly wrenched from a place they had come to see as their home:

I was happy at the fact that I had my own space. I was unhappy that I had to move so quickly and that I didn't have a TV or furniture, etc.

[I was unhappy about] going it alone! I didn't have any social or independence skills from my first carers, my second gave me a quick brush over as they did not have enough time, but I needed more.

Losing all my friends was terrible. I spent years with some friends. They were part of my life until I HAD TO MOVE. [Capitals in original.] I was slightly looking forward to independence.

The final group of 19 cases differed from the other two in that they defined the reason for the move as essentially a quarrel. They did not like foster care or their foster carers. In some cases they saw the disagreement as a natural part of growing up and their own desire for independence. Such cases differed little, if at all, from those we have described as 'positive':

I got on well with my foster carer but there was a lot of arguments with the other foster kids what was there. I left because I wanted my own independence and I wasn't getting enough there… It was a new start for me and I learnt how to cope by myself but I was sad to leave my foster carer.

In most cases, however, they thought that the antipathy was mutual and they placed at least as much emphasis on the prospect of moving away from foster care as they did on the potential joys of independence:

[I left because] I did not like the foster placement I was in.

[I left because] I was 18 and my care order had come to an end THANK GOD.

[I left because] I had had enough of mental abuse. It was the best thing I'd ever done. Life in care for me has and always will be a nightmare.

The results of such moves were variously experienced. The young adult last quoted felt that the results were thoroughly positive:

I was happy about every aspect of moving. I felt the chains had been released, I felt free and relieved.

Others were happy about the results even if not about the way they were achieved:

[I left foster care] because I was being blamed for something I did not say. [I was happy] because I could see my family more and take driving lessons. I was unhappy about the way I was treated.

Got chucked out. [I was happy about] place of my own. My own space. No one to tell me what to do.

Others were more dubious:

I was asked to leave. [I] was not ready to move. Did not want to live with mum.

[I left because] me and my foster carer had an argument and because we were really close it upset me a lot.

Some experienced the results as disastrous:

I was growing up and it was difficult between me and my foster mum because I wanted to go out more. My social worker looked into finding semi-independent living for me... I had led a very sheltered life... I missed my foster mum and the other young people in the hostel took advantage of my innocence and corrupted and bullied me.

Unsurprisingly these categories were related to experience of disruptions. Two-thirds of the 'quarrel group' had experienced at least one placement disruption (since 1998) as against less than one in six of the 'positive' group.

Carers' and social workers' views of the moves

We explored how the social workers and carers evaluated the moves from foster care and how these views related to those of the young people. We look at various aspects of the move: whether it was planned, whether the young person was seen as ready for it, whether the new environment was seen by the foster carer as appropriate and whether the young person was seen as wanting the move.

We defined a planned move as one which occurred when:

- the young person was said by the foster carer to leave as a result of a planned process

- the social worker said the move had been planned for a considerable time

- the social worker said that the move was not sudden and unexpected.

Where we had information from either social worker or foster carer but not both we judge the move planned or otherwise on the basis of the information available. Out of 89 cases on whom we were able to make a rating, just over a third (35%) had a move which was on our definition fully planned.[6]

Almost by definition those who did not make planned moves were more likely to have experienced a disruption or the breakdown of a family placement. Two-thirds of them (67%) had had one or other of these experiences. By contrast this was true of only 13 per cent of those whose move was, on our definition, fully planned. In keeping with our earlier discussion, planned moves were more common among older young people. Those making planned moves left foster care on average a year later than those making unplanned ones.

We asked social workers and foster carers whether the young person was *ready to move* and also whether he or she *wanted to move* at that point. In between a fifth and a quarter of the cases on which they commented they felt that the young adult was not ready to move. In only four out of ten cases were they sure the young adult was ready. In around half the cases they felt the young person wanted to move but in a fifth they thought he or she definitely did not want to move.

Generally foster carers took a rather bleak view of the move from foster care. They were less sanguine than social workers about whether the young adult was ready to move. In 57 per cent of the cases on which they commented they were sure this was not the case. In nearly four out of ten cases (half those where they were prepared to express an opinion) they thought their former foster child was going to a place where he or she would not be safe. In half the cases they felt the foster child would not get proper guidance and in a further fifth they were not sure. In a quarter of cases they said the move involved a change of jobs or schools. The foster carers' open-ended comments reinforced these rather negative perceptions. Generally they felt that moves should be better timed (neither frustratingly delayed nor done in a rush), and that there should be a greater choice of placements:

> [Long wait for flat] during which behaviour deteriorated dramatically – found place determined on the basis of emergency need [so moved suddenly].

> …there should be a lot more planning into moving children back to their birth parents and moves should be taken much more slowly over a longer period of time.

> The difficulty is not having enough placements available to enable us to move placements on without many reservations.

Foster carers could also be critical of the lack of support on leaving:

> As a foster carer of 18 years experience and always having difficult teenagers I find this a continual problem that teenagers leave care without support…most of mine have been OK because I have been there for them. One went to a drug squat but is OK now. Two went to hostels and struggled. One went to a house but had support.

> …more support on leaving care – particularly financial help – managing money and budgeting. Needs to continue for some while. More help in finding work and encouraging her to seek employment.

> I felt social services were glad to get him off their hands.

Our questions about readiness to move were matched by a question to the young people. We asked them whether they moved before they were ready. Three out of ten said 'yes', two out of ten said that this was partly true and just under half said it was not true. So according to all three groups less than half those who left were definitely ready to do so.[7]

We asked the foster carers to sum up their views of the move by saying how happy they were about it on a five-point scale. Predictably they were happiest when the young person fell into our 'positive group', rather less happy when he or she fell into the 'no choice' group and least happy when he

---

Box 9.3

Keith (who has already appeared in Chapter 2) had spent five years in the same foster placement. On reaching 18 his social worker was anxious that he moved to supported lodgings. Keith himself did not wish to move. The foster carers were unwilling to agree to the suggested compromise that he remained (in the foster home as a 'supported lodger') with strict rules, requiring that he did his own housework, budgeting, etc. They felt this was unrealistic. The result was unhappy. The social worker felt that the foster carers should realise they were not real parents. The foster carers felt criticised. Keith felt rejected, did £2000 worth of damage to the carer's car, drank a bottle of vodka and was picked up by the police, and ended up in an informal placement with a friend's family while refusing to see the social worker.

---

or she fell into the 'quarrel' group. The groups were also related to our rating of planning. Forty-one per cent of those in the positive or no choice groups were seen as being planned moves as against less than 10 per cent of the 'quarrel' group.

Could the move have been delayed or avoided?

All sources seem to agree that at least a substantial minority of these young people did not want to move and that many of them were not ready to move. Was there any way in which precipitate or unwanted moves could have been avoided?

One way would have been through adoption. Around a fifth of the young adults who replied to the questionnaire said that they had wished to be adopted by their foster carers. Nearly a quarter said that this was 'partly true'. This was a higher figure than we found for children currently with their foster carers, a difference that may reflect chance, the time at which the later judgement was made or the ability of the care leavers to consider all their foster carers as potential adopters and not just their latest one. Be that as it may, the possibility of adoption is clearly something that would normally have come up at an earlier stage if it was going to be considered at all. The possibility is therefore discussed in an earlier chapter.

A different option would be that the young person stayed on beyond the age of 18. This was a current possibility. Moreover in both our surveys of current foster children between four out of ten and five out of ten of the children said that this was something they wanted. In practice, however, staying on for any length of time appeared to be something which occurred rarely except, perhaps, among disabled young people. So would the foster carers have been willing to keep the young person? And if so were these the young people who wanted to stay? We have already considered these issues for those currently in foster care. What is the position for those who have left?

In half the cases the foster carers said they did not want the young person to stay. In just over a third of the cases they wanted her or him to stay. In around one in seven cases they were unsure.

We looked at these preferences in relation to our three groups of care leavers. The numbers were small but, as far as they went, the results were not encouraging. Eleven cases fell into the positive group. In six of these the carer wanted the young person to stay. By contrast they were certain they wanted only one out of seven cases to stay in the 'no choice' group and only 3 out of 13 cases to stay in the 'quarrel' group.

We also asked the carers if any of a number of factors might have influenced their views about keeping the child. Of the 63 carers who answered one or more of these questions, nearly half (46%) identified at least one factor which would have influenced them a great deal. Less than a third (30%) indicated there was nothing that would have influenced them. Unfortunately, as can be seen from Table 9.2, the clearest factors seemed to be a better relation-

Table 9.2 Would any of the following have influenced your views about keeping the child?

	n	No	Perhaps	Very much so
Better relationship with child	51	28 (55%)	13 (26%)	10 (20%)
Agreement of SSD	44	30 (68%)	9 (21%)	5 (11%)
Extra financial support	44	33 (75%)	8 (18%)	3 (7%)
Other SSD support	49	29 (59%)	14 (29%)	6 (12%)
Other personal circumstances	46	29 (63%)	7 (15%)	10 (22%)

Source: Questionnaires to foster carers at sweep 3.

ship with the child and the personal circumstances of the carer – issues which it may be difficult for the social services to control. Nevertheless just under a quarter (23%) of those responding said that their views would have been very much influenced by one or more of three factors: the agreement of the social services department (SSD) that they should keep the child, extra financial support or other SSD support. Just under a third (31%) said that one of these factors might have influenced their views.

These three inducements would apparently have made little difference to those in the 'positive group' of care leavers. Five of the seven carers involved said they would have made no difference to them. By contrast 10 of the 15 carers involved with the other groups said they might have made a difference. Five of these said the difference would have been considerable. In short, there is probably some scope for enabling at least some young people to stay on longer.

Conclusion

One reason for this research was to explore the possibility that more young people could stay on in foster care and thus avoid the accelerated and compressed transitions which have been shown to be characteristic of leaving care (Biehal *et al.* 1995; Stein 2004). These findings suggest the following:

- Staying on beyond 18 is rare.
- Only a minority of those who move on do so as a result of a process planned over some time.
- Inevitably moves raise the issues implicit in many young people's accounts of foster care which have to do with 'being an outsider', 'rejection', loss of birth family and an inability to control one's own fate.
- In around a third of the cases these issues were, from the point of view of the young people, handled well but in others the young person either felt pushed out or saw the ending as the result of a quarrel.
- Foster carers were particularly critical of the moves, feeling that in many cases they were premature, and to inappropriate settings where the young person was ill-supported and dubiously safe.

Strategies for addressing these problems would seem to involve:

- reducing the number of breakdowns of placements when the young people were 16 or 17 – something we considered in our last book (Sinclair, Wilson and Gibbs 2004)

- changing the expectation that young people inevitably move by 18, thus increasing the number of positive moves

- increasing support to foster carers after 18 thus reducing the number of 'forced moves'.

These strategies may not make a large difference to the numbers staying on. As we have seen, the cases where there seemed to be the strongest reasons for keeping the young person with the foster carer tended to be those where the foster carer was least open to this possibility. Steps therefore need to be taken to reduce the sense of rejection and isolation which may follow a move. This could involve:

- involving foster carers as much as possible in the planning of moves and in supporting the young people when they have left – as will be seen in Chapter 12, this may be possible even when a placement has officially 'broken down'

- ensuring that the placements to which the young person moves are in other ways adequately supported

- working with the young people's common wish to have their own place and manage their own lives.

The degree to which these strategies might bear fruit are an issue for the next chapter.

Notes

1. For a recent summary of this literature see Stein (2002).

2. Biehal and her colleagues (1995) similarly found that disruptions were more common among those aged less than 17 on leaving the care system.

3. Biehal and her colleagues (1992, 1995) suggest that around 10 per cent of children stay on with foster carers, and in the older age range leave care to live with their birth families. The latter kind of arrangement did not last in their study so the numbers living at home in our study were higher than this previous work would suggest.

4. One study (Rabiee, Priestley and Knowles 2001) suggests that the difficulties facing disabled young people leaving the foster care system means that they have 'abrupt and delayed' transitions from it.

5. A striking and unpredicted finding was that all those remaining had been fostered by couple carers in 1997. In most cases these would have been the same carers as in 2001 – 13 out of the 16 were with their index carer. This finding was highly significant

($p<0.01$) but was not predicted. It may be that couple carers are better able to stand the financial loss of continuing to foster or that lone carers are uneasy at looking after adults. The finding may be a chance one but would be worth testing in any further research.

6. Biehal and her colleagues (1995) defined two-thirds of their moves from 'care' in their study as 'planned'. The difference from this study may well reflect differences in the criteria used.

7. In practice the concept of 'readiness' was probably interpreted differently by the young adults and their former foster carers. Where we had questionnaires from both, their views of 'readiness' were quite unrelated. Perhaps the young people's answers reflected willingness or otherwise to move while the foster carers were concerned with the young person's perceived maturity. By contrast there was a significant correlation between the young person's view of readiness and that of the social worker. Similarly, the young person's view that he or she had no choice over the move correlated with the social worker's view that the young person was not ready ($r=0.52$, $p=0.02$).

Chapter Ten

Living Independently: What Makes A Difference?

I'm still moving around at 18 years of age and I've been moving since I was a little girl and I've got nobody apart from my dad but he's poorly and so that's that. Guess that's how it's always going to be. (Former foster child)

I am getting on better with my family and have my own flat. I have maintained a steady job and have two beautiful children. (Former foster child)

Introduction

We have seen that the way older foster children graduate to independence is not, in many cases, ideal. Does this matter? Is it the manner of their leaving that determines what happens after? Or the quality of the support or lack of it to which they move? Or is all determined by earlier events – the degree to which the young people are emotionally damaged, their genetic inheritance, their prior relationship with their birth families or foster carers, or the skills and qualifications they acquired or failed to acquire at school? These are the kinds of question with which this chapter is concerned.

The questions we have just posed are, of course, simplistic. They imply that there may be a small number of variables – e.g. Goodman score – which determine subsequent outcomes. More likely what is at issue is a complex unravelling of events – earlier histories make more likely subsequent events and environments which in turn lead on to other histories. Or perhaps there is a difference between short-term and long-term outcomes. In the short term, environment is what makes the difference. In the longer term, the young person's basic resilience or lack of it wins out. Despite these probable complexities, the limitations of statistical analyses mean that we begin with the simpler questions. So we will be concerned with:

- the current situation of the young person
- the degree to which this situation is desirable or not (outcomes)
- the relationship between the young person's account of their experience of fostering and their outcomes
- the other correlates of outcomes
- the explanation of these correlations.

As in the last chapter we will be visiting territory that others have already explored. Our main comparisons are with the study by Biehal and her colleagues (1995).

Method

We use the same sub-samples and sources of evidence as in the last chapter. We use this evidence to describe the situation of the young people, to provide measures of outcome and to predict them.

Where were the young people living?

As will be seen later the young people's accounts of their experience gave considerable importance to housing. Briefly, they valued safe housing from which they did not have to move. At its best their housing was a source of self-esteem, gave a sense of security, and was close to important family or friends.

Box 10.1

The next chapter gives the history of Tara and Alistair. Tara's high-standard housing, coming as it did packaged with a committed social worker, was probably an important element in her success. Alistair's housing was a more ambiguous asset. He invested much in decorating it, valued its closeness to his aunt but was worried by the youths who gathered outside it.

Against this background we asked the foster carers, social workers and young people where the young person was on 1 January 2001[1] (see Table 10.1).

Table 10.1 Living situation of young people according to different sources

Situation	Source of information	
	Social worker or foster carer	Young person
With foster carers	13 (13%)	3 (6%)
With birth parent(s)	9 (9%)	4 (8%)
With other relatives	2 (2%)	1 (2%)
Residential accommodation or hostel	7 (7%)	6 (12%)
Lodgings	10 (10%)	2 (4%)
Flat with partner	13 (13%)	8 (16%)
Flat with friends	3 (3%)	2 (4%)
Flat on own	24 (24%)	17 (35%)
Other	16 (16%)	5 (10%)
Not known	2 (2%)	1 (2%)
Total	99 (100%)	49 (100%)

Overall about four out of ten of the young people were 'independent' in the sense that they were living on their own or (in about a third of these cases) with a partner. Another four out of ten were living with older people with roughly equal proportions in lodgings, with foster carers, or with birth families/relatives. The remaining two out of ten were not known or in a variety of 'other' accommodation (e.g. prisons or university halls of residence).

Surprisingly there was not a significant difference in the average ages of the young people in these different types of accommodation. The youngest on average were those who were in lodgings or in residential accommodation.[2]

We asked the young people about changes of address. Those who answered our questionnaires told us that they had left foster care on average 21 months earlier. On average they had lived over that period at more than three different addresses. There was, however, a considerable variation in how stable their accommodation had been. Just over a quarter had had only one address and a similar proportion had had six or more.

Box 10.2

Out of our six case studies of young people in independent living two (Tara and Alistair) seemed to have stable accommodation. One (Sunita) was at university but living with her foster carer in the vacations; one had just moved to a friend's house after social services and the foster carers had failed to agree on arrangements for him to stay; one had reached 18 and moved as an 'adult fostering' from a hostel to a foster carer with whom he had had respite; and one had just moved from his foster carer to a flat she owned down the road. It was not certain if he would stay there long term.

Unsurprisingly the number of addresses tended to be greater the longer the time since the young adult had left foster care. Allowing for this a third of the sample seemed to have quite stable housing careers. They had had no more than one address for every ten months out of foster care. At the other end of the scale 29 per cent of this small sample had more than two addresses every ten months. Those who left foster care at a younger age tended to have rather more addresses per month out of foster care, possibly because they had periods in residential care or supported lodgings. Half of those replying to our questionnaire had been at their current address for less than six months. Only a minority (9 out of 37) appeared to have achieved stable independent accommodation in the sense that they had had no more than two moves and were living on their own or with a partner.

What was their employment situation?

The employment situation of young people can be hard to describe. They may be securely employed; marginally employed in short-term, part-time or 'black economy' jobs; on the verge of employment (in training schemes or undertaking voluntary work); or definitely unemployed as a result of lack of capacity or choice. They may also be full-time students.

We tried to capture this rather elusive situation in two ways. First, we asked the foster carers and social workers to rate the young person's involvement in work on a four-point scale from low (out of work and not trying to get it) to high (in stable work and committed to it).[3] We used the individual ratings or their average where both had replied to create an overall rating with three categories: 'out of job market', 'verging on work' and 'in work'. We also asked the young people what they were doing at the time they answered the questionnaire.

Box 10.3

One of the young people in our case studies (Alistair) had had a relatively stable job, initially in catering and subsequently as a care worker. Three others had temporary or part-time work in the fast-food industry, one was at university, and one (Tara) was looking after her baby. Of the six the last two, who had no current contact with work, were by far the most settled.

Our ratings were available on 83 young people (72% of the potential sample). According to these:

- just under a fifth (18%) were in steady work and committed to it
- just over half (51%) were out of the job market, not in work and not seriously looking or preparing for it
- around a third (31%) were in intermediate situations.

According to the young people themselves:

- just over a fifth (23%) were in paid work
- nearly half (44%) were out of the job market – either looking after a child (13%) or unemployed (31%)
- a third were receiving training (three cases), at school, college or university (11 cases), or in other situations (e.g. on an agency's books).

As can be seen the different sources of evidence are roughly agreed on the proportions of young people who are in work.[4] Again only a minority – probably between a fifth and a quarter – could be said to have achieved a successful transition to work.[5]

How much support were they getting from foster carers?

As we will see in our next chapter, foster carers can be significant sources of support to their former foster children. How far is this common? Overall we had questionnaires from foster carers on 76 (two-thirds) of the young people in independent living and we asked them about the support they provided.

Just over a fifth (22%) of the carers said they saw the young people on at least a weekly basis. A further four out of ten saw them once every two to three weeks or – more commonly – in occasional bursts. Just under four out of ten said they either saw them less frequently than this or (in a quarter of the cases) never saw them at all.

We suspected that carers would be more likely to return questionnaires about young people who had left if they were interested in them and continuing to support them. Table 10.2 may therefore overestimate the amount of support provided. For example, it is conceivable, if highly unlikely, that all those who did not return our questionnaires had provided no support for the young people. Even on this assumption, the proportion who received at least some help would be 47 per cent while around a fifth of the young people would have stayed at least a night with their carers after leaving foster care.

For their part the young people were generally more positive than negative about the help they were likely to get from foster carers. A quarter said they saw their carers at least weekly. Just over a quarter said they never saw them at all. Nearly four out of ten said their foster carers would always help if asked, a third said they would not and the remainder gave equivocal answers. As we contacted a number of young people through their foster carers these figures may also be rather too encouraging.[6]

Social workers also gave a high estimate to help given by foster carers – at least in some cases. In just under a quarter of cases they said that this was 'a lot'. However, in nearly half the cases they estimated the help as 'none'.[7]

In general the help provided seemed to reflect the previous relationship. Our measures of it were generally lower when the young person had had a placement disruption since first contact, when they had a comparatively negative view of their fostering experience or had scored comparatively high on our rejection score at first contact. Those who left foster care at a younger age were also more likely to have relatively little support from their foster carers, possibly because they had left for reasons of poor relationships rather than age.

The young people's perception of support also appeared to be related to their personalities and, possibly, other sources of support. Those who scored

Table 10.2 Proportion of foster carers reporting different kinds of support

Form of support	%
Had them to stay overnight	33
Had them to stay for a longer period	23
Done washing for them	23
Had their friends in the house	30
Lent or given them money	29
Given them a present	59
Talked over things that happened when they were fostered with you	60
Talked to them about things that matter to them now	63
Calmed them down in a crisis	34
Talked to other people on their behalf	36
Given them a meal	59
Taken them out	40
Helped them with school work	7
Helped with a job application or job problem	30
Sent them a card or letter	51
Other	16
None of the above	26

high on our measure of childlike attachment and also on our measure of Goodman score were significantly less likely to perceive their foster carer as ready to help. This association held when we allowed for the amount of support the foster carers had apparently given.

Overall all our sources agreed that a significant minority of foster children got considerable support from their foster carers. At the other extreme a sizeable number – nearly half according to the social workers – got none. The actual amount of support seemed to reflect previous relationships. Perceptions of support were also influenced by the former foster child's willingness to acknowledge it, by the foster carer's readiness to offer it, by the existence or otherwise of support from the young adult's family, and by the length of time out of the care system.

How much support were they getting from other sources?

We asked the young people to list the people to whom they turned if they got into difficulties. They cited around 110 different people or groups of people to whom they would turn for support and advice.[8] Family members were most commonly mentioned (36 mentions), followed by partners (fiancées, boyfriends etc.) and their families (21 mentions), youth, residential and social services teams or workers (21 mentions), foster carers (18 mentions), friends (17 mentions), doctors and health visitors (five mentions) and various others (four mentions). Two young people said they would turn to no one, although a number qualified their lists (e.g. by saying that a boyfriend or mother was only 'sometimes' helpful or that they thought it best to lean on no one but the leaving care team had been helpful).

A striking feature of these lists was their diversity. In the case of families the young people usually only listed one or two members out of what was clearly a large potential range. Mothers (13 mentions) were the most commonly listed but fathers (six mentions), siblings (eight mentions), aunts and uncles (seven mentions) were all included as were a cousin, a family friend and a grandmother.[9] Similarly, the 21 mentions of youth and social services included a bewildering array of support workers, social workers, leaving care teams, staff groups in hostels, youth workers, key workers and teams of (to us) uncertain provenance. The nature of this support was no doubt equally varied. For example, some may well have got good support from one or two members of their family while they found others a source of stress.

In an attempt to get some purchase on the extent of support provided we asked the foster carers and the social workers how far the young person was 'clearly attached to at least one adult' or 'not attached to any adult'. The rating was made on a four-point scale and we expected it to be made on the latest information available. We averaged the two ratings as a measure of the degree to which the young person had at least some emotional ties. As an additional measure of informal support we averaged the ratings given to us by the young people of the degree of support they received from friends, family or partner, and other people.

The two summary measures were quite highly correlated ($r=0.51$, $p<0.001$). Inspection of them suggested that overall just over a quarter of the young people were clearly well supported, scoring at or near the top of the scale on both measures. Around a fifth were clearly poorly supported. The remainder, around half the sample, were in an intermediate position with contradictory scores on one or other measure or medium scores on both.[10]

The young people themselves were generally more positive than this assessment would suggest. Half were quite clear that they 'had good friends'. Six out of ten were quite clear they were getting on with their family or partner. Four out of ten were definite that there were a lot of other people to help.

How did the young people feel they were getting on?

In general the young adults took quite a positive attitude to their time out of foster care. A quarter said that things had been going 'very well', six out of ten said they had been going 'well on the whole'. The remainder said they had been going badly or, in one case, very badly.

Some young people's lives were clearly going very well. Chloe, for example, reported that her foster carers had encouraged her to get her GCSEs and a GNVQ in Health and Social Care. Without them she would not have been working in a nursing home on an EMI unit. She reported on her life with justifiable pride:

> ...bought my own house on a quiet and nice street, had a baby son (now four months old), got my own dog (English bull terrier), I pay all my bills (with boyfriend), keep in touch with foster carers and their family.

By contrast other ratings seemed rather optimistic. One for example said that her life been going well on the whole:

> I have a nice house now with all my material needs. Going to college in September and have two children and boyfriend.

The foster carer was not so enthusiastic:

> Since leaving me she has had two babies, social services put in a lot of help...but both have been taken into care. Her boyfriend is in prison...no really good friends. She came and stayed with me for two weeks. I was happy to have her but I think social services should have provided support...

Another who felt life was going well on the whole valued his independence but regretted his lack of money and losing his flat. His social worker responding earlier to our questionnaire was highly committed to him but struggled to find positive features in the situation:

> He is vulnerable and is abusing alcohol and drugs and is facing eviction because of rowdiness and damage in his flat…however this shows signs of getting better…lots of work went into finding a college placement to do NVQ art and he only attended four times when given a lift…

In this case at least the social worker and the young person seem to have differed over what counts as 'life going well'. Such differences may reflect themes which recurred in the young people's questionnaires and which seemed to represent both the criteria against which they assessed their lives and the goals which motivated their behaviour.[11]

One goal or criterion explicitly mentioned by a number of young people was 'independence'. This was a matter of 'having your own place', 'your own space', keys and freedom to come and go. It implied accommodation, enough money to pay bills, the maturity and skills to be able to manage these things and friends to ward off loneliness. The achievement of these subsidiary goals was a matter of pride and self-esteem. Failure to achieve them was deplored. Answers to questions about what had gone well or badly included:

> …my own space, freedom and my own independence – I am still working, paying all bills on time, keeping clean and tidy…

> I have made a lot of new friends and I am a lot happier in myself. I feel not as different from everyone else now.

> I'm lonely living by myself. I have to pay the bills which I can't.

A further goal implicit in what many (not all) the young people wrote was the need to establish themselves with a family. This could involve sorting things out with their own family, an area where some seemed to have unfinished business:

> He was always close to his sister – moved to family in North, coped with both 'acceptance and rejection' from his mother – moved back to live with sister. (Social worker)

The goal of acquiring a family could involve adopting a new family (e.g. a partner's) or establishing that their former foster family was now in a sense theirs. Things that had been going well for two respondents were:

...having my foster carer around and seeing her every day and staying overnight and spending Christmas with her and the family...

We now live in a nice house with my boyfriend and I'm expecting another child. His family are now my family and we couldn't be looked after any better.

Finally, (but not exclusively of the above) it could also involve establishing a family of one's own:

Main thing is I have got a son of my own and got engaged and my girlfriend and I have got my own place with my girlfriend and my son.

Others, however, had none of these things:

Family problems, no friends, bad job for two and a half years...

A third criterion for doing well was that the young person had acquired a respected social role. This could variously be being a 'housewife' or mother, doing a college or university course, or getting a decent job. So the young people reported:

...being a homemaker makes me happy. I love cooking.

...job well – college course started to suffer...

...unable to return to college to finish A levels.

We asked the young people about how far they had experienced a long list of troubles over the last six months (see Table 10.3).

Only three of those responding to the questionnaire reported that they had experienced none of these troubles. The remainder were not so fortunate. Loneliness, depression, shortage of money and periods of unemployment were each reported by more than half the sample. A third had had rows with their family and over a quarter had fallen out with an important friend. Other troubles over homelessness, drink, drugs, unwanted pregnancy, abuse, bullying, or with the police or living in a frightening area were less common but sufficiently frequent to constitute a recognisable risk. On average the respondents reported four troubles each.

Despite these difficulties the young people were often positive about their lives. Eighty-five per cent said that they were currently happy or very happy. Only in relation to money did this optimism generally fail. No more than one in six said unequivocally that they had enough of it. Four out of ten were quite clear they did not.

Table 10.3 Experience of troubles over last six months

	n	%
Being lonely	25	52
Being homeless	6	13
Always being short of money	27	57
Having debts you couldn't pay	12	25
Regularly drinking more than you should	8	17
Having rows with your family	17	35
Having a bad experience with drugs	4	8
Getting into trouble with the police	6	13
Being unemployed	31	65
Living in a frightening area	8	17
Getting into trouble at school	2	4
Being bullied	2	4
Falling out with an important friend	14	29
Being depressed	27	57
You or your partner getting pregnant when you did not want this	3	6
Being abused	2	4
Other bad troubles	8	17

Source: Questionnaires to young people at sweep 3.

How did we measure outcomes?

We had three measures of outcome.

First, we asked both the social workers and the foster carers how well the young people were doing on their latest information about them. They could make three responses: very well (1), as well as could be expected (2) and not very well (3). Among these young adults the correlation between the two ratings was low but significant (r=0.34, p=0.037). So there is, at best, some agreement between these two different kinds of rater on this measure of outcome.[12]

As in our earlier study, we constructed one composite rating (the 'outcome score') by taking the most pessimistic assessment available. On this basis a fifth (22) of the 91 cases rated were said to be going 'very well', just under a half were going 'as well as could be expected' and between a quarter and a third (29%) were not going very well.

Our second measure (the 'trouble score') was simply the number of troubles the young person said they had experienced in the previous six months.

Our third measure (the 'well-being score') was the average rating (from 1 'very true' to 3 'not true')[13] which the young person gave to the following set of statements:

- I have been doing well at school or work.
- There are lots of things I enjoy in my spare time.
- I have good friends.
- I am getting on with my family or partner.
- I have enough money.
- My health is fine.
- I am feeling confident.
- I am pleased with the way my life is going.

Although these measures were conceptually distinct and reflected different viewpoints they were nevertheless quite strongly correlated. The trouble score was negatively correlated with the well-being score ($r=-0.63$, $p<0.001$). The composite foster carer and social worker rating (the outcome score) was also correlated as expected with both the well-being score ($r=0.35$, $p=0.026$) and the trouble score ($r=-0.45$, $p=0.004$). These associations suggested that we were tapping, albeit inexactly, some underlying dimension of 'doing well'.

What correlates with outcome? The experience of foster care

Our case studies suggest that the experience of leaving care – and perhaps the consequences of that step – need to be related to the experience of foster care. What accounts did those responding to our questionnaire give of foster care? How did they see this as related to their new lives?

As can be seen from Table 10.4 most of the young adults had quite positive views of their fostering experience. Just over half said that they got on well with their foster carers and a similar proportion said they got a lot out of being fostered. Nearly a third said they missed their foster carers 'a lot'.

Table 10.4 Young people's response to their time in foster care

	n	True (%)	Partly true (%)	Not true (%)
I got on really well with my foster carers	48	54	29	17
I would have liked my foster carers to adopt me	46	22	24	54
I wanted to see more of my family	45	36	28	38
I got a lot out of being fostered	46	52	22	26
I got on well with my social worker(s)	44	48	35	17
I miss my foster carers a lot	44	30	34	36
I got on well at school	46	35	30	35
I moved about too much	46	46	17	37

Note: Percentages add up to 100 across the rows.

The young people were evenly divided over whether they wanted to see more of their families. Just over a third would have wished to see more of them, just over a third would not and just under a third had mixed views on the matter. These views were quite uncorrelated with their attitudes to foster care and even with whether they wanted to be adopted. Views about how well they had got on at school were similarly divided and similarly unrelated to views of fostering. The young adults were quite positive about social workers. Just under half said they got on well with them.

The replies given by the young people emphasised themes implicit in our earlier chapters. Some wrote of the difficulty of making any overall comment on foster care:

I really got on and liked one set of foster carers but not the other.

Some carers were good some were not.

Box 10.4

Sunita left foster care for university but was able to return out of term time. She spoke very highly of her foster family:

> ...for the first time I could actually talk to someone without feeling nervous, and talk to someone if I had a problem with something. I mean for the first time I came here, and I think I must have broken a glass or something and then when I did they said 'it's OK, things like that can be replaced'.

She thought the experience had helped her understand her own culture and religion and was grateful this had not been forced on her:

> Religion is basically choice, and something you find in yourself...because if you get forced to do something, the more you reject it.

At its best foster care provided a sense of permanence, opened the eyes of the young person to a new way of life, enabled them to acquire the skills to support it, and gave them a perspective on their family with which they could live:

> ...with the help of my foster carers I passed all my GCSEs, went to college and achieved a GNVQ in Social Care... If it hadn't been for my foster carers I would not have passed my GCSEs or been interested in work at a nursing home or doing a college course.

> I got on well with the family I lived with and it sorted my head out and made me realise why I didn't get on with my natural parents.

These 'positive' replies differed from those given in earlier chapters because they commented on the capacity of foster care to help the young person grow up as well as on the support it offered. By contrast negative replies told an already familiar story. The young person did not have a family to which they belonged. Instead they experienced a confusing set of placements, and felt excluded from family life, jealous of the carer's children or foster children and unable to control events:

It was really bad because you was always second best to the foster carers' family. Even if they try not to make you feel second best they did. Getting left out of family things when all you wanted was to be part of a family, to belong. But somehow you just didn't fit in. Also when you move from home to home you have to live by lots of different rules, that messes your head up because you are just trying to get it right and fit in to the family.

…lots of moving about – different sets of rules, never knew where I stood…no control over my life – everyone making decisions about me without me.

I didn't like the other girls who stayed with us. I think I was possessive of my foster mum.

In such cases foster care had not provided the young people with an alternative family. On the other hand their own family might not be available to them:

…not seeing family or being with them.

…by the time I left care my mum was dead.

Equally sad were those who felt that they had islands of love in their otherwise bleak lives in the care system. One whom we quote later had moved many times. On leaving she remembered one foster carer, 'Jane', of whom she carried a photograph in her wallet. She wrote she had lost Jane's address but would remember her throughout a life which she expected to be full of moves.

This yearning for love was sometimes obliquely expressed in comments on payment for foster care. For one young person the main thing about this care was:

Always knowing at the back of your mind that your foster 'parents' are being paid to be nice and make us better children.

This issue also surfaced when a young person had to leave foster care because, as they saw it, no money was available for their care. As a minority of young people saw it, the fact that their foster carers would then no longer keep them cruelly exposed the commercial nature of the relationship.

Box 10.5

According to John:

> I've had so many foster placements from the age of four…[my first placement] I don't think I was very happy there because the foster parents actually got banned from fostering. Because they actually hit me. Quite a lot… I was in adoption care for about a year and a half…then I moved on to a foster placement [for four years] – lovely people, a bit strict… And you know you go through a phase of taking things – I done that which I am ashamed of and so I moved on to Alison's…which was temporary…I was [in next placement] for about two years…they didn't trust me…they hated my girl-friend at the time…and I ended up disobeying everything they said…and I moved in with people called Stockman… I didn't feel at home at all… I got back from school at half past three, they wouldn't come back till eight o'clock so I would have to wait outside and I had no friends there…one day I came back and I was told to pack your stuff… I've had two good placements…Alison's and Jane.

Fortunately Alison (temporary placement) had stayed in touch and John was delighted to be going back to her as an adult fostering.

One young person framed her complaints about foster care in terms of abuse. She wrote:

> All my foster parents were either perverts or psychopathic maniacs.

This rather extreme account of foster care was endorsed by the social worker:

> This young person had a catastrophic care history…foster carer one (male) sexually abused at least her older sister – disruption. Foster carer two – neglect/emotional abuse issues – disruption (ran away) – foster carer three harsh, high achieving upper middle class expectations – emotional abuse – end of placement.

Given their vulnerability and the difficulty they experienced in controlling their lives it is not surprising that some complained about lack of visits from their social workers, having a bad social worker (it seemed that social workers, like foster carers, varied), having too many social workers, or having a social worker who did not listen to them.

Box 10.6

Sunita had had a previous foster carer who had tried to cut her off from her sister and family and had, as she saw it, bullied her:

> I just described it as hell, sometimes…because I don't think you should make a child feel nervous and things in your own house, and not knowing what was right and what was wrong, and everything they did was wrong – they couldn't do anything right… I think that has an effect on me now because I am still quite a nervous person, and shy…which is very bad.

Throughout this five-year placement she felt frightened and that she did not belong. However, she felt she could not talk to her social worker who told the foster carer what she said and that she was spied on by a foster sibling who went to the same school. So she was cut off from all outside support and she still relived the experience in her dreams. Yet at the time she had half accepted it. 'I just thought it was love in a weird way.'

We explored the relationship between the young people's answers to our questions about foster care and our measures of outcome. Briefly:

- None of the answers related to the 'doing well score' derived from the foster carers and social workers.

- Young people who said that they had moved around too much had higher trouble scores (tau b=0.3, $p=0.02$) as did young people who said that they had not got on well at school (tau b=0.28, $p=0.07$).

- Young people who said that they had got on with their foster carers had higher well-being scores (tau b=0.32, $p=0.01$) as did those who said they 'got on' with their social workers (tau b=0.27, $p=0.03$).

These correlations do not necessarily show cause and effect. None of them were significant if we took account of the young person's level of measured disturbance (Goodman score) at sweep 1. They do, however, suggest that current experience is, in some sense, partly of a piece with previous experience. Those who did not do well in their social lives at school went on to have troubles after foster care. Those who had had a good experience in foster care felt that they were doing well after they had left it.

What correlates with outcome? Some other hypotheses

Our other hypotheses were that outcomes would be related to:

- the young person's individual characteristics[14]

- development in foster care, particularly educational performance and social skills[15]

- involvement in work and stability of housing[16]

- relationships with family of origin[17] and general informal support[18]

- support from foster carers[19] and social services[20]

- willingness to leave foster care and whether ready to move at that point.[21]

We look first at the associations between our measures of these variables and our three main outcome variables. Table 10.5 sets out the results. In this table the correlation between, say, 'work involvement' and 'doing well' could therefore arise in a number of ways. It could reflect the respondents' assessments that involvement in work was a *criterion* of doing well. It could reflect a 'halo' effect (the fact that respondents who saw the young person as doing generally well were also more likely to see her or him as doing well in particular respects). It could reflect the influence of some intermediate variable – disturbed young people are unlikely to do well at work and in other respects. Or it could reflect a causal relationship – success at work underpins success in other respects.

Given these difficulties perhaps the most striking feature of Table 10.5 lies in the persistent and strong associations between measures of the young person's personality collected from foster carers in 1998 and the young person's own account of their difficulties and well-being three years later in 2001. The Goodman score, its main sub-scales other than emotional problems, and our measure of childlike attachment were all strongly and consistently associated with the young person's accounts of their well-being and of the number of troubles they had experienced in the last six months. These associations cannot be explained on the grounds of 'halo effect'.

A second feature of Table 10.5 is that the pattern of associations with the first two outcome measures is not the same as that found with the third. For example, there are no significant associations between the personality variables and the doing well score. We will argue below that one reason for these differences lies in the different perspectives of the social workers and foster

Table 10.5 Selected correlates of outcomes

	Trouble score		Well-being score		Doing well score	
	r	n	r	n	r	n
Personality variables						
Goodman total Score (FC 98)	0.54***	34	-0.63***	34	-0.23	62
Hyperactivity sub-scale (FC 98)	0.67***	37	-0.52***	37	-0.10	67
Emotional problems sub-scale (FC 98)	0.08	35	-0.25	35	-0.13	67
Conduct sub-scale (FC 98)	0.58***	36	-0.51***	36	-0.12	68
Peer problems sub-scale (FC 98)	0.38*	36	0.56***	36	-0.16	67
Stoicism score (FC 98)	0.10	39	-0.23	39	0.13	75
Childlike attachment score (FC 98)	0.56***	39	-0.46**	39	-0.13	73
Development variables						
School performance (FC/SW 98, 99)	-0.07	46	0.11	44	0.26*	86
Personal skills (FC/SW 98, 99)	-0.19	47	0.14	47	0.06	88
Overall development score (FC/SW 98, 99)	-0.34*	47	0.31	47	0.21*	81
Move from foster care						
Ready and willing (YP 01)	-0.16	43	0.12	43	0.29	39
Ready and willing (FC/SW 01)	-0.27	32	0.13	32	0.55***	74

Table 10.5 cont.

	Trouble score		Well-being score		Doing well score	
	r	n	r	n	r	n
Work and housing:						
Work involvement (FC/SW 01)	0.03	38	-0.15	38	0.31**	77
Housing stability (YP 01)	-0.16	41	-0.06	41	-0.17	33
Informal support						
Family rows (YP 01)	0.49***	48	-0.27	48	-0.22	40
Adult ties (FC/SW 01)	-0.45**	40	0.43**	40	0.25**	77
General support (YP 01)	-0.43**	48	0.55***	48	0.15	40
Support from carer and SSD						
Count of carer support (FC 01)	-0.08	31	0.14	31	0.06	67
Carer in contact (YP/FC 01)	-0.26	46	0.28*	46	0.21	67
Carer ready to help (YP 01)	-0.40**	46	0.44**	46	0.22	39
Rating of support from SSD (SW 01)	0.26	25	-0.22	25	-0.26	48
Has a social worker (YP 01)	0.37**	48	-0.12	48	-0.35*	40
Can get support from SW (YP 01)	0.29*	46	-0.08	46	-0.42**	39

* significant at 05 level; ** significant at 01 level; *** significant at 001 level.

Key: FC = Foster carer; SSD=Social services department;
SW=Social worker; YP=Young person

carers on the one hand and the young people on the other. However, another reason is undoubtedly the fact that the foster carers and social workers were often unaware of the young people's situations. For this reason we carried out similar analyses looking at the pattern of associations when we looked separately at the foster carers' and social workers' ratings and we restricted the analyses to cases where on our evidence either the social services or the foster carers were currently in touch.

The new analyses produced a much more consistent pattern. For example, in one analysis we looked at all cases where either the foster carer was in at least monthly touch, or the social worker responding was the young person's worker or said that the latter was getting at least some support from social services. In this analysis the Goodman score was significantly associated with the foster carer's assessment of outcome ($r=0.45$, $p=0.02$), the social worker's assessment ($r=0.37$, $p=0.053$) and the combined assessment ($r=0.34$, $p=0.044$).

In other respects the pattern was similar to the one displayed in Table 10.5, except that the associations were, despite smaller numbers, more likely to be significant. We will call the sample where we omitted those without recent contact the 'restricted sample'.

Overall the main consistent patterns appeared to be as follows:

- Our measures of disturbed behaviour from 1998 predicted poor outcomes.

- The overall Looked After Children development score from 1998 and 1999 predicted good outcomes (more strongly in the restricted sample).

- Adult ties predicted good outcomes (more strongly in the restricted sample).

- Contact with a social worker and other measures of social services support predicted high trouble scores and poor 'doing well' scores.

- Contact with the carer and perceptions that the carer was ready to help predicted positive scores, although the associations were not always significant.

The main inconsistencies were the following:

- Social work and foster carer ratings of good school performance, high involvement with work and good moves from foster care predicted high 'doing well' scores but not the scores based on the young people's replies.

- The young person's accounts of family rows and informal support predicted the young people's 'trouble' scores[22] but not the 'doing well score'.

What combination of variables predicts outcomes best?

Many of the variables just discussed are highly correlated with each other. For example, the Goodman score is correlated 0.6 with our childlike attachment score and -0.63 with our general development score. Interpretation would be easier if we knew whether each was, in a sense, a proxy for some underlying measure of disturbance or whether they made independent contributions to predicting outcomes. For this reason we used multiple regression to reduce the number of variables and produce predictors of each outcome.

Table 10.6 gives our most efficient predictor for the trouble score. As can be seen this was higher when:

- the Goodman score was high (young person disturbed)
- the young person was more involved with work
- the young person did not have at least one strong adult tie.

Table 10.6 Predicting the 'trouble' score

	Beta	t	p
(Constant)	–	1.568	0.129
Goodman score	0.530	3.469	0.002
Involvement in work	0.342	2.284	0.031
Has adult ties	-0.392	-2.587	0.016

The same set of variables predicted the 'well-being' score. In fact they did so even more strongly, with work involvement and adult ties being highly significant (p =0.002) and the Goodman score even more highly so (p<0.001).[23]

The paradox is that involvement in work predicts not well-being and an absence of trouble but rather the reverse.

There is less a paradox about the predictors of the 'doing well' score (derived from carer and social worker replies). The main predictors are:

- adult ties (positive)
- involvement in work (positive)
- ready and willing to leave foster care (positive).

Table 10.7 gives the results for the restricted sample.[24]

Table 10.7 Predicting the 'doing well' score

	Beta	t	p
(Constant)	–	10.885	0.000
Ready and willing to leave foster care	0.430	3.660	0.001
Involvement in work	0.246	2.080	0.044
Has adult ties	0.393	3.480	0.001

So on balance it seems that the presence of a strong relationship with another adult predicts good outcomes as judged by both the young people and the foster carers or social workers. Involvement in work has a more ambiguous relationship with outcome. From the point of view of the young people it seems to predict trouble and a lack of well-being. From the point of view of the social workers and foster carers it predicts doing well.

Conclusion

Some of those who had left foster care for independent living were clearly, on any definition, doing well. They were, however, in a minority. Many more had not achieved stable housing; were marginally, if at all, involved in employment; and were vulnerable to a wide variety of troubles, including, pre-eminently, loneliness, unemployment, depression and lack of money. These results are in keeping with those produced by a long line of research. These produce minor differences in proportions – a result presumably of differences in definition, the time at which the study was undertaken, and the inevitable bias introduced by problems of following up a rather elusive group. The broad thrust of the results is, however, remarkably consistent and clear. Although some of those leaving care have jobs, housing and adequate support, most do not (Biehal et al. 1992, 1995; Broad 1998; Stein and Carey 1986).

In these circumstances anyone would need support and for most it was – in some form – forthcoming. It was provided by a very wide variety of people including members of birth families, partners and their families, foster carers, friends, youth, health and social services and members of the community. Within this range of support, foster carers provided an important, financially unacknowledged and sometimes highly significant source of encouragement and back-up.[25] The existence of this resource was not consistently associated with outcomes, partly perhaps because where it was not forthcoming other supports often were, partly because it was rarely as intensive as would be necessary if it were to have an impact.[26] By contrast formal support from social services, while sometimes appreciated and praised, tended to be associated with trouble. No doubt the young people asked for it because they were in difficulty.

Three variables distinguished those who were doing well from those who were less successful.

First, a high degree of disturbance in 1998 was associated with poorer outcomes on all our measures. Our main measure of disturbance, the Goodman score, was itself correlated with other key variables – performance at school, placement disruption, low involvement with work, a high degree (as we measured it) of childlike attachment. So it is hard to know if it is a young person's personality – a product presumably of genetics and early upbringing – which brings difficulty or the cumulative effect of this and the situations into which he or she gets. Most commonly, perhaps, all these things apply.

Second, and unsurprisingly, a strong attachment to at least one adult was associated with good outcomes. This finding no doubt reflects the success of those who had achieved good relationships with their partner and their partner's family, who had found a member of their family from whom they could get genuine support or who had a continuing relationship with their foster family.[27] In one or two cases this latter relationship had been formalised so that, for example, a foster carer was paid a retainer while a young person was at university and then full board when the young person returned.

Third, and paradoxically, involvement in work was associated both with trouble and low well-being and with high ratings of success from foster carers and social workers. It seems most likely that the latter finding reflects the fact that involvement in work is a criterion of success. It is what parents expect of their children. It is not surprising that foster carers and social workers expect the same of former foster children. At the same time the work in which these young people are likely to be involved is marginal. The money earned may raise their rents sharply. If they fall out of work they may fail to act quickly enough to sort out their benefit position. Financially they are little, if at all, better off than university students, who have support officially provided for them and who can feel they are going somewhere, or lone parents on benefit, who have regular money, however meagre it is, and whose role, however stressful, does at least have meaning and promise.[28]

A fourth variable – whether the young person was, in the view of social workers and foster carers, ready and willing to leave foster care – was associated with 'doing well' but not with our other outcomes. Arguably this is a case of being wise after the event. If a young person did not do well, he or she was probably not ready to leave. This hypothesis cannot be disproved. For the moment the most sensible response to this finding is one which most would in any case approve on other grounds – to wit, to try to avoid removing young people from foster care before they want to leave and are capable of managing when they do so.

More generally our findings raise a question for current policies over the aftercare of these young people. Emphasis is rightly placed on education, employment and the development of leaving care teams and various forms of mentoring. However, the things that are likely to matter most to young people are their relationships, their well-being and the troubles which come upon them. These outcomes are not in the short term affected positively by the kinds of jobs they are likely to get or even, in many cases, by their previous school performance. Contact with social workers and similar professionals is certainly an index of trouble. It is less clearly an effective antidote to it.

Some steps have been taken to make this period easier for those who go to university. They have support available to them, they may be able to go back to their foster families when necessary, and there is at least some expectation that what they are doing will lead somewhere. Somehow similar resources need to be provided for those who are in marginal jobs. Generally, this means that these jobs have to be less 'dead end' and exploiting. More specifically in the case of former foster children they need to have someone, often a former foster carer, on whom they can fall back, adequate income guarantees when the job goes sour, a guarantee that they will be supported to get the training and keep the accommodation they require, and a chance to talk over the often difficult and confused relationships that continue to trouble their lives.

Summary of Chapters 9 and 10

1. The majority of young people leaving the care system for independent living either moved before they felt ready or did so as the result of a 'quarrel'. In independent living they commonly faced a wide variety of problems, including loneliness, depression, unemployment and debt.

2. Their success in these circumstances depended partly on their personal qualities, particularly their degree of attachment difficulties, and partly on whether they could call on reliable relationships. Involvement in the job market made life, as the young people experienced it, more difficult.

3. Experiments should be made in minimising the abruptness of the transition from foster care to independence, enabling more to stay in foster care or to continue to draw support from it, and in providing as much support for those in or looking for work as is currently available in the best schemes for those going to university.

Notes

1. The question to social workers and foster carers asked for the situation at 1 January 2001. The questionnaire to young people was 'where are you living now?' The first column in Table 10.1 gives the situation of the young people, combining information from both social workers and foster carers and giving, for the sake of a clear rule, priority to the former where there was a discrepancy. Statistical analyses in this chapter use the information in this column except for three cases where there was no information from foster carer or social worker and we used information from the young person.

2. A slight bias is introduced because Table 10.1 only includes young people under the age of 18 if they are living independently. Their exclusion, however, makes little difference. For example, the proportion living with foster carers increases to 15 per cent, while the proportion living on their own decreases to 22 per cent. As the table covers 86 per cent of the care leavers in the sample, it is likely that it gives a fair enough picture of their accommodation within two or three years of leaving care. These figures are difficult to compare with those of Biehal et al. (1995). In their study young people became increasingly likely to have their own tenancies the farther away they were from their exit from care. At 18–21 months after this 59 per cent of them had their own tenancies.

3. Where both rated the same individual they agreed in 54 per cent of cases and differed by one point in a further 29 per cent. The correlation was 0.7 ($p<0.001$).

4. In 38 cases we could compare the information from the young people with our rating of work involvement derived from the foster care and social worker questionnaires. Out of the 15 who said they were unemployed (11) or caring for their child (4), 12 were 'out of the job market' and three on the verge of it. Of the 13 who said they were in 'intermediate positions', five were 'out of the job market', six on the verge of it and two in it. Of the

ten who were in paid work only two were on the verge of the job market and eight were in it.

5. These figures are rather more optimistic than those from other surveys (Biehal *et al.* 1992, 1995; Broad 1998) which give proportions in work varying from 9 per cent to 13 per cent. On the other hand our figure for those securely involved in work (18%) is very close to figures given by Biehal and her colleagues for those taking the 'work route' (as opposed to the routes characterised as 'insecure', 'parent' and 'academic').

6. Other studies suggest that around a third of care leavers receive some support from foster carers around nine months after leaving the care system but that the proportion diminishes over time (Biehal *et al.* 1992, 1995; Fry 1992). Our findings support the idea that support 'tails off'. Half those who had left for less than a year reported seeing their foster carer at least weekly. Among those who had left for two or more years none reported seeing their carers this frequently and half said they never saw them at all.

7. There seemed to be a considerable degree of agreement between foster carers, young adults and social workers about the degree of support provided and the frequency of contact. The correlation between the foster carers' and the young persons' estimates of contact frequency was 0.8 ($p<0.001$). Our measure of the amount of support provided by the foster carers was based on the foster carer questionnaire. Nevertheless it correlated 0.55 (p=0.003) with the social worker's rating of foster carer support and 0.68 ($p<0.001$) with the young person's estimate of the carer's readiness to help.

8. Strict counting was not possible as some mentioned 'teams' or 'my foster family' whereas others listed individual names. Some also named individuals whose roles we did not know.

9. Other research (Biehal *et al.* 1992, 1995) suggests that more than three-quarters of care leavers have some contact with their families on leaving the care system. This rarely amounts to living with them for an extended period but around half of Biehal and her colleagues' (1995) sample had lived with a member of their extended family for at least a brief period over 18 to 24 months. In addition relationships between care leaver and mother could improve with the birth of a baby and some drew strength from knowing that their families were 'there for them'.

10. Strict accuracy is again inappropriate as the sample is small and the scales dependent on subjective judgements.

11. Social workers who commented on these cases generally felt that it was important to work within the constraints imposed by the young person's goals even if it was against the young person's interests to do so. So 'failure' might occur because the young person wanted the wrong things or they wanted the 'right things' which could not be provided because of financial or other constraints.

12. As already pointed out social workers were more optimistic than foster carers, making the best rating in four out of ten cases (38%) and the worst in one in eight (12%). The comparable figures for foster carers were 20 per cent (doing well) and 33 per cent (worse than expected).

13. For reasons of clarity we have reversed this score so that 'high' equates with 'well-being'.

14. Goodman score, measures of stoicism and childlike attachment – all gathered from foster carers in 1998.

15. Average ratings for these two 'looking after children' dimensions based on information provided by both social workers and foster carers in 1998 and 1999 and also an average score for all looking after children dimensions added together. The latter score has a very high reliability.

16. Scores already introduced.

17. Whether young person reported rows with family.

18. Rating of adult ties and young person-based measure of informal support which have been introduced earlier.

19. Count of number of different kinds of support mentioned by carers (see Table 10.2), whether young person felt he or she could turn to foster carers, and whether they were still in contact.

20. Whether young person said they had had contact with social workers, ratings by social workers of extent of support from social workers and other colleagues.

21. Composite average rating of these variables added together based on social worker and foster carer information in 2001 and a separate score based on replies from young person in 2001 and covering whether the move was chosen, when young person was ready and after her or his views had been sought and listened to.

22. The correlation of rows with the trouble score is exaggerated since a row is counted as a trouble. The association remains significant if the score is recalculated with 'row' not counted. The association of 'rowing' with well-being is not significant but in the predicted direction.

23. The childlike attachment score is an almost equally efficient predictor of both outcomes, but is highly correlated with the Goodman score. In predictions of trouble it does slightly better than the Goodman score when both are entered together and in predictions of 'doing well' rather worse. Overall both models account for a higher proportion of the variance (45% and 66%) when the Goodman score is entered. Numbers with all relevant data are low (n=28) because outcomes are based on the young people's replies and the predictors on those from social workers and foster carers.

24. The results for the larger sample were similar although involvement in work just dropped below significance. These results are based on numbers of 43 (restricted sample) and 62 (larger sample). In predicting the 'doing well score' both the dependent and independent variables are derived from the same sources. Knowledge of the outcome could therefore have influenced ratings of the predictors. However, analyses using the social worker questionnaires for the outcome variable and the foster carer ones for the dependent variable produced similar results. They account for 46 per cent (restricted sample) and 39 per cent (larger sample) of the variance. One of the variables in this model (ready and willing to leave foster care) is not included in the earlier models which predict trouble and well-being. Another – involvement in work – is included in this model but in the opposite direction. Only one variable – 'adult ties' – operates in the same direction in all the models that we have introduced.

25. Our figures on this are rather more optimistic than those from Fry (1992) and Biehal and her colleagues (1995). This may well reflect the date at which we carried out the research or the way we acquired our sample. In any event the differences between their findings and ours are not large.

26. For example, in the case studies given in Chapters 11 and 12 Alistair's carer acted towards him in an altruistic and committed way. She was not, however, in sufficiently close touch with him to be aware of or head off the various problems that came upon him. Tara had fewer problems and much closer support.

27. Biehal and her colleagues (1995) emphasise the importance to some care leavers of having a family member who was 'there for you'. Quinton and Rutter (1988) similarly emphasise the importance (for good or ill) of partners for young women leaving care.

28. Contrast Alistair's and Tara's cases in the next chapters for an illustration of these points.

Chapter Eleven

Tara's Story: A Case Study

Introduction

This study has tried to integrate three very different kinds of data: quantitative measures, quotations from questionnaires and case studies. Our tables refer to large numbers and to statistical relationships among them. They deal with groups of individuals who often appear as acted upon by external factors rather than as choosing their fate.[1] By contrast our case studies are concerned with particular individuals who are influenced by circumstance but also make their own destinies. These different approaches are likely to interest different people. Managers and administrators necessarily have an interest in statistical regularity. Social workers are necessarily concerned with individuals. There is a question, however, over how far and in what way statistical research can inform work with a particular person.

Our next three chapters represent our final struggle with the integration of these different kinds of data. The first two of these chapters consider two cases with contrasting outcomes. The young people involved have left the care system and are living independently. They do not represent the very young children who were adopted or went home. Both, however, represent in our eyes a number of key themes which are foreshadowed in our findings on younger children and have occurred repeatedly among older children variously returning home, in foster placements or leaving the care system. In our third chapter we pick up these themes, remind readers of earlier findings relevant to them, and see how they are illustrated in our cases. The intention is not to explain the cases. For that more detail and a wider range of concepts would be needed. Rather we use the cases to bring out themes which are relevant both to the cases themselves and to the wider arena of foster care.

Tara

Tara was 20 when we met her, a young parent of Indian descent, living on her own in a predominantly Asian part of the city where she grew up. Her two-bedroom flat was spotlessly clean and well furnished with the help of her boyfriend's parents. Her child of 15 months played happily during the interview. Tara was very well supported. Her character, resilience and achievements inspired affection and admiration among those who talked to us about her.

Tara had been voluntarily accommodated at her mother's request at the age of 15. Family relationships had not been happy for some time and Tara's mother and father had recently separated. Tara had remained with her mother, more perhaps because this was expected than because it was what she wanted:

> My mum had the right to us…me and my mum never bonded. I was more close to my dad… I left my dad for my mum and it still hurts me thinking 'I left my dad for you and I get back nothing'. She favours my brothers more than me. You can see it, you can tell.

There were other problems. Tara felt that her mother and father took out their disagreements on her, that she tried to protect her mother against her father but got no thanks for it, and that her father was angry and her mother strict:

> It was not nice to be told off for everything that I did.

This rather unhappy situation had already brought Tara to the attention of social services. However, the immediate reason for Tara leaving home was that she had been found to be having sexual relations with her boyfriend.

At first it was assumed by Tara that the admission would be short term, a matter of two weeks to allow things to blow over. However, her mother made it clear that she did not want Tara back at the moment and a foster placement which had been intended to last two weeks lasted for three years.

On our measures Tara was potentially quite difficult – she scored above average for her age on our measure of Goodman score and above average on our measure of stoicism score. Only on our measure of 'childlike attachment' did she score lower than her peers. Despite this her foster carer felt that she had been, like her only other foster child, 'easy'. The interviewer felt this reflected the way the carer treated them.

Tara's foster carer lived on her own with her son, although she was in close touch with her two daughters, one of whom was at university at the time.

She was on all our measures exceptional – scoring as high as possible on our ratings of foster carer quality and above average on our measure of 'child orientation'. At our first contact both she and her son were apparently very glad that Tara was there.

Despite this welcome Tara was at first wary. The situation was strange and unwanted:

> It was odd – it was just totally odd because after 15 and a half years you end up moving somewhere where you don't even know anyone... I wanted to go to my house – you know in your house with your mum, or whatever, and your brothers. I mean, I didn't say much then, at the house, I didn't say much at all.

Nevertheless trust grew:

> After about six months then I started talking to them properly – we met both fifty-fifty, then we actually got somewhere... I could tell her anything and she'd understand. And even whatever happened in my past before I moved in, why it happened we even talked about that. A couple of times we went halfway through a conversation and then I just said 'I don't want to talk about it any more'. Then I actually had a good conversation about it and then I thought 'now I can open up'.

Even then trust was not total:

> But then I always had this insecurity in me. I always keep my distance with her. And I still do that – I keep my distance with women or someone whom I'm getting close to...it's just that I'm scared that if this goes wrong again, I'm not taking it. I can't take it every time it goes wrong with a female, or somebody I trust...she understood why I kept my distance from everybody. It's just my insecurity.

This developing relationship was based on what the foster carer did as well as on her empathy. As Tara said she met her half-way, insisting for example that Tara did not smoke in the house, encouraging her to cut down on smoking but not banning her from smoking altogether.

> She just said 'look cut down on smoking, it ain't good for your health'. And when the time came I quit. [She used to say] you can drink but don't get pissed and come home. I got pissed about twice when I came home but she didn't say nothing. She just told me 'Learn from it. Learn from your mistakes.'

In Tara's eyes she was, in contrast to her own mother, very modern and permissive:

> I knew her ground rules, her limits, but then I knew how much freedom she gave me on top of those ground rules. I mean fifteen and a half – no one lets anyone go clubbing at fifteen and a half. I got to go clubbing… I didn't mess up. If I told her I would be home by two o'clock I would be home by two o'clock. She gave me that trust and with that trust I think I felt better… My parents are more old fashioned, she's more modern.

The carer was also totally committed to treating Tara as one of the family. On one occasion her son got into quite serious and uncharacteristic trouble in Tara's company. Despite what must have been a temptation to blame Tara for this, the carer insisted that both had equal responsibility. On another, the family had been invited to an important family wedding but Tara had not been invited. They risked a family rift by refusing to go unless Tara went too. They made her feel involved and welcome by involving her in their weekly visits to the cinema and to bowling:

> It was nice. I did fit in the family. Maybe not blood but I was important to them. So we always had that relationship. It's like her kids are [my child's] aunts and uncles.

Against this background Tara felt that she learnt things that were still with her. Her foster carer was religious within the Hindu tradition. Tara started to pray – something she still does and in which she involves her son – whereas she had previously felt that she ought to pray but was 'too angry' with God to do so. Her foster carer's children had gone to university. This became something that Tara, who had previously avoided school as much as possible, wanted and wants for herself:

> I didn't want to go to college when I was at my mum's house. I didn't even want to study at all. But now I really want to study…I really miss homework. Do you know that? I actually do. I actually miss it! I used to love my homework. I was so interested, I used to love it and I miss it so much.

There were, however, additional reasons for wanting to go to college:

> I see my mum walking around. I see so many women work so hard, do ten, fifteen hours a day and they don't get nowhere. I'm not going to do that. I want a decent job, a government job, so he [child] can have everything and I want my big house. That's my dream.

And she felt she acquired a different way of bringing up children:

> My foster carer doesn't shout at her kids. She sits down and talks to them. They don't rebel. I never rebelled then neither. Now I'm trying to teach [my boyfriend] to do what [my foster carer] did, just sit down and talk to him. Because I don't want him hit the way we got hit when we were young, because that's the Indian way.

Despite her acquisition of these benefits Tara had still felt that she wanted to leave when she reached 18. In part this seemed to be because this was what was expected and in part it reflected her own need not to depend on others:

> A: I think they were warning the foster carer that when the foster child reaches 18 it has to be independent living... So I had a choice. [My foster carer] says you can stay here if you want or you can go and get your own place, and I thought go and get my own place. Because I wanted to be independent – not dependent on anyone else – I need to depend on myself...
>
> Q: So your foster carer offered you to stay with her basically. And how did you feel about that?
>
> A: I don't know. I was really happy because I thought she'd say 'you've been really lucky, time's up now'. You know, you feel like that, but I knew she wouldn't say it but then I had this little insecurity that she might just, and then she went 'she can stay here if she wants', and then I said 'no'.

Asked about what she would have felt if she had stayed Tara said she would have been happy, have gradually taken on more responsibility and gone to university. As it was, her departure was planned over about six months and she moved into a special housing project with her younger brother, who was also having trouble at home. The arrangements were negotiated by the social worker associated with the project, who was to become a strong support to her.

Although she chose to move, Tara found it sad to do so:

> I cried when I left. I cried. Three years you are together and then you separate...and then she used to come and see me and I used to cry even more [laughs].

Quite soon, however, her foster mother was puzzled at not seeing her:

> ...but she had lost touch – deliberately, she wasn't in touch with me after she left. She was for a couple of months, but you know, when she fell pregnant,

she did not know how I would react, because she wasn't married... I really tried my hardest. I used to leave messages through the doors, I used to ring her brother...but even before she told me I could suss out she must be pregnant. But then I made an effort to show her that I don't mind what's happened, I'll still be there for her. So she got all that trust back in me.

The arrival of the baby had a major effect on Tara's relationships and views of the future. Her new social worker became involved in discussions about what should happen with Tara and her boyfriend. At the time of the interview over a year later he was still visiting weekly and along with her boyfriend assisted with DIY. The boyfriend's parents became major supports and in due course she re-established contact with her foster mother:

> It's been good. Good. It feels lonely sometimes but now I've got the little one he keeps me busy all day long... But I do still see my foster carer. We go out every Monday, we ring up every week, see each other. We've got a really good relationship like that – we discuss everything and this and that. I don't feel lonely in that way – I've got somebody there, you know, that I can talk to about anything. It'll be alright...and my boyfriend's family – they don't come down because they are always working, but I tend to go down there, and leave him there sometimes to go out, and I take him to see them and they love him too. He gets spoilt.

This support was perhaps necessary, for Tara did not find the responsibility easy:

> I'm only 20 and I look back and I think, oh my God, I've been through so much and right now I've got a kid, and I do so much for a 20 year old, and I take so much stress on. And I don't like it sometimes, and I don't want it. I don't want the responsibility. But at the back of my head, there's always going to be, he's there... But I want to do what 20 year old people do. I want that life, but then I know I can't get it.

But in practice Tara did manage. She organised her routine and life round her child:

> My first responsibility is him now. And my priority is him. When I've got to decide, I'm deciding what he's going to be doing at the same time. I've got to put him first. So everything revolves around this little one.

She planned her life in the expectation that she would go to university. Her foster carer encouraged her in this and Tara had worked out how she would be able to ensure that her child was properly cared for while she studied. She thought she would be finished with university when he was six or seven. She could then rely on her in-laws to manage while her son was at school. This would allow her to work 'nine hours a day'.

Despite her reliance on her 'in-laws' she was not planning to marry for at least a year. The explanation was again her 'insecurity':

> I know how I got hurt with my friends splitting up. It affected me. It affected me a lot. [I don't want to get divorced.] Because frustration…the only way we take our frustration out is on someone close to us, someone we love and is close to us, and it'll be [my son]. And he'll get everything. He'll get told off for no reason, and we just end up…we don't realise we're taking it out on people, but we end up doing it. And I don't want that. I don't want him to learn that it's alright to shout at your wife or your girlfriend for no reason.

One issue had been only partially resolved. For three years after her arrival in foster care Tara's mother did not speak to her although her father and brothers had some contact. Following the arrival of the baby her father initially broke off relationships. Her elder brother also felt that his prospect of marriage had been badly damaged by Tara's behaviour, which, in his eyes, brought disgrace on the family. Despite his impending marriage he maintained this attitude, shunning Tara when he met her in the street.

Things with her parents were now somewhat better. Tara's father had been to see the baby; according to her social worker, he wanted to be part of his grandson's life. Tara's mother had swallowed her pride and come to see Tara. She had also returned from India bringing gold for Tara and presents for the child. Tara was hurt by the initial rejections and was glad of the improvements. She also respected her mother's courage in coming to see her and saw too that her mother was sad that Tara had a better relationship with her foster carer than with the mother herself.

At the same time the relationships were, as the social worker pointed out, 'on Tara's terms'. She denied that her own status as a lone parent would damage her brother's marriage prospects and saw his attitude as old-fashioned. She waited for her father to visit her and set the rules for his visits:

> His pride was so big that couldn't even see his own grandchild. I said 'OK, fine'. Then I waited and he came to me… Dad doesn't like it sometimes when he's late and I start getting angry. 'If you're going to come, you come on time otherwise just ring and tell me.' Even his friends – I think dad's friends are really scared of me. They are!

This was part of a more general attitude:

I like to have a good relationship with everyone. But if people get on the wrong side, I get on the wrong side myself as well. I just say 'don't mess me about, because I'm not going to take it any more, that's not me'. OK I used to take it, but not any more – because of [my son]. I don't want him thinking that it's all right for people to walk all over you and use you and you can have a happy life like that.

She was clear that her mother was her mother, while she respected her foster carer 'as a mother' and as a kind of grandmother to her child. For these reasons she had not wanted to be adopted. Nevertheless, she felt that she was not dependent on her mother:

It's like I don't really need her...because she hasn't been there for the past five years and I've coped without her. If she came back, I wouldn't really need any help... She might need me, but I don't think I'd need her as much in return.

So Tara accepted the situation as it was and wanted, at it were, to move on:

I know she's never apologised for what happened between us. But I don't mind. I don't want an apology. I just don't... I forgive her but I don't forget what she's done. I'll never forget. It hurts, but I can forgive her, just leave it.

Tara's ability to see her family on her own terms stemmed in part from her feeling that she had other family available to her:

Do you know what? I was thinking what a big family! I've got my dad's side. I don't get on with them, my mum's side, I don't talk to them at all. I've got his dad's side – mum and dad – they love me. And then I've got [my foster carer's] whole side – her sisters' and her husband's side. So I've got like families everywhere. That's what I feel like I've sort of got families and families and families, and I've got my own family now. Even my leaving care worker, I've met his wife and kids in town, and that, so we have a good relationship.

Another reason may have been Tara's remarkable resilience and personal qualities. Her leaving care worker was quite clear about her contribution:

I've got a lot of time for her. I honestly care for her quite a lot. And her little baby. Obviously I'm there a fair amount. No, hopefully, you know, she'll turn out to be whatever she wants to be, and she has got aspirations, and why not? Let's go for it. If we can help, we'll help her. If not, fine, because she's great.

Tara herself felt that she had been lucky:

> From every single foster child there is, I was the luckiest one. Everything on one plate and not to worry. In a way it makes me happy, thinking kids go through so much, right, but I just went through a little bit but everything came out good in the end. And there are good bits in life. There are good bits in life and they are still to come. Everything doesn't come in one go.

Note

1. Regression equations are typically described as explaining a 'dependent variable', in our case often the future state of an individual in terms of independent ones (e.g. the 'child orientation' of the carer). What sociologists seem to call 'agency' is usually implicit rather than explicit in these models and sits uneasily with the whole approach.

Chapter Twelve

Alistair's Story: A Case Study

Introduction

Alistair, like Tara, was 20 years old when we met him. Of West Indian origin he was living alone in a council flat which he kept immaculate. His interviewer described him as a stylishly dressed, well-mannered, pleasant and competent young man.

According to his last foster carer Alistair arrived in foster care with much emotional baggage. His early history had been complex and confused, and his step-father used family secrets against him. He was his mother's first child and although he had a number of siblings, none of them were by his father. His immediate situation was distressing. According to Alistair:

> I was physically abused by my step-dad. Basically I was treated like a little slave.

Rebelling against this treatment he went to live with his aunt, returned shortly after to live again with his mother, and was told that if he was going to go, he should do so. He then fled to a police station and at the age of 12 entered his first foster placement.

Alistair's initial impression of this placement was much more favourable than had been Tara's of hers:

> The first day we talked about everything, and no one had ever talked to me before. And like made me a cup of cocoa. And I had my own room, because I never had my own room before, which is nice, isn't it?

After a while, however, things went 'sour'. Unlike Tara he did not feel he was part of the family:

> I think it was when the other foster kid came… It was like a girl – she was a bit older than me. I had no problem with that, but it was like…different standards. Like she would ask me to go shopping with her, then she stopped when a girl came along…it was like she forgot about me.

To outsiders, however, it clearly looked different. To them it appeared that Alistair was excluding himself:

> They started reviewing [the situation] and they were saying that I was differentiating myself from everyone else. And I found that odd, because I am always sitting in the sitting room and there's no one in the sitting room except for me, or I'm in my room – everyone kept themselves to themselves and that made me really angry.

Alistair's behaviour started to worry his foster family, and they took to locking their bedrooms. Tara had been delighted with the trust she experienced. The lack of trust upset Alistair and made him feel even more the odd one out:

> Everyone had a key to their bedroom and that made me feel funny because I never had a key. It was like everyone was thinking I was a thief… And everyone's locking their doors and I just had to shut my door. And I just felt so left out at that time – I felt so left out at that time.

In the end the placement broke down. The final straw was said by Alistair to be an incident when he was blamed for something that had actually been done by a member of the family. He left during a birthday party for the other foster child. According to Alistair the first he knew of this was the sound of people singing 'happy birthday'. After 'enduring that' he was asked to come to join the party but refused:

> I said 'I'm fed up of living here…being ignored'. The girl's [room] next door was done up and she arrived ages after me and her room was done up and my room was an antique kind of. So I just packed all my stuff and started going down, and she says 'where are you going to go?' and I says 'I'm going'.

In practice he went to a children's home, which he liked, and from there in a short while to the foster placement from which he first entered our study. Here once again things started off well. He liked his room and:

> She tried to make me feel part of the family, so that was good.

At the same time Alistair was sensitive to the possibility of rejection:

She tried to make me be a bit more independent, and maybe go out on a trip, and do all sorts of things for myself, and that helped in a way, but kind of moved me away from her, so we didn't talk much and I did my own thing.

On one occasion the foster carer took Alistair away with her to a concert in a different city. This was a highlight of Alistair's life.

That was brilliant that. Yeah, so she was very good to me, in fact. It was like the talking stopped. Because I was like on my own again, always…but I still talked to her, but I still like her now, you know what I'm saying?

Sadly, however, a disagreement over a minor delinquency further ruptured relationships:

Q: She was annoyed with you for not being straight?
A: Yeah, exactly that was it. But everything was all right after that. It was just everyone was separate again.

For the foster carer, however, things were not all right. She confirmed that in some ways the placement started as had the last one:

For the most part it was just me and Alistair. So most of the time Alistair had me to himself. We'd cook together. Sometimes he'll cook, he'd want to cook for me, make soups and that…every Tuesday we'd go out for a meal together, we'd go to the cinema, when we shopped we were shopping for us. You know. It's Alistair's biscuits. They're Alistair's. That's Alistair's juice. These are Alistair's. He didn't have to share anything with anyone.

Into this idyll, however, others intruded. When relatives came Alistair would shut himself in his room and have nothing to do with them. At times he would lock his foster carer out. Another foster child (again a girl) came. Alistair said they got along well but the foster carer reported otherwise. And the foster carer found Alistair's demands increasingly suffocating:

You know, he didn't like anybody coming round, he didn't like me going anywhere, he didn't like to go out.

His behaviour drew a reaction from his foster carer:

I think we got into this relationship – tit for tat…that psychological game. He'll go into his room… I said 'right you can stay there, because you're not even going to see me because I am going to come in late from work'.

In the end the foster carer felt she could take no more. She tried to explain to Alistair that this did not mean that they did not get on. Alistair, however, wanted none of it. His removal came as a shock to him:

A: We weren't talking when we left and she'd gone to work and I didn't know I was leaving, because she didn't tell me I was leaving, and I'd come home…and [the social worker] just came and he was like 'aren't you ready?' and I goes 'what are you talking about?'

Q: So why weren't you talking?

A: That's what I can't remember – that was so odd – there were lots of mixed feelings in ourselves going on. But it was strange.

Like Tara, Alistair cried about his departure, although he returned to the children's home he liked. After about a month he sought his foster carer out:

She was brilliant… So when I told the social worker, he was like, 'what? What do you mean went?' And I was like 'yeah, she wasn't that bad: we just weren't talking for some reason'.

Alistair's story now becomes quite hard to follow. It seems that he was going to college to learn catering – something which according to his foster carer he had organised for himself when he was with her. He continued to do this in his new placement which was some kind of hostel or supported lodgings. He liked the hostel where he made friends with a girl upstairs:

I used to love that place. The blokes were on my level and the women were upstairs and I just got on with everyone – everyone was always in my flat – they were cooking for me, I was cooking for them, and it was brilliant.

This was a welcome change for Alistair who had previously had no friends to invite to his birthday party and who had been called hurtful nicknames at school.

What was less welcome was Alistair's financial situation. The hostel was some way from Alistair's college and he was in any case anxious to earn money. Social services tried to dissuade him:

The social workers – they were sitting round a big table and they said 'we don't want you to do this', and I go 'it's up to me, I want to work – do you know what I am saying – I want to buy nice things'. So they said 'don't go', so I left anyway and I got a job.

Unfortunately what the social workers did not, according to Alistair, tell him was that this step would have dramatic effects on his rent. This increased from £3 to £88 a week. Tara, who was also in supported lodgings, had faced a similar dilemma when first moving from foster care and had cut down the work she was doing to avoid it. Alistair felt the rent was grossly unfair and refused to pay. His arrears increased and reached, according to him, £1000, and were only finally paid off by the use of his leaving care grant.

Alistair's financial situation was, he said, exacerbated by his generosity. Some of this was towards his new-found friends:

> And my friends, they were all good. I was paying all their rent. That's what I'd say – they were all at college, or on the dole, or whatever, and I was paying their money.

More importantly Alistair paid a large sum of money to his step-father:

> I'm the kind of person that would give people money to borrow, whatever, and my step-dad, he said he's having trouble with the house, with my mum and that, and he needed some money to borrow, so I lent him some money – that must have been about £400 altogether.

Alistair did not apparently get this money back. Despite this, and in great contrast to Tara who dealt with her family strictly on her terms, Alistair was persuaded by his step-father to take in a woman and her children who turned out to be his step-father's mistress. This, as will be seen, further complicated his relationships with his family.

Immediately, however, Alistair was advised by his former foster carer and decided on his own account to leave the hostel. He involved the leaving care team and was offered a council flat. Although he immediately found it 'disgusting', a friendly girl at the hostel helped persuade him to move into it. Initially the move did not go well:

> For a month I was just there, with no fridge, no cooker, no bed, just lying on that thing because the social worker was on holiday…and then they were starting to write to me, and that, and I was saying, 'I don't want nothing to do with you' because I was…that was a horrible time for me. It was like being homeless in a way – it was like the bunk room, and a bed in the middle of it, and I was just lying there and that was horrible.

Fortunately, his aunt was living down the road and from now on becomes the bright point in this story. She was according to him his 'salvation' at that time and 'doing everything for him'.

Less positive was his job as a trainee chef. His foster carer, who was then in touch with him and even had him to stay on one or two occasions, felt that the hotel where he worked exploited him. He agreed:

> That chefing job – oh God, I was there for two and a half years and I just thought, I've had enough. Them lot was just taking the mick. I was doing two people's jobs. I was a trainee chef – I was doing the job of a professional chef…and I wasn't getting paid for that either. So I left that job.

This departure led to further debt:

> I was working for an agency and I was earning £50 a week and they didn't tell me 'oh you can still sign on' and I could get housing benefit [which took] about two months and they wouldn't sign it and all the time I was being charged full rent and I was trying to eat on £50 a week. When I left [the job] I was in arrears by about £500.

These financial troubles seem to have coincided with the complicated situation with the other woman involved with his step-father. Apart from his aunt and her husband little support was available. His foster carer had gradually lost contact with him. When we interviewed her she was surprised to think she had not seen him for a year. She noted that Alistair made few demands on her and that perhaps she had not sought him out:

> …maybe it's just me being childish, thinking OK then don't contact me then, I won't contact you then.

Nevertheless she mused about him with affection:

> I don't know. Alistair's just amazing – one of my other foster children saw him earlier and he goes, he saw this big tree coming down the road… Alistair went out and bought the biggest Christmas tree he could find – a real one! And [the other foster child] says 'when I looked, peeped, and, I thought, God, what's that? And it was Alistair!' He's a very homey person.

Alistair himself, however, remembered this time with less affection:

> I couldn't work it out [why mother was behaving as she was] and then the pressure got worse and worse and then at Christmas, I was on my own for Christmas so that made it even worse… I was thinking of all the bad things that happened at home, and I thought, whoah. That man did so many bad things, how could I let him get away with it? And I thought, well there's no point in me living – what's the point? Every part of my life was messed up, I can't get a girlfriend, I can't trust anyone…so that's when… I tried to top

> myself. A bit of whisky, about 60 paracetamols, and I was just lying there the whole day, vomiting, going to sleep, fainting, until I just thought, I have to call an ambulance.

It was at this point that Alistair's story began to turn. After a brief spell in a psychiatric hospital, which he hated, he returned home:

> My stomach was still playing up, but they let me go. And when I left there my aunt was at my flat, waiting for me. She was waiting there for me. My mum doesn't know nothing about this. My mum still doesn't know nothing about this...

There were medical or perhaps psychiatric consequences of these events. At one time Alistair found himself stuck on his bed unable to move:

> And that was the worst bit, but apart from that, everything went all right after that. I left the job. I was signing on for a few months... So things have got better since then. I've got older. I had a bit of counselling.

The counselling seems to have been arranged by his doctor prior to his admission to hospital:

> I said everything... It was like, deep, and I had to talk about what happened and I was like... I never talked to anyone like that before and that really helped me.

The interviewer asked if he could have used this kind of help before:

> I think for me it was like trying to come to terms with it at the time, when all this was going on, I was in another world, I cut myself off from everybody... [I thought this was] normal, I thought these things happen. It's only when you get older and you live on your own that you think 'whoah'. I dream of things, I remember things that he did to me, and that was on my mind...so I remembered how wicked that bloke was, and how everyone I come across is not really nice, do you know what I am saying? They're always up to something but I'm really glad that I got that help from those people.

Alistair got a job, one that he preferred and where he worked easier hours. He ensured that his step-father's other woman moved out of his flat. He had another meeting with his mother, a strange encounter, whose pain he conveyed to us but whose substance was unclear. He has not seen her since. He talked of his birth family:

They don't exist now… It's not them – it's not their fault, it's just the things the man is doing. I'm a very forgiving person, but the things that lot did to me – I could have killed that lot, seriously.

From time to time he saw an older male relative – a somewhat ambiguous figure from his past. More importantly he saw his aunt and her husband regularly and frequently. They supported him in his dealing with some threatening local teenagers who were hanging about his house, and the counselling seemed to have freed him up to talk to his aunt:

> It's dealt with the issues at home, that I've had to deal with at home, yeah it's dealt with that because like I say I can talk to my aunt about it, and I speak to her, and it's like I speak to her about everything, she tells me everything, things that I wouldn't even know about my family. Do you know what I mean?

With other people, however, Alistair remained, like Tara, cautious. He did not contact his foster carer. He had a history of quarrelling with key workers. He rejected the offered help of a girl he had known at his hostel because he felt he had to sort things for himself. He thought his history set him apart and that there were things that would shock people if they came out:

> I'm on my own, and I don't have a girlfriend, so even though I want a girlfriend, I know you can't trust anyone, do you know what I mean?

Chapter Thirteen

A Common Explanation?

Introduction

These cases are on the face of it very different. One involves a determined, well-supported young woman with academic and social aspirations, whose Asian culture is relevant to much in the case – for example, to the significance of religion, of refusal to attend the family wedding, of being 'modern' or 'old-fashioned' and of having a child when not yet married. The outcome seems conspicuously successful. Another involves a young West Indian man who is not obviously academic or ambitious and who until recently had little support in the community. The outcome at the time of our study may or may not be seen as a success. Certainly much of Alistair's life had been very sad.

Despite the differences between Tara and Alistair there are also striking similarities. Both came from families in which they felt they were harshly treated; where siblings were, in their eyes,[1] preferred to them; where they felt their role was to meet the needs of others rather than their own; and where they were in the end rejected. These aspects of their previous history helped define the problems with which both foster carers and young people had to wrestle.

In what follows we explore the relevance of the concepts we have used in this research to the cases we have just described. In doing so we are not seeking to provide a complete explanation for the way either case turned out. Rather we are aiming to highlight key processes which seem to us evident in these cases, in those of other care leavers, and – more widely – among those in foster care, returning home or being adopted. We explore these issues under the headings of permanence, relationships with birth family, attachment status, school and work, and working things out. We then consider why the outcomes of the two cases differed and what the implications of these stories might be.[2]

In illustrating these issues we have deliberately repeated some of the quotations used in Chapters 11 and 12.

Permanence and the foster family

> We'd go to eat about three times a week. We used to go to the cinema every week. We used to go bowling… Every week, we did something with the family. And do you know what, that made me feel more welcomed, and more wanted…that's how you bond with a child. We'd just bond by doing things together. We used to go out, and gossip about anything we could think of! [laughs] When we get together, we gossip about anything we can! News, or anything… Once they had a family feud, or something, about this wedding, one of their nephews' wedding. And all her kids said, 'you can come, [or] we're not coming'… It was nice. I did fit in the family. Maybe not blood, but I was important to them. (Tara)

> Yeah, she always tried to make me feel part of the family, so that was good. [tape paused]…a certain atmosphere. I think…that's it – she tried to make me a bit more independent, and maybe go out on a trip, and do all sorts of things for myself, and that helped in a way, but that kind of moved me away from her, so we didn't talk much, and I did my own thing. (Alistair)

Foster care is family care. Unsurprisingly the foster children in our study generally wanted from their foster carers some of things that are the 'rights' of family members – acceptance, fair treatment in comparison with foster siblings, even love. Where they differed was over the implications for their relationships with their own family. Were they being cut off from their roots? Was 'being cut off' what they really wanted? Was family loyalty something that could be shared? In keeping with the salience of 'family', our statistics suggested that the parental qualities (e.g. child orientation) of the foster carers had an important bearing on placement outcome. This, however, was an effect that was not limited to foster care. Children returning home did better if their parents scored high on our 'parenting score'. Young people leaving for independence did better if they had at least one solid close relationship with another adult.[3]

Against this background a key aspect of fostering was the degree to which it did or did not offer 'permanence'. For good or ill, birth families are 'for life'. Foster care is for a limited period. For most children 'permanent foster care' is only on offer for those aged four or over and less than 18. For this group it appears as a curious anomaly – half family care and half bureaucratic provision. Where else do people get paid to parent and have to ask social services if their child can go on a school trip? Does all this matter?

In our first chapter we distinguished between various aspects of permanence. These included 'objective permanence', 'subjective permanence', 'enacted permanence' and 'uncontested permanence'. These concepts have guided much of our further analysis. For example, we have tried to describe how far children achieved 'objective permanence', staying in foster care for as long as they needed, and to find correlates of and explanations for this. In general the statistics suggest that most of those in the sample seemed to settle but that 'contested permanence' could translate into a wish not to be fostered and hence to breakdown. Similarly a high 'rejection score' (the opposite in a sense of enacted permanence) was associated with breakdown.

The case studies suggest that these concepts are useful in that they capture aspects of a foster placement that are important to the young people.

- *Objective permanence* – Alistair had two fostering breakdowns. In this sense he experienced less 'objective permanence' than Tara. The first, in particular, was etched in his mind as an extremely unpleasant experience and is likely to have made him less trusting in the future.

- *Subjective permanence* – Tara had clearly come to conceive of her foster family as in a sense her family. She commented on this and on how at home she had felt there. It was clearly now part of her internal sense of security. Equally Alistair commented on how initially he had felt at home in both his placements but how he had come to feel out of place and excluded. Again this was significant to him.

- *Enacted permanence* – Both Alistair and Tara were acutely sensitive to the way in which they were treated as part of the family and commented on this. For example, Tara was aware that her foster carer had risked a diplomatic breakdown with the carer's extended family over whether Tara could be invited to a wedding. By contrast Alistair, initially delighted at the way he was treated in his first placement, felt finally that everyone else had a key and was locking their doors against him.[4]

- *Uncontested permanence* – Neither placement was under pressure from relatives that it should end. In Tara's case her mother's blank refusal to have her back may well have been an important element in her own decision to settle down and make the best of what was on offer. Lacking this clarity Alistair continued to involve himself with his family as discussed below.

Perhaps the crucial difference between Alistair and Tara lay in the degree to which what was on offer corresponded to what was wanted. Tara seems to have expected little and to have been correspondingly delighted with what she got. Alistair by contrast wanted a lot. He threw himself into both his foster placements with an enthusiasm that his second carer at least found daunting.[5] For him these were golden times, shopping with his carers, going on trips with them and enjoying their exclusive attention. These times did not, however, survive the arrival of another foster child or, in the second placement, what sounds like attempts at independence training. And so the loneliness which underlay the initial enthusiasm returned.

These differences seemed to have wide implications. Tara came to accept her foster family as one of a number of families that she had. She did not see her carer as her mother – 'to me mum is mum' – but she did see her as someone whom she greatly respected and who would always be available to her. On this basis she was able to re-evaluate her own relationship with her family and her goals in life (which became more like those of the foster family). Alistair by contrast remained vulnerable to his family. His time in foster care remained in a sense isolated from his life. He looked back on parts of it with fondness. It did not, however, provide him an adequate base from which to review and construct his life.

Relationships with birth family

Yeah. But after about a year, it didn't really bother me about my mum. Even right now, it doesn't bother me. It's like I don't really need her. Sometimes I do think, I don't really need her. Because she hasn't been there for the last five years, and I've coped without her. If she came back, I wouldn't really need any help... Do you know what? I was thinking what a big family! I've got my dad's side. I don't get on with them, my mum's side, I don't talk to them at all. I've got his dad's side – mum and dad – they love me. And then I've got [my foster carer's] whole side – her sisters' and her husband's side. So I've got like families everywhere. That's what I feel like I've sort of got families and families and families, and I've got my own family now. Even my leaving care worker, I've met his wife and kids in town, and that, so we have a good relationship. (Tara)

Q: Are they [brothers and sisters] family or just theoretical family?

A: Not any more. They don't exist now. The things that…not them – it's not their fault, it's just the things the man is doing. I'm a very forgiving person, but the things that lot did to me – I could have killed that lot, seriously! And it's just like, I've got over it, I think – because I've been on my own for so long… (Alistair)

Fostering involves a break with a previous family as well as a temporary sojourn with a new one. Inevitably the relationships of foster children with birth family and with foster family are intertwined while the children variously view these relationships as compatible or mutually exclusive. Arguably it is only if the relationships with the foster family are secure that it is possible to take a cool look at those with the birth family.

Statistically, contact with birth families was associated with problems. Children who returned home were more likely to be re-abused and did worse in other ways. If there was no control over who visited previously abused children, their placements were more likely to break down. Yet at the same time many children yearned for their families or for particular members of them. If this yearning was translated into a wish to be at home rather than fostered, this too could threaten the placement.

Some of these themes were illustrated by our case studies. Out of the two only Alistair had been clearly abused. His contacts with his family were fraught and ambivalent. He complained about them, thought obsessively about them, loaned them money which was not repaid and seemed somehow under a compulsion to return to them and be hurt again. His counselling and his contact with his aunt and uncle seemed to be enabling Alistair to re-evaluate his relationships with his family.

Tara by contrast had, on the face of it, been treated less badly. She was clearly hurt by her family and was sad about the way things had turned out. She had considered returning to them on leaving foster care but decided against it. Now she dealt with them on her terms, had no wish to placate them, and while in no way vindictive was perfectly capable of telling them off when occasion demanded. Now she felt that she could forgive, if not forget, and move on.

The Dartington group have rightly pointed to the potential of birth families and relatives to provide support to children ceasing to be looked after (see Bullock et al. 1998). Nevertheless the lesson, both from the case studies and the statistics, may be that the families of these children may also retain the power to harm them. In such cases the aim should perhaps be not so much to bring about reconciliation and re-unification as to enable the children and young people to come to a '*modus vivendi*' with their families and psychologically 'move on'. If in doing so they can also understand and forgive, so much the better.

Attachment

> But then I always had this insecurity in me. I always keep my distance with [my foster carer]. And I still do that – I keep my distance with women or someone whom I'm getting close to…it's just that I'm scared that if this goes wrong again, I'm not taking it. I can't take it every time it goes wrong with a female, or somebody I trust…[my foster carer] understood why I keep my distance from everybody. It's just my insecurity. (Tara)

> But then the other girl, the other foster kid was…she was always with them as well, and then when I was on my own a lot, that's when them lot would go out, and I wouldn't know anything about it – they'd organise it, and they'd go out and forget about me, but then the last thing was the birthday party, and no one said a word, and they were all singing Happy Birthday, and I thought, what's going on? So after I had to endure that, then someone calls me, so I said, 'I'm staying up here – no one called me before', so she said, 'why are you acting like this? Why are you acting funny?' I said, 'I'm fed up of living here, you know what I'm saying? Being ignored.' (Alistair)

> I think we got into this relationship – tit for tat…that psychological game. He'll go into his room…I said 'right you can stay there, because you're not even going to see me because I am going to come in late from work'. (Alistair's second foster carer)

Separation is intrinsic to foster care. Some foster children have been repeatedly separated from adults on whom they depend. Many are likely to be separated in the near future from their current foster home. These past or impending separations coloured their relationships with both foster and birth families and raised issues of attachment. Children were variously wary of relationships or so keen on closeness that they demanded exclusive relationships or aroused feelings of claustrophobia in their carers by continually following them around. We had two measures of attachment status: 'childlike attachment' and 'stoicism'. Both were associated with our other main measure of disturbance, 'the Goodman score'. Childlike attachment in particular predicted difficulties in adoption, fostering and among care leavers.

In keeping with this analysis, attachment issues seemed to us to be prominent in both our cases. Both Tara and Alistair were sensitive to the possibility of rejection, describing themselves as cautious and holding back in relationships. This was how Tara explained her reluctance to open up to her foster carer, her half-belief that the carer would not want to keep her beyond 18 and her decision not to get married immediately. It was how Alistair explained why he had few friends and no girlfriend. Together they pick up the theme of wariness which has recurred throughout our case studies, which we have associated with the concept of compulsive self-reliance (Bowlby 1979), and which we have tried to capture through our stoicism measure.

A second key form of disturbed attachment – referred to by Bowlby (1979) as anxious attachment – was displayed most clearly by Alistair. In his foster placement he demanded an exclusive relationship, and was threatened by the arrival of new foster children. Yet his distrust made it difficult for him to ask directly for the love that he craved. Instead he was quite capable of locking his second foster carer out and trapping her at times into a cycle of mutual rejection. A central theme of Alistair's interview was loneliness – a feeling of being on the outside as others sang happy birthday or took part in a family Christmas. His desire to be close led to a feeling of claustrophobia on the part of his carer. His anxiety about relationships between others and those to whom he desired to be close contributed to the breakdown of his placements. In Bowlby's (1979) view jealousy is almost another name for childlike attachment. Alistair's anxious attachment, like his stoicism, can therefore be seen as characteristic.[6]

These differences seemed in part to reflect the success of the foster placements in building trusting relationships. This was difficult. Tara felt that her foster carer was likely to have had enough of her at 18. Alistair and his carer reached an impasse when neither talked to the other. Both our foster carers were, as far as we could see, good, perhaps even exceptional.[7] Where the two cases differed was in the 'fit' between child and family and in the benign or negative spirals which developed. Tara was amazed at the trust which her foster mother showed in her and did her best not to abuse it. Her one act of delinquency was firmly but sympathetically dealt with. She did not feel alienated by the way she had been handled. By contrast the history of both Alistair's placements was similar. He began by bonding but something went wrong with the arrival of a new foster child. In both his placements he felt that he was excluded by the foster family. In both placements his behaviour made the exclusion come to pass. His one act of minor delinquency led, in his eyes, to further exclusion. In his last placement he managed the contradictory feat of making his foster carer feel suffocated, unable to go out or have friends to stay, and also rejected when Alistair locked himself in his room or her out. She reacted humanly by withdrawal and counter-rejection. Whereas Tara and her foster carer talked, Alistair and his ended by not speaking at all.

Perhaps because of their previous rejections, both Tara and Alistair found the experience of leaving their foster carers a sad and troubling one. In both cases the relationship with the previous foster carer was threatened and in both cases it was retrieved, at least in part, by the skilled and committed behaviour of the foster carer.[8] This was true even in Alistair's case where the placement had effectively broken down. It is hoped, therefore, that neither had given up on the possibility of human relationships. Tara loved others and was cautiously contemplating the possibility of marriage. When Alistair returned from hospital to his flat to find his aunt waiting for him, his life seemed to change.

So the implication seems to be that foster care is an arena in which the dramas of attachment are played out. This can lead to mutual rejection. More positively it seems to offer the opportunity for resolving previous issues. It may also require a recognition that the relationships forged in foster care are real and important. In the case of adoption there was some evidence that continuing contact with a foster carer lessened the likelihood of childlike attachment behaviour. Contact with the carer on return home or on leaving care may also be important.

School and work

Because her oldest daughter has just graduated Masters in psychology, and her second daughter's just graduated in psychology, doing a BA, or something. And they're both looking for jobs. I think I never wanted to go to college before... I didn't want to go to college when I was at my mum's house. I didn't even want to study at all. But now I really want to study... I really miss homework. Do you know that? I actually do. I actually miss it! I used to love my homework. I was so interested, I used to love it and I miss it so much. (Tara)

The first three years at school was all right. It was only till I left home, and I was on my own. I was on my own for about two years...the last two years at school. I spent my whole life just walking around, and going to the music room. (Alistair)

It's been good. Good. It feels lonely sometimes but now I've got the little one he keeps me busy all day long… (Tara)

That chefing job – oh God, I was there for two and a half years and I just thought, I've had enough. Them lot was just taking the mick. I was doing two people's jobs. I was a trainee chef – I was doing the job of a professional chef…and I wasn't getting paid for that either. So I left that job. (Alistair)

Attachment, permanence and relations with birth family are bound up together. The concepts are connected almost by definition. It would be odd to say, for example, that a child had a normal attachment status but no attachment to her or his birth family or foster family. It would also be odd to say that a child was permanently settled with foster carers but wanted to be with a birth family. By contrast school and work are conceptually separate from family. There is nothing odd about saying that a child is doing well at school but is unhappy at home.

In practice our statistical analyses suggested that life outside the current 'placement' – school for foster children, work (or the lack of it) for care leavers – was very important for life within the placement.[9] Children who were happy at school did better in their placement. They were also less likely to exhibit social problems such as delinquency. The relation between well-being and work seemed more problematic. Care leavers who were working were more likely than others to be seen by social workers and foster carers as doing well. They themselves were more likely to feel that they had a wide variety of troubles.

In keeping with these analyses Tara enjoyed her time at school, delighted in her homework and, in great contrast to her earlier behaviour, developed academic ambitions. By contrast Alistair was lonely at school, felt the odd one out there and was bullied. It was only the interest of a music teacher that enabled him to develop an interest in music which was still a solace. His willingness to lend money to friends at a hostel and his later anxiety about the youths gathered outside his house may both have reflected his early school experience.

A striking difference between the two case studies lay in the degree to which school was in a sense 'part of a package deal'. For Tara school came to be seen as part of a way of life, a route to the kind of house and lifestyle that she wanted for herself. She identified with her foster carer's daughters who went to university. She had plans for achieving this and she almost certainly had the support she needed to bring this about. By contrast Alistair did not see school as a route to anywhere. Nor did his subsequent work require expertise in school subjects other than perhaps an ability to read and do arithmetic.

In practice life outside foster care involved severe practical problems for both Alistair and Tara. Both found that their supported accommodation charged rents to those working which made it financially very difficult to work. Alistair's longest job was low paid, gave him no training and involved unsocial hours and a very difficult journey. His fortunes started to improve when he dropped some agency work and signed on instead. Tara loved her new baby and was delighted by its arrival. Nevertheless, even she was daunted by the responsibility it involved. A striking feature of these difficulties was the speed with which potentially serious difficulties could develop. Alistair's two failures to pay his rent quickly resulted in debts of £1000 and £500 respectively. Within two months of leaving foster care Tara was out of touch with her loved foster carer and wrestling with the implications of pregnancy.

Managing these problems involved competence – something which both, as it happened, had in considerable quantities (Alistair's ability at cooking, ironing and managing money greatly impressed his foster carer) – but also reliable, trusting relationship(s). Because of the speed with which troubles could arise it was important that these relationships were immediately available. The job market is often precarious for young people. Those with supportive families have, however, a safety net when jobs turn sour. Tara had support available to her. She discussed her pregnancy with her boyfriend and her social worker and worked out its implications. Subsequently she also made great use of her foster carer and her in-laws. Alistair, until recently, wrestled with his problems on his own.

So what is the relevance of school and work? Much may depend on the context. It may help if school is seen as part of a way of life, so that children participate partly because this is what people in their kind of family 'do'. It may help if qualifications are meaningfully related to what the child wants to do. It may help if this work or the training needed for this future is supported financially and in other ways. It may also help if work in turn complements a young person's life. Tara was happy with her life partly because she was clear that she was carrying out a meaningful task. She had the support she needed to do this. Alistair by contrast did not see his job as meaningful, nor did it provide him with the money he needed to manage his life as he wanted. It seems unlikely that additional qualifications would have made his life go better.

Working things out

> Well, I still talk to my birth family. I don't know about my mum's side of the family, but I do talk to her when I see her, but then, I'm going to…by the time he's about six or seven, I'm going to make him understand why he's got two grandmothers on my side. (Tara)

> I think, for me, it was like, trying to come to terms with it, at the time, when all this was going on, I was in another world, I cut myself off from everybody. [tape paused]…normal, I thought these things happen. It's only when you get older, and you live on your own, that you think, whoah! (Alistair)

Foster care confronts children with questions of blame. There is the question of why they are looked after. There are the related issues of whose fault this is and what this implies for the future and for the relationship with the birth family. Does it mean that the child has never been loved, or that he or she brought this about, or that he or she will never amount to much? Children's answers to such questions may inform their decisions about where they wish to be and what they want to do.

Such issues are about ways of conceiving of the world. For attachment theorists they are involved with 'working models' – ways of conceiving of oneself and one's relationships. For others they may be conceptualised as 'family myths' or 'scripts' or as central features of identity, self-concept or self-esteem. We did not measure these concepts and so have no statistical data on them. Case studies, however, illustrated the effort some families put into allocating blame and the concern some children felt when they could not understand or accept the reason for which they were looked after. What these two case studies illustrate is the effort some children and young people put into reworking their views of the world.

In working out their own salvations Alistair and Tara used the materials to hand. Tara acknowledged that her foster carer had opened her eyes to things that she now wanted for herself – education, a comfortable style of life and new ways of handling relationships. She had also learnt to talk to her foster carer, something which she felt she had been able to do because she had first talked to her social workers. Her new relationships had perhaps made her less dependent on her family. Her ability to talk to her carer had helped put her past in perspective. Against this background the arrival of her son seemed to have enabled her to develop a coherent philosophy of life. She had worked out views on religion, on what it was to be a 'modern Indian', on her current priorities, her obligations or otherwise to her son and her birth family, the kind of job she wanted, and the way she expected her life to go.

Interestingly, Alistair seems to have used relationships outside foster care much as Tara used fostering. While in foster care he had developed a good relationship with a music teacher. This had opened his eyes to music, something which he still found a major consolation. His counselling had enabled him to put some of his past life in perspective. He was now able to use his aunt for discussions much as Tara had used her foster carer. Prior to this his needs seemed more often to have been expressed in what he did than in what he said. As a result behaviour which may well have expressed a great loneliness and a need for love was experienced by his carers as strange, threatening, constricting and possibly indicative of mental ill-health. Now he was making some kind of sense, if not necessarily of where he wanted to go, at least of what had happened to him in the past.

So the suggestion in the case studies is very similar to the one put forward by Downes (1992) and the one implicit in the model of successful placements developed in our second book (Sinclair, Wilson and Gibbs 2004). The role of foster care is to enable a reworking of earlier views and anxieties about the world. This is a creative act. For this reason it is not something that another person can bring about. Nevertheless like all creative acts it can be enabled or made virtually impossible. Foster placements which offer committed parenting along with permanence as we define it and which support safe access to birth families and achievement at school and subsequently at work may provide the conditions in which young people can work out their own futures.

Reasons for differences in outcome

Why were the outcomes for Tara and Alistair initially so different? No doubt there are many reasons, but some pick up themes from elsewhere in this book.

One reason may have to do with differences in the degree to which the two individuals had been damaged by their former experience. On our measures Alistair was more disturbed. In 1998 he scored very high on our measure of overall Goodman score (higher than Tara who in turn scored higher than her peers), very high on our measure of childlike attachment (where Tara scored lower than her peers) and very high on our measure of stoicism (where Tara scored lower than Alistair but higher than her peers). So Tara may have found it easier than Alistair to ask for support and establish relationships which the other party did not find claustrophobic.

These differences probably affected the foster placements. Both young people were, in our view, lucky in their last foster carers who were skilled, committed and ethnically matched with the foster child. However, in Alistair's case a placement that was initially going well was allowed to spiral out of control. Faced with his extremely disturbed attachment behaviour, his carer felt simultaneously locked out and stifled. Despite her skill and insight she was not given the kind of support which she may have needed. The best of foster carers may be, as Alistair's carer felt she had been, sucked into ways of dealing with the young person that are not helpful.

The progress of the placement affected the young people's well-being at school. As we have seen, Tara became committed to her carer's way of life, changed her view of school and found that she was rewarded with success there. By contrast Alistair found it difficult to mix. Although there was no evidence that foster care was responsible for his difficulties at school, it was not obviously helpful either. Tara's self-esteem was therefore likely to be enhanced by school. Alistair's was not.

It might be thought that these differences in school performance explain subsequent differences on leaving care. Neither our case studies nor our statistics suggest such an easy equation. Tara's outcome seems directly attributable to the support she received from her carer, social worker and in-laws, her own resilience, and the reliable if meagre housing and financial support available to mothers with babies. Alistair's difficulties were attributable to the difficulties of those clawing their way into the job market and his initial lack of support. Both support our statistical conclusion that the key to successful leaving care is a close relationship and – unfortunate though this is – a role that does not immediately require getting a job.

Finally, the security which Tara drew from her placement enabled her to re-evaluate her life in general and her relationship with her family in particular. She was no longer vulnerable to them. By contrast Alistair remained vulnerable. Angry as he was with his step-father he nevertheless loaned him money and involved himself in his plots. This was certainly one of the major reasons for his difficulty on leaving care.

Conclusion

In statistical analysis, variables, although often associated, are in a sense discrete. A measure of attachment in such analysis differs from a measure of 'permanence' or a measure of conflict with birth families. In histories such as those we have described these concepts are more fluid. The nature of 'permanence' is informed by a child's attachment status and relations with their birth family. The meaning of school is informed by the way the family regard it and so on. Despite this fluidity, it may be helpful to draw boundaries, as it were, to sketch out a pattern, which, while it is inevitably false to life, nevertheless can inform the way we think and act.

In essence then we suggest that the aim of long-term foster care should be to offer a placement which is permanent as judged against all the criteria given in Chapter 1 (i.e. 'objective', 'subjective', 'enacted' or 'uncontested' forms of permanence). It would not be an alternative to a birth family. It would, however, be on offer after 18; it would not be subject to disruption; it would feel like a family; those in it would behave with the commitment expected of family members; and it would not involve a continual conflict of loyalties. In this situation a child will be happy with where they are and happy to stay there. As we have seen, the wish to be in the placement is almost certainly central to the success of both foster care and rehabilitation.

Such a placement is likely to be enabled by skilled committed foster care, probably backed by consultation so that placements are not destabilised by spirals of rejection, and by social work that is able to deal with the difficulties of contact and is sensitive to issues of attachment. Work with the child might also make it easier for her or him to make sense of their background and talk about such issues with their carer.

Work with the child's school would, it is hoped, ensure that this key area of life was a source of strength rather than difficulty. It would be concerned with whether the child was happy at school, what they liked doing there and their successes there beyond the purely scholastic. There would be a recognition that the move from school to work is stressful and that the initial stages of entering the world of work are often ill-paid and insecure.

Young people would move from their foster placements in consultation with their carers and with the possibility of maintaining close relationships. Because of the difficult roles young people have to play on leaving care it is vital that they have strong supportive relationships available to them. Foster carers can supply such relationships (as did Tara's foster carer). However, they have to be strong, the young people need to be able to call on them easily and the foster carers need to maintain them proactively.

This model sees success in all settings as primarily determined by the child's individual difficulties, by whether or not they want to be in that setting, and by the quality of 'parenting' and schooling they receive there.

Successful transitions between one setting and another may be enabled by work with the child's yearning for the previous family and by enabling the positive relationships built up in earlier settings to continue in the current one.

Against this background some of the attachment difficulties of children may be assuaged. Patterns of relating learnt in birth families are likely to be rehearsed and may be changed. Young people may, like Tara, use the opportunity to make sense of their own lives, forgive if not forget, and move on. On leaving foster care they may well stay in touch with their foster families. Certainly they need support – for the lives they have to lead would be easy for none of us.

Summary of Chapter 13

1. Both our case studies and our statistics support the view that long-term success in foster care requires:

    -   achieving objective and subjective permanence in the placement

    -   managing relationships with the birth family

    -   dealing with disturbed attachment

    -   enabling success at school and/or work.

2. This in turn is likely to require:

    -   skilled committed foster care

    -   a willingness by the carer to provide post-placement support

    -   social work which deals with issues relating to attachment and birth family

    -   support for child or young person in their school or work.

3. Such conditions, it is hoped, enable the children and young people to resolve their often ambivalent feelings of attachment and come to their own settled views about their relationship with their family and the kind of person they wish to be.

Notes

1. Strictly speaking this is an inference for Alistair – he did not say his siblings were preferred to him but his self-description as 'family slave', his anger against his step-siblings and his behaviour on the arrival of foster children make it likely that this is what he felt.

2. In our second book (Sinclair, Wilson and Gibbs 2004) we used case studies to illuminate the day-to-day transactions between carers and foster children (see Wilson *et al.* 2004). The patterns we identify in what follows are very similar but on a wider scale. So, for example, issues of attachment are evident both in the daily dealings of foster carers with their foster children and in the wider arena of the foster children's careers.

3. This obviously need not necessarily be their family of origin. Quinton and Rutter (1988), for example, found that the quality of new marriage or partnership was crucial for the outcomes for the young women in their sample.

4. Both Alistair and Tara felt that they were the odd one out in their own families and this may have made them particularly sensitive to the possibility of being unfairly treated. This sensitivity may be common among rejected children who have siblings at home with their parents (cf. Quinton *et al.* 1998; Rushton *et al.* 2001; Sinclair, Wilson and Gibbs 2004).

5. In this respect he resembled those adoptive children who were professing undying love for their new parents before the latter had even had time to like them.

6. Attachment theorists commonly put individuals into types. The assumption seems to be that a child is likely to show one type of disturbed attachment behaviour in preference to others although mixed and disorganised patterns are allowed. This does not seem particularly helpful in this sample. The evidence for this is partly statistical. There was virtually no correlation between our stoicism variable and our childlike attachment variable. High scorers on one were no more or less likely to be high scorers on the other. In addition it was obvious in the case studies that a child could show one type of behaviour towards, say, the mother and another towards the father. They could also change their behaviour so that, for example, a child who had been very wary of her foster carer became very anxiously attached to her following an illness. It seemed easier to assume that both stoicism and childlike attachment were different responses to the fear of being let down. Which was employed in a given situation would depend on learning and particular features of the situation concerned – for example, as others have pointed out, the degree to which children are exposed to threats arousing attachment behaviour towards the threats' source.

7. This may seem grudging acknowledgement of their efforts. In the context of foster care, however, it is difficult to rate any foster carer 'exceptional'. The commitment of most foster carers was, to us, very impressive indeed.

8. This is in keeping with Downes (1992). Her thesis is that the threat of renewed separation implicit in fostering teenagers allows old traumas to be revisited and re-appraised from the 'secure base' provided by the foster carer.

9. Bullock and his colleagues (1998) may express a similar idea with their concept of the importance of a teenager's 'complementary roles' outside the family for his or her successful re-union with family on ceasing to be looked after.

Chapter Fourteen

Conclusion

I think Samantha's mum, I don't know much about her but I think she was a very damaged person too, but she loved her daughter, I'm quite sure of it, in her own way but she was useless at mothering. (Samantha's foster carer)

Q: If they'd have said to you, 'We've got a family that's interested in adopting you', or something like that...?
A: Oh no, no...
Q: But why would that have been a no no?
A: Cos it just would. I wouldn't be able to see my mum and it would do me head in really, I'd flip if they offered me adoption, I'd flip, so. (Samantha)

I had been fighting for her to come back... But the day I, the day she come back to me... I think they put, locked me in prison and threw the key away... I told her the other day...I feel as though I'm on a life support machine, just lifeless, nothing there...cos you've took everything away from me. That's just how I feel. I've got nothing, no [pause] well, I've got nothing anyway. (Samantha's mother)

We never did really, we never did address the issues. (Samantha's social worker)

Introduction

Foster care has many strengths. The reasons for it are usually unhappy – separations, family breakdowns and abuse. Its existence is a repeated demonstration that in the face of such origins there is room for love, good sense, skill, good humour, commitment and resilience.

Despite these strengths official initiatives concerned with foster care concentrate on the difficulties of foster care itself – for example, the undoubted need to recruit more carers and the turnover of foster children. These are serious problems. Nevertheless, the key problem highlighted in this book concerns the relationship of foster care with other parts of the care system. Foster care is not conceived as a permanent solution to a child's problems, nor in most cases does it operate as one. In many ways the Achilles heel of the system lies not in what happens in foster care but in what follows it.

Against this background the purpose of the conclusion is:

- to provide a brief overview of this dilemma
- to provide an analysis of the reasons for it
- to suggest ways forward.

Our research cannot produce a clear-cut set of recommendations which we can be sure will work.[1] It is 'observational': we have not intervened in such a way that we could tell whether or not the intervention causes a good result. Moreover, the variables we find to be influential most commonly have to do with practice. We have not shown that particular policies or administrative actions will produce better results. We have shown, for example, that child-oriented carers had better outcomes. This result, however, does not show how to select child-oriented carers or how they can be helped to practise in a child-oriented way.

These difficulties have not stopped us from making suggestions. Social work research is not rich in evidence of effectiveness. Any evidence on what might work needs to be garnered and, if possible, codified. In this way it may in time be possible to benefit from the hard-won insights of practitioners and others involved and turn them into trial teaching material, practice guides and so on. They can then be subject to rigorous empirical test.

In general, and even if all our suggestions are appropriate, we will not have resolved the dilemmas of foster care we discuss below. In our view there is no final solution. It is, however, possible to reduce dilemmas through good practice, a modification of priorities, and the wise use of resources. Much of this must take place in arenas other than foster care itself. We have summarised our suggestions under the main headings of adoption, foster care, return to birth family and leaving care. As it seems likely that some will read this chapter and not the earlier ones we have sometimes repeated the concluding sections of earlier chapters.

The dilemmas of foster care

This research is not about short-term foster care. The children we studied were in foster care at a particular point in time. They thus stayed on average much longer than the larger number of other children in need who enter and leave the system, commonly within eight weeks, and, in the majority of cases, within a year. At the same time our sample should represent the children who occupy the great majority of places in the foster care system at any one time and thus consume the lion's share of fostering resources.

Although the children in our study are in a sense the 'bread and butter' of fostering, they present it with a dilemma. In the past, residential care was seen as a mechanism for change. Foster care was not. Very few of the children in Rowe and her colleagues' study (1989) were in anything that could be called treatment foster care. This situation persists. Hardly any (1%) of the children in this study were seen by their foster carers as placed with the hope that fostering would somehow help to bring about change. So treatment, if it happens, happens in the context of foster care through outside specialists. It is not usually seen as involving the foster carers themselves, although in our case studies both here and in our previous report we have identified foster carers who in many respects could be said to be providing treatment (Wilson *et al.* 2004). As a result foster care seems to be seen as a caring environment, not essentially as something which prepares you for life elsewhere.[2]

In the past this may not have mattered. Foster care was then conceived as a kind of quasi-adoption. Children fostered on Scottish farms who pulled their weight could remain there into adulthood and many apparently did (Ferguson 1966). Undoubtedly some children in our study were in quasi-adoptive placements, which in a minority of cases would persist beyond 18. Effectively, however, foster care only offered 'permanent' placements to those aged between 4 and 14 when we first met them in 1998. With younger children every effort was made to get them adopted or get them home. Children aged 15 or over in 1998 were over 18 when we followed them up in 2001. Fewer than one in seven of them were with their former carers.

In practice, foster care itself offers a rather fragile permanence even among those aged between 4 and 14.[3] Fewer than four out of ten in this age group were still with the same foster carer in 2001 as when we first contacted them in 1998. Long stays in foster care were indeed quite common among the younger children. If they remained in foster care, however, they had to surmount the hurdle of their teenage years. Among those who were aged 11 to 15 when we first met them 48 per cent had had, on our definition, a disruption by the time we followed them up three years later.[4] It was only a minority, probably between one in six and one in seven of the whole sample, who had achieved permanence in foster care in the sense that they were still with their original carers and they wanted to use the foster home as a base. This minority, however, was vulnerable to disruption and subject like others to the expectation that they move at 18. Our case studies show that foster care can offer permanence. The statistics suggest that it rarely does.

A further, and perhaps more serious, problem is that in most cases the environments other than adoption to which children move from fostering are not ideal. In less than a fifth of cases was a residential home seen by the social workers as fully satisfactory, materially adequate and safe. As only 4 per cent of the sample were in residential care this may raise questions about the resources consumed by this form of provision. From the point of view of the foster children its deficiencies were, however, less serious than the difficulties confronting the much larger numbers who go back to their birth families or leave for independent living.

Among those aged 4 to 14 the most likely route out of foster care was to go home. Sometimes this was planned. Commonly it was not, a consequence brought about by disruption, the wish of parent and child to be together, and acceptance by the social worker that nothing else was likely to be better. In less than a third of the returns home did the social worker feel that the environment was fully satisfactory, materially adequate and safe. Returning home was associated with re-abuse, with a failure to improve at school, and, among older children, with an incidence of difficult behaviour that was greater than that found for residential care and almost certainly not accounted for by the children's initial characteristics. As argued in Chapter 1, a sizeable body of research now suggests that children who are vulnerable enough to be looked after but who remain with their parents on return often do worse than those who are adopted or those who are looked after on a long-term basis.

Those graduating out of foster care to independent living encountered the problems already documented by others (Biehal et al. 1995; Broad 1998; Stein and Carey 1986). In less than a fifth of these placements did the social worker feel that the young people's situations fully met our criteria of being satisfactory, safe and materially adequate. Among those on whom we had information around a third had reasonably stable housing careers, less than a fifth were in steady work, and only 1 in 16 had none of a long but nevertheless serious list of problems about which we asked them. Some care leavers were doing well on any criteria. Those who had babies had at least a regular income (however small), a meaning for their lives (however difficult these were), and sometimes strong support from their 'in-laws', partners or mothers.[5] Those who also went to university might also be supported by their former foster carers on special schemes.[6] The most severe problems were faced by those at the mercy of the job market. The jobs available were typically unskilled and insecure. Getting a job raised rents dramatically. Losing one and failing to get immediate social security assistance could lead quickly to severe debt. Involvement in work was associated with success as defined by social workers and former foster carers. For the care leavers themselves it predicted a higher than average number of severe difficulties and a lower than average sense of well-being.

Such findings might suggest that the aim of policy should be to cut the umbilical cord. Fewer children should return home. Those who cannot return home should be quickly adopted.[7] Implementing such proposals raises serious ethical and political dilemmas. On our evidence they would often cut across the views of children and birth parents. As we have seen the ties with birth parents are often strong, if ambivalent. Many children in our sample yearned for their mothers or for other members of their families. In addition half the sample first entered the care system when over the age of five and were thus too old to have a realistic chance of adoption. Even if adopters were available, fewer than one in ten of the children appeared to want adoption.[8] Many were vehemently opposed to it. We have shown that the wishes of children to be or not be in a placement have an important effect on its outcome. It is likely that this holds good in adoption as well as in foster placements and at home. If so, it follows that in most cases adoption would not work.

So in a sense long-term fostering is a compromise. It is not family life at home. It is not full adoption. It is not treatment.[9] It is not accompanied by systematic attempts to change the environment from which the child has come.[10] Only in the case of those young children placed for adoption does it commonly seem the ante-room to a better life.

In what follows we suggest ways of reducing this dilemma. Essentially we argue that it is necessary:

- to somewhat increase the number of adoptions where this can be done ethically
- to reduce the difference between fostering and adoption (e.g. by reducing breakdowns and enabling more children to stay on after 18)

- to improve the support available to birth families in such a way that enabling children to return home when they want is no longer so intimately connected with worse outcomes

- to improve the support for children when they leave for independent living.

Most people would agree that these would be desirable goals. It would be surprising if research concluded that there should be more breakdowns in foster care. It is, however, easier to state the goals than to say how they should be pursued. Before discussing this we need a more grounded analysis of the problems of the foster children themselves.

The problems of foster children

Some of the problems of foster children may be genetic in origin. Some, however, are undoubtedly environmental. Most have been stressed by abuse. All have been separated from those to whom they might be expected to be attached. These losses and separations often pre-date the removal to the care system.[11] Such moves are often produced by abuse and would be expected to result in attachment difficulties (Howe *et al.* 1999). In Chapter 3 we argued that re-abuse was a causal factor in worsening mental health as was heightened anxious attachment (our interpretation of the 'childlike attachment score').

The first key problem faced by such foster children is that they are likely to have difficulty in relating to others. This difficulty predicts others. We have shown that our childlike attachment score measured in 1998 predicts subsequent difficulties in adoption and (very strongly) fostering breakdown. We have suggested that in many cases changes in this score pre-date changes in the Goodman score and can be seen as 'causing them'.[12] The score was also a very strong predictor of a measure of difficulties on leaving care (loneliness, delinquency, drinking too much and so on). Subjectively those exhibiting this childlike attachment may have felt excluded and their clinging behaviour tended to induce feelings of claustrophobia and suffocation in others. Faced with such demands the carers often reacted by retreat or even rejection – a pattern likely to make the situation worse.[13] Only birth mothers may have been immune to this vicious circle, possibly interpreting the clinging behaviour of their children as affection rather than anxiety.

Difficulties in relating to others are only part of the problem facing foster children.[14] A second key problem is their performance at school (Aldgate

1999; Aldgate *et al.* 1992; Cheung and Heath 1994; Essen *et al.* 1976; Jackson 2001; St Claire and Osborne 1987). This study is perhaps unusual in emphasising the impact of school on fostering rather than lamenting the lack of impact of fostering on educational progress. Unhappiness at school as assessed in 1998 was a strong predictor of fostering breakdown as well as of subsequent truancy, running away, delinquency, trouble with drink or drugs, problems over sexuality and self-harm. It remained so when the other variables we had found to predict were taken into account. So unhappiness at school is not only an indicator of trouble but also, arguably, a source of it.

The third key problem facing foster children is the continuing involvement of their birth parents. Undoubtedly this is what many of them want.[15] To deprive them of it arbitrarily would breed resentment and infringe their human rights. Nevertheless, family contact is not necessarily very good for them.[16] Where there was strong evidence of previous abuse, uncontrolled contact with families (i.e. contact which was permitted for all family members) was, in keeping with our earlier study, associated with breakdown over the three years.[17] It was also associated with re-abuse. This was for two reasons. Abuse could take place on contact, and contact was associated with return home, itself a risk factor for further abuse. So, many children were, in a sense, in limbo. The pull of home meant that they could not fully commit to the foster home. At the same time they could not return home safely.

A fourth key problem facing foster children is that environments for which they leave often do not support any gains they have made in foster care. We have already rehearsed the difficulties of those returning home and of care leavers.[18] A problem facing children in all settings is that their personal difficulties do transfer. Thus there is a high correlation between children's child-like attachment scores in one setting and their scores in another. By contrast the benign effects of good parenting in one foster care setting do not necessarily transfer to another. For example, the parenting skills of carers at the first sweep were not significantly related to the parenting skills of carers in other foster placements at sweep 3 or to the subsequent behaviour and well-being of the foster children. So there is a danger that the main legacy of one setting to another is negative. The children bring their problems with them but may also yearn for the previous setting and fail to settle in the new one.

In tackling these problems it is important to address:

- the child's immediate environment – particularly the quality of caring provided by their parents or foster carers, their schooling and the availability to them of key positive relationships with other adults

- the connection between the child's previous environment and their next one.

In what follows we consider practical ways of doing this in the different settings: adoption, foster care, home, and independent living.

What might be done: adoption

Our questionnaire to adoptive parents produced an unusually high response rate of 82 per cent. At the conclusion of it they made a large number of suggestions for improvement. Many of these recommendations have to do with procedures and support. In what follows we concentrate on other issues more central to this book. In this respect our data suggest to us the following.

First, there is scope for some increase in adoptions among younger children. The chance of adoption drops rapidly with age. Only three of the children who were six or over when we first met them were adopted. In some cases it appeared that attempts at rehabilitation continued despite the birth mother's wish to give up the child or evidence that it was not going to work. Some adoptive parents complained of this and some children complained that their plight had not been heard. In a minority of cases a greater willingness to recognise the inevitable might have resulted in an adoption rather than long-term foster care.

Second, there may be scope for diminishing the distress and accompanying disordered attachment behaviour among adopted children. Delays in the adoption process (which it is in any case desirable to reduce) meant that many children spent much longer with their foster carers than with their own parents. Some adoptive parents complained that some foster carers failed to dispel the impression that the child was moving because of naughtiness. Carers might also not keep in touch with foster children who missed them, even if the adoptive parent wanted this to happen. Statistically, contact with previous foster carers was significantly associated with a reduction in one of our measures of attachment difficulties, after allowing for such variables as we could, albeit on small numbers. In general, contact with foster carers reduced over time as the child 'moved on', whereas in other cases it was irrelevant because of age, or impossible because of a poor handover. Until there is further research the safest assumption is probably that there is a benefit in continuing but diminishing contact, provided it is conducted with skill and goodwill on both sides.

Third, there is probably scope for continuing cautiously with the encouragement of contact with birth families. Infrequent low level or postbox contacts with various members of birth families was common and did not appear to have any serious detrimental effects. Where birth families behaved in the eyes of the adopters inappropriately, the latter seemed able to terminate contact or change the means by which it was conducted. Obviously this research can say nothing about the long-term effects of contact.[19] It would, however, suggest a need for caution. Uncritical enthusiasm for contact between abused children and their families could result in some of the difficulties associated with this in foster care.[20] Failure to recognise the wish and need for contact could make it harder for some children to come to terms with their situation and 'move on' (Fein, Maluccio and Kluger 1990).

Fourth, there is scope for increasing the number of adoptions by foster carers.[21] These seemed to take place because foster carers and children 'bonded', there were difficulties in getting the child adopted by 'strangers' (e.g. because they were disabled), and the local authorities agreed, sometimes grudgingly, that the child should be adopted. In practice, carer adoptions seemed to work out, if anything, even better than 'stranger adoptions', a result apparently in keeping with American research (cited in Sellick and Thoburn 1996), although it might not hold with a longer follow-up. In particular, attachment status appeared to be negatively affected by moves either to an adoptive home or another foster carer. Such moves were obviously avoided by carer adoption.

According to social workers, foster children and carers, carer adoption was almost the only likely route to adoption for those over six at first contact. This group contained some foster children who had spent a very long time with their foster carers. They naturally wanted their effective membership of this family recognised. To judge from the children's replies the upper limit of older children who might be adopted in this way would be 10 per cent. As not all those wanting to be adopted had carers wanting to adopt, a more likely figure would be 5 per cent. This proportion could be slightly increased if authorities met carers' anxieties about continuing financial and practical support (cf. Kirton, Ogilvie and Beecham 2003).

In general, adoption appears in this book as a considerable success. Its failures were, if anything, administrative. Its major limitation was its restricted age range. The suggestions made above are intended to slightly increase the numbers benefiting from it, while minimising the trauma inherent in the separations associated with it.

What might be done: foster care

The first requirement for increasing permanence in foster care is to reduce the incidence of breakdowns. This is easier said than done. Both the statistical data and the case studies suggest that what is required are the abilities to:

- handle disturbed behaviour, particularly disturbed attachment behaviour, on the part of the foster child which can otherwise alienate the carer and lead to a vicious circle of mutual rejection

- minimise interference with the placement from birth parents who cannot easily tolerate their child being either with them or away from them

- enable the child to come to a *modus vivendi* with their parents so that they are not torn in their own minds between yearning and rejection

- enable the child to adjust to school and enjoy her/himself there.

To these requirements we can add evidence from the children's questionnaires. As we have seen, foster children see foster care in different ways. Some see it as essentially family care, some see it as a safe and satisfactory alternative to a bleak life and some see it as a threat to their family bonds. There is diversity on whether they want to be the only child in a placement or would value other children and if so whether they would be children of a similar age, babies and so on. There is, however, no disagreement that carers should care for you, perhaps even love you, treat you fairly and as a member of the family, listen to you, do things with you, offer advice, and perhaps, although there is less agreement here, provide rules and control. At older ages at least they should relax the rules, negotiate, and listen to the teenager's side of the story. These basic provisions should be supported by adequate material goods, a room of your own, holidays, activities and encouragement of your interests.

The ability to meet these requirements probably depends first on the qualities of the foster carer. Child-oriented carers do better in these respects.[22] Success requires social workers and carers to see difficult behaviour as something other than a personal attack.[23] Carers have also to develop ways of dealing with the anxieties that may underlie behaviour without reinforcing the behaviour itself. They may require methods of behaviour management.[24]

Social workers may need to act as a go-between interpreting child to carer and vice versa.[25] They may need to act authoritatively towards the birth family, recognising that contact with one family member may be helpful and that with another the reverse.[26] Prohibiting a family member contact was associated with a lower risk of breakdown when there was strong evidence of prior abuse. Both carers and social workers require the co-operation of school and perhaps an educational psychologist. Happiness at school was probably a determinant of outcome. In the last study we showed that contact with an educational psychologist was associated with a reduced risk of breakdown over 14 months.[27]

These practices are elusive – matters of skill, timing and professional judgement – things not easily brought about by administrative fiat. That said, they would seem to require a philosophy which pays heed to attachment issues, makes use of the principles of social learning,[28] gives due importance to the school[29] and successfully manages the ambivalent attachment of children to their home. The case studies suggested that even the most skilled carers could find themselves trapped in negative spirals. Social workers are the obvious people to prevent these spirals or minimise their impact. So it would be important that the training of carers is consonant with the training of social workers. It may be they should be trained together. In this way supervision would reinforce training. It may also be true that administrative means could help ensure that the educational needs of children are not overlooked and that there is collaboration with school and educational psychology.[30] Contact also needs to be handled in ways that recognise the genuine risks, the complex views of children, the probable need for contact if children are 'to move on', the rights of those involved, and the changing nature of the situation.

The second task in increasing permanence is to change the assumptions surrounding foster care. In the children's eyes arrangements outside the foster family should be adapted to make it less out of the ordinary. It helped if the child knew the family before arrival or came with a sibling. Relative placements, while not always ideal, certainly had this advantage. Rules which singled the child out in relation to their friends were widely resented. Most parents do not have a family police-checked before they let their child spend the night there. Most do not have to ask a social worker before they can agree to a child going on a school trip. The foster children did not see why they should be made conspicuous by having to go through these time-consuming hoops.[31]

The key assumption that has to be challenged is that foster children effectively have to move out of their foster homes at 18. Strictly speaking this is not true. Some do stay on. It is perfectly legal for them to do so. Nevertheless, both foster children and foster carers seemed to feel that moving on was expected. In some authorities this expectation seems to be reinforced by a visit from the leaving care team around the age of 16. Yet as we have seen, social workers, foster carers and care leavers concurred in thinking that less than half of those who did move on were fully ready to do so.

In practice the scope for enabling staying on was limited by breakdowns – around a third of those who returned our questionnaires defined themselves as leaving because of a quarrel – and by a paradox – the more the foster carer defined the child as not ready to move the less willing they were to keep them. So much acknowledged, there did seem to be scope for changing the incentives so that staying on became less financially disadvantageous for foster carer and child and for continuing much the same level of support. The assumption would be that the young person would indeed move on but when they were ready and with flexible support.

What might be done: birth family

We failed to get statistical evidence of anything working when children returned to their birth families. Some returns clearly worked better than others. This, however, commonly seemed to have to do with changes that did not originate with social services. A violent partner moved out. An ill woman became less ill. A father or grandmother stepped into the breach. Such developments are difficult to bring about through intervention.[32] For this reason we can make no firm suggestions as to how matters should be improved. Instead we rely on suggestions made by our interviewees. These, however, were at least compatible with what we have found. Five suggestions can be made.

First, foster carers might more often be used to provide support for both mother and child combined with occasional respite care. The relationship between foster carer and child provides emotional capital and a potential force for good that too often lies unused. Respite stays in residential care (as suggested by one of the children in the case studies), short breaks in specialised foster care, or even day support in the successors to the former settlement houses might be used for teenagers in the same way. It is hoped that the effect would be to make the situation less desperate for both parent(s) and child. The arrangement might also offer a safety net at times of crisis, enable the carer to 'parent the birth parent' and provide the child with some ordinary, enjoyable experiences. One of our case studies provided an outstanding example of how such an arrangement can work.[33]

Second, children within these difficult ambivalent situations need to have access to adults whom they trust and with whom they can talk on a regular basis. The counsellor at the school provided a lifeline to one of the children in our case studies. The education social worker had done so earlier to another. Former foster carers were providing a listening ear to two others. An important feature of these arrangements was that they seemed to have rather little to do with formal qualifications and be available to children in the context of their ordinary lives.

Third, there should be experiments in making training available to birth parents in how to deal with teenagers. The one parent who had been on such a course found it helpful. There is American evidence that an effective approach is to train parents and foster carers in the same methods (Chamberlain 1998b). In this way there would be continuity between what is learnt in foster care and what is expected on return. Such experiments would challenge the assumption mentioned at the beginning of this chapter that foster care is not about change. They would also widen the foster care net making it more suitable for difficult teenagers who cannot temporarily live at home and for whom there is at the moment no alternative to residential care.[34]

Fourth, and contrary to the views of earlier researchers, it might be helpful if social services were less wary of care orders. A number of the placements in the case studies had been undermined by parents who, for example, authorised their children to stay out way beyond the time the foster carer thought appropriate. Similarly, some social workers felt that accommodated children should not go home. In these cases they sometimes resorted to subterfuge, pretending to parents that they had more power than they really had. A care order might clarify some of these situations. It need not mean that the child should not go home. It would, however, encourage clarity over what would have to change if return were to take place.

Fifth, and finally, it is illogical to offer less support to birth parents than to foster carers. It is true that many of them do not want to take up support. However, support and change do not often seem to be discussed as part of a return package. A surprising number of returns are experienced as sudden, rushed and presumably without much discussion at all. Moreover birth parents could justifiably complain that the level of support on offer does not amount to a realistic response to their problems. Contact with a social worker may well seem more likely to result in the detection of one's failures than in the promotion of one's success.[35] Many birth parents do seem to care about education while not being particularly good at promoting it. A determined and straightforward offer to help with admittedly difficult children, tackle depression and practical difficulties, and ensure that all concerned promote the child's schooling might well be more acceptable.[36]

What might be done: independent living

We think it would be desirable that more foster children should stay on beyond 18. For reasons already given we do not think it likely that many will. Steps therefore need to be taken to reduce the sense of rejection and isolation which may follow a move. Again, we lack statistical evidence on what might work. On the basis of the qualitative material we have suggested:

- involving foster carers as much as possible in the planning of moves and in supporting the young people when they have left – our case examples suggest that this may be possible even when a placement has officially 'broken down'

- ensuring that the placement to which the young person moves is in other ways adequately supported

- working with the young people's common wish to have their own place and manage their own lives.

Some steps have been taken to make this period easier for those who go to university. They have support available to them, they can go back to their foster families when necessary, and there is at least some expectation that what they are doing will lead somewhere. Somehow similar resources need to be provided for those who are in marginal jobs. Generally, this means that these jobs have to be less dead-end and exploitative.

More specifically, former foster children need to have someone, often a former foster carer, on whom they can fall back, adequate income guarantees when the job goes sour, a guarantee that they will be supported to get the training and keep the accommodation they require, and a chance to talk over the often troubled and confused relationships that continue to damage their lives. Our case examples provided impressive evidence that foster carers can meet this need. Our statistics failed to show that support from carers was effective – arguably because other support was available when that from foster care was not or, perhaps more plausibly, because the impressive degree of support that was offered was simply insufficient. Continuing support from former foster carers is unlikely to be enough on its own.[37]

Conclusion

Long-term foster care is about enabling children to grow up safely and happily in the face of what is for many an agonising dilemma. The children can neither live with their parents nor without them. As a result they want a wide variety of arrangements to exist between foster care and family. These range from living with family with no contact with foster care, through living there with frequent contact, living in foster care with contact, to living in foster care without any contact with family at all.

Foster care has to encompass these various possibilities. It also has to enable children to grow up safely, with support, reasonable education and as a happy a childhood as may be. In this context[38] the children may come, as many do, to a *modus vivendi*, a way of relating to and thinking about their families with which they can live and whereby they are no longer vulnerable to exploitation by them. Some may then return home. Others may stay on with their carers until they leave. A few may be adopted.

In all these situations adequate support has to be provided. In this respect a key potential resource is the carers themselves.[39] Some foster placements do not work out. Nevertheless many carers form important relationships with their foster children. The challenge is to profit from these relationships not only while the children are there but also once they have left.

Summary of Chapter 14

1. Viewed as an isolated experience foster care is often impressive. Viewed as part of a career it too often offers a truncated, tantalising and disrupted experience of family life followed by stressful and ill-supported moves to birth family, residential care or independent living.

2. This situation reflects the difficulties of the children and their families; their real, if often ambivalent, love for each other; the lack of resources for social services and of proven ways of effective intervention; and the current difficulties of young people entering a difficult job market.

3. Nevertheless there seems to be scope for:

- slightly increasing the proportion of children adopted

- reviewing philosophies about return home, which is not the touchstone of improved family relationships

- increasing the permanence offered by foster care in line with that offered by residence orders but without reducing support to carers

- delaying or making less drastic the transitions to independent living.

4. These changes in what happens to foster children would need to be accompanied by changes in practice and in the amount of support offered. Particular attention would need to be paid to:

- the obstacles to adoption

- relationships with and visits to/from birth families

- the child's/young person's attachment difficulties

- the child's/young person's happiness in school or at work

- the need for purposeful work with child and family both prior and subsequent to re-unification.

5. Experiment is required to discover reliable ways of delivering effective practice and, in particular, of benefiting after the placement from the strong relationships that arise between carers and foster children while the latter are fostered.

Notes

1. The definition of 'what works' requires a definition of 'good outcome'. Unfortunately, there can be legitimate disagreement on what a good outcome is. Is it better that a child is safe within a foster home or where he or she wishes to be with its parents? Research is relevant to these dilemmas but cannot resolve them.

2. The Looked After Children (LAC) system and the new performance indicators do now embody the expectation that children should develop (e.g. improve their education). However, the potential of foster carers to act as key agents of change is arguably less recognised than it should be.

3. American evidence also seems to suggest that whereas foster care may feel permanent, in practice it offers less continuity of care than either birth or adoptive families (Lahti 1982).

4. The rate was not much lower (40%) among those who had already spent two years in placement. Similar difficulties may apply in adoption (Rushton *et al.* 1996). Late

adoptees seem to have similar rates of fostering breakdown to late foster placements (Fratter *et al.* 1991). This may not apply to those becoming teenagers having been adopted young. However, none of our sample were in this position.

5. Clearly some of these mothers were not supported and ran into severe difficulties.

6. Similarly going to university could end in failure, debt and discouragement.

7. For the research case for adoption see Rushton (2000).

8. A point already made by Sinclair, Garnett and Berridge (1995).

9. Treatment does take place in the context of fostering. Our last study suggested that contacts with all professionals other than educational psychologists were, if anything, associated with poor outcomes rather than good ones.

10. This statement is based on our case studies which certainly support it. The only statistical evidence is indirect. In only 9 per cent of cases were social workers planning return home in 1998. They were then seeing the birth family weekly in 9 per cent of cases. It therefore seems unlikely that social workers were seeing change at home as a priority in a high proportion of cases.

11. We did not collect evidence on the frequency of moves between families before entry to the care system. By 1998, however, only 13 per cent had a birth family including both their natural parents. The case studies provided abundant evidence of children being shunted between families before they started to be looked after. American evidence on this comes from as long ago as 1972 (Jenkins and Norman 1972). For British evidence see Fisher *et al.* (1986) and Sinclair and Gibbs (1998).

12. This rather tentative conclusion is based on the fact (discussed in Chapter 3) that it predicts worsening in the Goodman score after allowing for the initial Goodman score. The importance we allocate to attachment difficulties distinguishes our hypothesis from the well-attested fact that difficult behaviour (of which childlike attachment is one form) predicts breakdown (for which see Berridge 1997; Sellick and Thoburn 1996; Sinclair and Wilson 2003; Sinclair, Wilson and Gibbs 2004).

13. There was a very highly significant correlation ($r=0.35$, $p<0.001$) between our measure of carer rejection in 2001 and our measure of childlike attachment at that point. The comparable correlation in 1998 was even higher ($r=0.47$, $p<0.001$).

14. There is a significant association between unhappiness at school and childlike attachment in 1998 but it is low ($r=0.17$, $p=0.002$). The associations discussed remain when attachment is taken into account.

15. There is now abundant evidence of this e.g. from Bullock *et al.* 1993; Kufeldt, Armstrong and Dorosh 1995.

16. The term 'family contact' disguises the fact that contact with one family member may be benign and wanted and contact with another the reverse.

17. For other evidence on re-abuse in the British care system see Farmer and Pollock (1998) and Hobbs, Hobbs and Wynne (1999). There has been a dramatic change in the frequency of contact with relatives (compare figures from this study with those from Rowe *et al.* 1984) and the proportion of children who are abused. Earlier findings on the benign effects of contact may no longer apply. Moreover, Quinton and his colleagues (1998) have reviewed earlier studies which allege a positive effect of contact on child

welfare pointing out serious methodological flaws. Recent work by Farmer and her colleagues (2004) points, like this report, to the dangers of contact. Cleaver (2000) is rather more positive. Schofield *et al.* (2000) found most contacts problematic to at least some degree. Our own work has suggested some negative effects on carers as well as on children (Wilson *et al.* 2000).

18. Neither group had much support from social services. In the case of birth families this was partly that they, like adoptive parents, were ambivalent about support — they welcomed concrete practical help but were reluctant to expose themselves to the judgements and interventions of social workers. Social services, short of time and resources, were not keen to press help on reluctant families. As a result birth families were clearly receiving far less support than even foster carers for dealing with the same children.

19. One difficulty is that the existence of and need for contact may vary over time, with, for example, children seeking or being helped to seek contact in their teens when they have not had it before (Thoburn *et al.* 2000; Thomas *et al.* 1999). A further problem is that benign contact with one member of a family may lead to less benign contact with others (Macaskill 2002).

20. For a recent balanced viewpoint based on a detailed study see Macaskill (2002). The Parker review argues for a balanced approach taking each case on its merits (Parker 1999). The review also makes a number of detailed recommendations designed to minimise the dangers of contact.

21. This recommendation is also made in the Parker review (1999) on the basis of adoption research.

22. The child orientation score predicts a variety of 'good outcomes' after other variables have been taken into account.

23. The effect of difficult behaviour on breakdown seems to be mediated by rejection. If carers did not respond with rejection difficult behaviour did not lead to a disruption. Quinton and his colleagues (1998) seem to make a similar point.

24. Evidence from the last study suggested that these were effective against particular behaviours but that their use did not ensure overall success.

25. This suggestion comes from the case studies. We have no statistical evidence for it.

26. Children may want to see some members of their family and not others or to have different kinds of contact (supervised/unsupervised, telephone/face to face, etc.) with different members.

27. There may be additional contributions from counselling and life story work. It was quite clear from the case studies that some counsellors were providing a lifeline to their clients. Others (including social workers) broke the ice and allowed the child to talk about difficulties which as a result they later found it easier to talk over with their foster carers. Life story work was the one form of intervention for which in this study no one seemed to have a bad word (one child described it as 'well decent'). Others studies do contain criticisms of life story work e.g. some adoptive parents find the books 'sanitised' (Thoburn *et al.* 2000) while some children may find them upsetting or fail fully to understand their content (Thomas *et al.* 1999).

28. As exemplified in the work of Chamberlain (1998a, 1998b), Webster-Stratton (1984) or Webster-Stratton and Herbert (1994).

29. The recent study of an intensive foster care scheme in Scotland also led the researchers to advocate an approach to fostering which combines attention to attachment with behavioural techniques (Walker *et al.* 2002). Earlier work involving the same team drew attention to the potential of residential education for difficult adolescents (Triseliotis *et al.* 1995).

30. For example, all children in foster care could be screened by an educational psychologist at key points in their careers to make sure that they were settled at school, not being bullied etc. and to make recommendations if they were in such difficulty.

31. Some but not all foster carers see more point to them. It can be worrying looking after other people's children particularly when some of their parents are quick to complain.

32. This rather gloomy conclusion from six cases may or may not be in keeping with other research. American research on re-unification is, as pointed out elsewhere, typically not conducted on the long-stay population considered in this research. Some British research does suggest that committed, skilful social work can lead to successful returns, at least if the children are under 11 (Bullock *et al.* 1993, 1998). However, this research may not apply to samples restricted to long-stay children. Moreover successful return may encourage committed social work and make it appear skilful.

33. Aldgate and Bradley's (1999) study of 'short-break' foster care showed that this was a highly valued service. What is suggested above is an extension of this approach building on relationships formed in longer-term foster care.

34. The only recent British experiment with treatment foster care (Walker *et al.* 2002) seems to suggest that the type of client envisaged (in that case those who might be in secure accommodation) requires a longer time than that traditional for treatment foster care. American studies of 'family re-unification' including the classical Alameida project (Stein *et al.* 1978) have focused on a potentially short-stay population. Social learning approaches such as those used by Chamberlain and her colleagues (see, for example, Chamberlain and Reid 1991) combined with a task-centred focus and the involvement of families may well be appropriate for such children. Children of the kind studied in this report may need an approach that takes more account of attachment principles.

35. This was clearly the fear of many of those who answered our questionnaires.

36. The evaluation of the 'Supporting Parents on Kids' Education' (Spokes) project, funded by the Department of Health and led by Stephen Scott and Kathy Sylva, may be highly relevant to this suggestion (see Ballie, Sylva and Evans 2000).

37. Aldgate and Bradley (1999) seem to have reached a similar conclusion in their study of the use of foster care to provide short breaks.

38. The idea that foster care provides a safe base within which children can explore their dilemmas is central to the work of Celia Downes (1992) and derives from attachment theory. Other British research on childcare has also taken attachment theory as central, most notably perhaps in work at the University of East Anglia (Howe *et al.* 1999; Schofield *et al.* 2000) – cf. Rutter (1995).

39. North American researchers also emphasise the potential of contact with former foster carers along with the difficulty of ensuring it (Fanshel, Finch and Grundy 1990; Kufeldt *et al.* 1995; Palmer 1996).

Sampling Bias in Sweeps 1 and 2

Introduction

Our sample includes a large number of separate surveys. Prior to 2001 we completed the following:

- a census of all carers in seven authorities in 1997
- a postal survey of the same carers in 1997
- a survey of children with those carers in 1998 with separate data from foster carers, social workers and family placement social workers
- a repeat of this survey with data from the same sources in 1999
- a postal survey of children in the sample in 1998.

In 2001 we carried out the following surveys:

- a postal survey from social workers of all 596 children potentially involved in 1998
- a postal survey of their current carer (adoptive parent, birth parent, foster carer) where they were neither over 18 nor in independent living
- a postal survey of the young people over 18 or in independent living
- a postal survey of their last foster carer.

There was an additional survey of the 22 young people in residential care. However we only had six replies and have not included the material in the report.

The various samples involved 596 children. These were fostered by carers involved in our 1997 survey of carers and present in January 1998. Children fostered as part of a series of agreed short breaks were excluded unless they had been in the placement for six months. Much of the analysis in the report has involved relating data collected on these children in 1998 to data collected on them in 2001. Bias may arise at either collection point.

Our previous books (Sinclair, Gibbs and Wilson 2004; Sinclair, Wilson and Gibbs 2004) have considered possible biases in our 1997, 1998 and 1999 samples. Briefly we found that our sample was, as far as we could tell, highly representative of children fostered at a particular point in time when we did our research. One exception was that minority ethnic children were under-represented in relation to the authorities in which we carried out the research, although probably not in relation to the national population of foster children. We also found that children fostered by relatives were under-represented, while our response rates from our two London authorities were considerably poorer than our response rates from others. As the variables in which our sample may have been biased were not related to our outcomes we did not think that the bias, if any, affected our analysis of outcomes.

In considering the 2001 surveys we use data from 1998. We compare those who responded and those who did not in terms of:

- social services area
- characteristics of child
- age
- sex
- ethnicity (UK and non-UK)
- Goodman score
- childlike attachment score
- whether said to be happy at school
- whether said to be abused prior to being looked after
- whether child said by carer to want to be in placement
- whether had weekly contact with a family member.

Characteristics of carer:

- child orientation score of original carer
- whether couple
- whether child rejected.

Outcome:

- whether disrupted by 1999.

These were the key variables in predicting outcomes. Our comparisons were between those who could have responded to a particular questionnaire (e.g. adoptive parents) but did not and those who could have responded and did.

Social worker questionnaire

The overall response rate was 60 per cent. The only significant differences were by social services area, ethnicity and whether or not carers were lone carers in 1997.

Response rates varied from 26 per cent in one area to 75 per cent in another. There were response rates for only 49 per cent of the lone carers as against 63 per cent of the others, and for 63 per cent of the 'white British' children as against 47 per cent of the others. These latter differences were largely an artifact of the low response rate from the two London boroughs. If these two boroughs are omitted the differences shrink (61% to 64% for ethnicity and 55% to 65% for lone carers). Neither of these differences is significant. Within the London boroughs responses were, if anything, more likely when the child was from an ethnic minority and there were no differences by whether or not the carers were a couple.

In summary the major bias seems to be a London one. London social workers were less likely to return questionnaires. Lone carers and black and Asian children were far more common in London. Hence their situations were less likely to be covered in the social work questionnaires.

Adoption questionnaires
There were 90 potential respondents. The response rate was 82 per cent. There were no significant differences between those who responded and those who did not.

Birth parent
There were 96 potential respondents and a low response rate of 26 per cent. We were reliant on the goodwill of social workers to introduce this questionnaire and responses varied by area as had the responses to the social worker questionnaire. Two areas dominated providing 18 of the 25 responses. The only other significant difference was that those who responded had children who scored significantly higher on the Goodman score ($p=0.011$). Our chapter on the difficulties of birth parents may therefore have tended to overestimate the difficulty of their children.

Current foster carer
There were 231 potential respondents and the response rate was 79 per cent. There were no significant differences on any variable.

Young person in independent living
There were 116 potential respondents. We had 48 replies, a response rate of 41 per cent. Respondents and non-respondents did not differ significantly on any of our variables.

Previous foster carer where child no longer in foster care
There were 365 potential respondents and a response rate of 62 per cent. The only significant difference was that couple carers were more likely to respond than lone carers (49% v. 66%).

Foster children still in foster care

There were 231 potential respondents and a response rate of 55 per cent. The major variation was by area (from 75% to 25%). The area with the particularly low response rate was one in which the authority insisted on questionnaires being given to the children by social workers. This seemed to have no effect on the nature of the responses but undoubtedly affected the number who responded. Children with high childlike attachment scores ($p<0.01$) and living with lone carers were less likely to respond.

Conclusion

Social workers had the major influence on response rates. The pressures on them meant they could give little priority to introducing the questionnaire to foster children (where this was required) or birth families or, in certain areas, to responding to the questionnaires themselves.

We found few other differences between respondents and non-respondents. Couple carers of former foster children were more likely to respond than lone carers of such children, as were children currently living with couple carers. Children with high childlike attachment scores were less likely to respond. Birth parents with children with high Goodman scores were more likely to respond. These differences could have led us to underestimate the extent of attachment issues in the children's questionnaires and to overestimate the difficulties of birth parents. It is unclear what the effect of the higher response rate of couple carers might be.

In general there are remarkably few differences between respondents and non-respondents in any of our surveys. We are confident that the differences that there are do not have a major influence on our conclusions.

Some Key Variables

Introduction

In the course of the report we routinely made use of a number of key variables. None of the variables, with the exception of the Goodman score, were measured through 'off the peg' instruments. This appendix gives some details on what we consider to be the most important of these 'home-grown measures' and their 'psychometric properties'.

In general it is desirable that measures should be reliable – i.e. that different individuals or the same individual at different times should give the same measure to the same thing. One criterion for reliability is 'inter-rater reliability'. This is concerned with the degree to which different individuals measure the same variable in the same way. For example, if one rater rates someone as having 'high educational ability', another rater should also rate the same person 'high'. Where appropriate we give the correlations between ratings between different raters.

A further criterion of reliability applies when what is being rated is supposed to be an enduring trait rather than a transient state. In these circumstances it is useful to assess the correlation between a measure at one point in time and measures of the same objects or individuals some time later. The assumption is that the correlation should be positive and significant. The degree to which this is so must depend partly on the measure and the degree to which it is precise and partly on the degree to which the thing measured actually changes in the relevant respect. Where appropriate we give the relevant correlation.

Where a measure is created by adding together scores on a number of different items, it is desirable for these items to be correlated together. This again suggests that each of the items is getting at 'the same thing'. The usual measure of the degree to which different items are getting at 'the same thing' is Cronbach's Alpha. We give this for each of our own 'home-grown' measures where appropriate.

Reliability is concerned with the repeatability of a measurement. An equally if not more important criterion of a satisfactory measure is 'validity', which is concerned with meaning. It is one thing to know that our measure 'childlike attachment' is reliable. It is another to know that it is valid i.e. that it actually measures something concerned with attachment. There are a number of different criteria for assessing whether a measure is valid. These include the following:

- *Face validity* – we give the items which together make up a measure. If their meaning seems to correspond with the concept we are trying to measure this suggests that the measures have face validity. We give the various items below.

- *Construct validity* – a measure has construct validity if it is associated with other measures in a way which 'makes sense'. The report has discussed the relationship between these measures and others. We do not discuss construct validity below.

- *Divergent validity* – it is desirable that measures are not so highly associated that they can be assumed to be measuring the same thing. There is a problem over divergent validity with our 'childlike attachment' variable and we discuss it below.

- *Criterion validity* – sometimes there is a 'gold standard' measure which can be used to test the validity of a new measure. We did not have this measure for any of our variables which was why we created them in the first place.

Foster parenting score

At sweep 1 we asked the social workers and family placement social workers to rate the parents on six four-point scales (caring, accepting, clear about what wants, not easily upset by child's failure to respond, sees things from the child's point of view, encouraging). The ratings were very positive but we took the lowest one by either worker and averaged the result to give a parenting score.

Reliability (Cronbach's Alpha) as measured at sweep 1 was 0.87. We examined the stability (test–retest reliability) of this measure over three years by correlating the score at sweep 3 with the score at sweep 1 for those carers whose children remained with them. It was significant ($r=0.34$, $p=0.003$) but not as high as we would have liked. Either parenting ability changes (e.g. because of transient stress, training, experience, 'burn out' and so on) or this measure is not particularly reliable.

As a check on reliability we calculated a score for 'parenting ability' based on replies from the social workers and a second score based on replies from the family placement social workers. The correlation was very highly significant but not particularly high ($r=0.36$, $p<0.001$). We would therefore see this score as not particularly reliable although certainly better than nothing.

Foster parent's child orientation score

This is a measure developed by Marjorie Smith of the Thomas Coram Research Unit. It contains ten items which refer to activities which the parent might undertake with the child and which the child might be expected to like (e.g. 'taking child to cinema';

'reading child bedtime stories'). The items were scored 1 (never), 2 (sometimes), or 3 (frequently) and the carers were also allowed to put 'not applicable' (e.g. child too young).

The items were added together. Reliability (Cronbach's Alpha) as measured at sweep 1 was 0.76. The test–retest correlation over three years was 0.45.

The child orientation score was significantly correlated with the parenting score at both sweep 1 and sweep 3. This is some evidence for the validity of both scores even though they are not meant to be measuring the same thing. It should be said, however, that the correlation is low (0.2 in both cases).

Rejection score

At sweep 1 we asked foster carers whether they were fond of the child, were unsure that they could go on living with/putting up with the child, felt there was no point to telling the child why they did not like her or his misbehaviour, liked or disliked having the child there, were quite sure that there was no point in asking the child why he or she misbehaves. Each of these questions could be answered on a three-point scale ('not at all true', 'somewhat true', 'to a large extent true') with the exception of the question about liking or disliking which was scored on a five-point scale. Carers were also allowed to indicate that the question was not applicable. The score was formed by addition with scores reversed as appropriate.

Reliability was 0.74. We did not repeat this score at sweep 3.

School experience

We measured this at sweep 1 by asking the foster carers to rate whether the child was happy at school (three-point scale). We also asked whether they had seen an educational psychologist. As described in the report we also asked carers and social workers for separate ratings of educational performance and involvement in school activities. The correlation between the carers' and social workers' ratings of the child's school performance in relation to their ability was 0.49 at sweep 1 and 0.28 at sweep 2. The test–retest correlation for this measure was 0.35 (for foster carers) and 0.63 (for social workers). Chapter 3 discusses some further properties of these measures and their relationship with each other.

Contact with birth family

We asked the carers whether anyone was forbidden to have contact with the child at sweep 1. We also asked about the frequency with which different members of the family had contact with the child at that point. A child was said to have frequent contact if any member of the family had, according to the carer, contact with the child at least once a week.

Family integration and exclusion scores

The family integration score was based on carer or parent responses to the following questions. How far would you say the child:

- feels part of your family
- trusts you
- feels you care about him or her
- feels encouraged
- talks to you about personal things
- fits in better than when he or she first came?

The exclusion measure asked similarly about whether the child:

- feels the odd one out
- wants to leave
- feels picked on.

The parents or carers could answer each question 'a great deal', 'to some extent' or 'not at all'. We counted the number of times a parent said 'a great deal'.

Reliability for the inclusion measure was 0.72, that for the exclusion score was 0.36.

These measures were not particularly stable over time, even when the child had not changed placements. Among this group of 'stable placements' there was a correlation of 0.32 ($p<0.001$) for the exclusion measure at sweep 1 and sweep 3. However, the correlation between the two inclusion measures over the same period was only 0.14. This low level of correlation may partly reflect unreliability in the measure. However, it was also true that both measures predicted breakdown. Thus children who felt excluded were only likely to remain in the placement if their feelings changed. The low level of correlation between these measures at sweep 1 and sweep 3 may therefore partly reflect genuine change.

Breakdown

A placement was counted as 'breaking down' by sweep 3 if:

- social worker, foster carer or family placement social worker said that it had broken down at first follow-up or
- the last foster carer (at second follow-up) said that child had moved after a breakdown or
- social worker at second follow-up said that child had suffered placement breakdown, an unsuccessful trial at home or a placement for adoption that had not taken place.

Attachment measures

We had two measures which we believed were related to attachment. These were the stoicism score and the childlike attachment score.

High scorers on stoicism were those who were said by their carers to bottle up emotions, show little affection, hide fears and hide feelings of sadness. Reliability at sweep 1 was 0.73.

High scorers on childlike attachment were said to seek attention by misbehaviour, be more friendly with strangers than the carer would like, seek a lot of attention and show affection like a younger child. Reliability at sweep 1 was 0.73.

The scales are taken from work by David Quinton, are scored between 4 and 12, have a low correlation with each other (0.09 at sweep 1 and 0.12 at sweep 3) and reasonable reliabilities (at sweep 3 alphas for stoicism score 0.7 (foster carers) and 0.69 (adoptive parents) and for childlike attachment 0.76 (foster carers) and 0.72 (adoptive parents)).

The correlation between childlike attachment as measured by carers at sweep 1 and by carers or adoptive parents at sweep 2 was 0.62. The correlation for stoicism was 0.57.

In our mind the scales relate to the concepts of childlike attachment and compulsive self-reliance (Bowlby 1979), but they have not been validated against other measures of these concepts. A problem with our measure of childlike attachment is that it is highly correlated with the Goodman score ($r=0.68$ at sweep 1 and $r=0.67$ at sweep 3). It also predicts the Goodman score at sweep 3 almost as well as does the Goodman score at sweep 1 ($r=0.56$ as against $r=0.62$). There is, therefore, a question over whether it is simply a measure of disturbance. For the present, our argument that it is not is simply based on its 'face validity'.

Conclusion

A number of our key measures are less reliable than we might have wished, although we would argue that all are usable. Our measure of childlike attachment has less 'divergent' validity than we would have liked. It could be argued that it is simply a measure of general disturbance. On balance we do not think that it is. All have in our view a reasonable degree of face validity and all are associated with other variables in a way that 'makes sense'. Overall our confidence in our results is based on the sensible patterns that they make. We may not have measured our target variables with great precision. We are confident that the great majority of the associations we have uncovered hold good 'in the real world'.

References

Aldgate, J. (1999) 'Social work and the education of children in foster care.' In M. Hill (ed) *Signposts in Fostering*. London: British Agencies for Adoption and Fostering.

Aldgate, J. and Bradley, M. (1999) *Supporting Families Through Short-term Fostering*. London: The Stationery Office.

Aldgate, J., Colton, M., Ghate, D. and Heath, A. (1992) 'Educational attainment and stability in long-term foster care.' *Children and Society 6*, 91–103.

Allerhand, M., Weber, R. and Haug, M. (1966) *Adaptation and Adaptability*. New York: Child Welfare League of America.

Arden, N. (1977) *Child of a System*. London: Quartet Books.

Ballie, C., Sylva, K. and Evans, E. (2000) 'Do intervention programmes for parents aimed at improving children's literacy really work?' In A. Buchanan and B. Hudson (eds) *Promoting Children's Emotional Well-being*. Oxford: Oxford University Press.

Barth, R. and Berry, M. (1994) 'Implications of research on the welfare of children under permanency planning.' In R. Barth, J. Berrick and N. Gilbert (eds) *Child Welfare Research Review: 1*. New York: Columbia University Press.

Berridge, D. (1997) *Foster Care: A Research Review*. London: The Stationery Office.

Berridge, D. and Cleaver, H. (1987) *Foster Home Breakdown*. Oxford: Blackwell.

Biehal, N., Clayden, J., Stein, M. and Wade, J. (1992) *Prepared for Living: A Survey of Young People Leaving the Care of Three Local Authorities*. London: National Children's Bureau.

Biehal, N., Clayden, J., Stein, M. and Wade, J. (1995) *Moving On: Young People and Leaving Care Schemes*. London: National Children's Bureau.

Bohman, M. (1971) 'A comparative study of adopted children, foster children and children in their biological environment born after undesired pregnancies.' *Acta Psychiatrica Scandinavica 60*, Suppl.221, 5–38.

Bohman, M. (1996) 'Predisposition to criminality: Swedish adoption studies in retrospect.' In M. Rutter (ed) *Genetics of Criminal and Antisocial Behaviour* (CIBA Foundation symposium 194). Chichester: Wiley.

Bowlby, J. (1979) *The Making and Breaking of Affectional Bonds*. London: Tavistock.

Broad, R. (1998) *Young People Leaving Care: Life After the Children Act 1989*. London: Jessica Kingsley Publishers.

Bullock, R., Good, D. and Little, M. (1998) *Children Going Home: The Reunification of Families*. Aldershot: Ashgate.

Bullock, R., Little, M. and Millham, S. (1993) *Going Home: The Return of Children Separated from their Families*. London: Dartmouth.

Chamberlain, P. (1990) 'Comparative evaluation of foster care for seriously delinquent youths: a first step.' *Community Alternatives: International Journal of Family Care 2*, 2, 21–36.

Chamberlain, P. (1998a) *Blueprints for Violence Prevention: Book Eight: Multi-dimensional Treatment Foster Care*. Colorado: Institute of Behavioural Science, Regents of the University of Colorado.

Chamberlain, P. (1998b) *Family Connections: A Treatment Foster Care Model for Adolescents with Delinquency*. Oregon: Northwest Media Inc.

Chamberlain, P., Moreland, S. and Reid, K. (1992) 'Enhanced services and stipends for foster carers: effects on retention rates and outcomes for children.' *Child Welfare 71*, 387–401.

Chamberlain, P. and Reid, J. (1991) 'Using a specialized foster care community treatment model for children and adolescents leaving the state mental hospital.' *Journal of Community Psychology 19*, 266–276.

Cheung, Y. and Heath, A. (1994) 'After care: the education and occupation of adults who have been in care.' *Oxford Review of Education 20*, 3, 361–374.

Cleaver, H. (2000) *Fostering Family Contact: A Study of Children, Parents and Foster Carers.* London: The Stationery Office.

Colton M. (1988) *Dimensions of Substitute Care: A Comparative Study of Foster and Residential Care Practice.* Aldershot: Avebury.

Cook, R. (1994) 'Are we helping foster-care youth prepare for their future?' *Children and Youth Services Review 16*, 213–229.

Department for Education and Skills (2001) 'Health Minister announces major review of fostering and placement services.' Press release. http://www.dfes.gov.uk/qualityprotects/doc/190302.doc

Department of Health (1993) *Children Act 1989.* Cm. 2144. London: HMSO.

Downes, C. (1992) *Separation Revisited: Adolescents in Foster Family Care.* Aldershot: Ashgate.

Ellaway, B., Payne, E., Rolfe, K., Dunstan, F., Kemp, A., Butler, I. and Sibert, J. (2004) 'Are abused babies protected from further abuse.' *Archives of Diseases in Childhood 89*, 845–846.

Essen, J., Lambert, L. and Head, J. (1976) 'School attainment of children who have been in care.' *Child Care, Health and Development 2*, 339–351.

Fanshel, D., Finch, S. and Grundy, J. (1990) *Foster Children in a Life Course Perspective.* New York: Columbia University Press.

Farmer, E. and Moyers, S. (2004) *Children Placed with Relatives or Friends: Placement Patterns and Outcomes.* Report to the Department for Education and Skills. University of Bristol.

Farmer, E., Moyers, S. and Lipscombe, J. (2004) *Fostering Adolescents.* London: Jessica Kingsley Publishers.

Farmer, E. and Parker, R. (1991) *Trials and Tribulations.* London: HMSO.

Farmer, E. and Pollock, S. (1998) *Substitute Care For Sexually Abused and Abusing Children.* London: Wiley.

Fein, E., Maluccio, A. and Kluger, M. (1990) *No More Partings: An Examination of Long-term Foster Family Care.* Washington, DC: Child Welfare League of America.

Fenyo, A., Knapp, M. and Baines, B. (1989) *Foster Care Breakdown: A Study of the Kent Family Placement Scheme.* Canterbury: University of Kent Personal Social Services Research Unit.

Ferguson, T. (1966) *Children in Care and After.* London: Oxford University Press.

Festinger, T. (1983) *No One Ever Asked Us: A Postscript to Foster Care.* New York: University of Columbia Press.

Fever, F. (1994) *Who Cares?: Memories of a Childhood in Barnardo's.* London: Warner Books.

Fisher, M., Marsh, P. and Phillips, D. with Sainsbury, E. (1986) *In and Out of Care.* London: Batsford in association with British Agencies for Adoption and Fostering.

Fletcher, B. (1993) *Not Just A Name.* London: National Consumer Council.

Fraser, M., Walton, E., Lewis, R., Pecora, P. and Walton, W. (1996) 'An experiment in family reunification – correlates of outcomes at one-year follow-up.' *Children and Youth Services Review 18*, 4–5, 335–361.

Fratter, J., Rowe, J., Sapsford, D. and Thoburn, J. (1991) *Permanent Family Placement: A Decade of Experience.* London: British Agencies for Adoption and Fostering.

Fry, E. (1992) *After Care: Making the Most of Foster Care.* London: National Foster Care Association.

Garnett, L. (1992) *Leaving Care and After.* London: National Children's Bureau.

George, V. (1970) *Foster Care – Theory and Practice.* London: Routledge and Kegan Paul.

Gibbons, J., Gallagher, B., Bell, C. and Gordon, D. (1995) *Development After Physical Abuse in Early Childhood: A Follow-up Study of Children on Protection Registers.* London: HMSO.

Goodman, R. (1994) 'A modified version of the Rutter parent questionnaire including extra items on children's strengths: a research note.' *Journal of Child Psychology and Psychiatry 35*, 1483–1494.

Harwin, J., Owen, M., Locke, R. and Forrester, D. (2001) *Making Care Orders Work: A Study of Care Plans and Their Implementation.* London: The Stationery Office.

Hazel, N. (1981) *A Bridge to Independence.* Oxford: Basil Blackwell.

Health and Social Services Committee (1998) *Children Looked After by Local Authorities. Report and Proceedings of Committee* (Vol. 1), London: HMSO.

Hensey, D., Williams, J. and Rosenbloom, L. (1983) 'Intervention in child abuse: experience in Liverpool.' *Developmental Medicine and Child Neurology 25,* 606–611.

Hobbs, G., Hobbs, C. and Wynne, J. (1999) 'Abuse of children in foster and residential care.' *Child Abuse and Neglect 23,* 1239–1252.

Howe, D., Brandon, M., Hinings, D. and Schofield G. (1999) *Attachment Theory, Child Maltreatment and Family Support.* London: Blackwell.

Hunt, J. (2002) 'Friends and family care: Current policy framework, issues and options.' http://www.dfes.gov.uk/qualityprotects/pdfs/friends-family-paper.pdf

Jackson, S. (2001) *Nobody Ever Told Us School Mattered: Raising the Educational Standards of Children in Care.* London: British Agencies for Adoption and Fostering.

Jenkins, S. and Norman, E. (1972) *Filial Deprivation and Foster Care.* New York: Columbia University Press.

Kahan, B. (1979) *Growing Up in Care; Ten People Talking.* Oxford: Blackwell.

King, J. and Taitz, L. (1985) 'Catch-up growth following abuse.' *Archives of Disease in Childhood 60,* 1152–1154.

Kirton, D., Ogilvie, K. and Beecham, J. (2003) *Remuneration and Performance in Foster Care.* Report to Department for Education and Skills. University of Kent at Canterbury.

Koluchova, J. (1976) 'Severe deprivation in twins: a case study.' In A. Clarke and A. Clarke (eds) *Myth and Evidence.* London: Open Books.

Kufeldt, K., Armstrong, J. and Dorosh, M. (1995) 'How children view their own and their foster families: a research study.' *Child Welfare 74,* 695–715.

Lahti, J. (1982) 'A follow-up study of foster children in permanent placements.' *Social Service Review 56,* 4, 556–571.

Lambert, L., Essen, J. and Head, J. (1977) 'Variations in behaviour ratings of children who have been in care.' *Journal of Child Psychology and Psychiatry 18,* 335–346.

Littel, J. and Schuerman, J. (1995) *A Synthesis of Research on Family Preservation and Family Re-unification Programs.* http://aspe.hhs.gov/hsp/cyp/fplitrey.htm

Lowe, N. and Murch, M. with Bader, K., Borkowski, M., Copner, R., Lisles, C. and Shearman, J. (2002) *The Plan for the Child: Adoption or Long-term Fostering.* London: British Association for Adoption and Fostering.

Macaskill, C. (2002) *Safe Contact? Children in Permanent Placement and Contact With Their Relatives.* Lyme Regis: Russell House Publishing.

Maluccio, A. and Fein, E. (1985) 'Growing up in foster care.' *Children and Youth Services Review 7,* 123–134.

Maluccio, A., Fein, E. and Olmstead, K. (1986) *Permanency Planning for Children: Concepts and Methods.* London: Tavistock.

Maugham, B., Collishaw, S. and Pickles, A. (1998) 'School achievement and adult qualifications among adoptees: a longitudinal study.' *Journal of Child Psychiatry and Psychology 39,* 669–685.

Maugham, B. and Pickles, A. (1990) 'Adopted and illegitimate children grown up.' In L. Robins and M. Rutter (eds) *Straight and Devious Pathways from Childhood to Adulthood.* Cambridge: Cambridge University Press.

Meier, E. (1965) 'Current circumstances of former foster children.' *Child Welfare,* April, 196–206.

Meier, E. (1966) 'Adults who were foster children.' *Children 13,* 16–22.

Minty, B. (1987) *Child Care and Adult Crime.* Manchester: Manchester University Press.

Moore, A. (1990) *Growing up with Barnardo.* Sidney: Hale and Ironmonger.

Napier, H. (1972) 'Success and failure in foster care.' *British Journal of Social Work 2*, 187–204.

Packman, J. and Hall, C. (1998) *From Care to Accommodation: The Implementation of Section 20 of the Children Act 1989*. London: The Stationery Office.

Page, R. (ed) (1977) *Who Cares? Young People in Care Speak Out*. London: National Children's Bureau.

Palmer, S. (1996) 'Placement stability and inclusive practice in foster care: an empirical study.' *Children and Youth Services Review 18*, 7, 589–601.

Parker, R. (1966) *Decision in Child Care*. London: Allen and Unwin.

Parker, R. (ed) (1999) *Adoption Now: Messages from Research*. Chichester: Wiley.

Parker, R., Ward, H., Jackson, S., Aldgate, J. and Wedge, P. (1991) *Looking After Children: Assessing Outcomes in Child Care*. London: HMSO.

Quinton, D., Rushton, A., Dance, C. and Mayes, D. (1998) *Joining New Families: A Study of Adoption and Fostering in Middle Childhood*. Chichester: Wiley.

Quinton, D. and Rutter, M. (1988) *Parenting Breakdown: The Making and Breaking of Intergenerational Links*. Aldershot: Avebury.

Rabiee, P., Priestley, M. and Knowles, J. (2001) *Whatever Next? Young Disabled People Leaving Care*. Leeds: First Key Leeds.

Rathbun, C., Di Virgilio, L. and Waldfogel, S. (1958) 'The restitutive process in children following radical separation from family and culture.' *The American Journal of Orthopsychiatry 28*, 408–415.

Rathbun, C., McLaughlin, H., Bennett, C. and Garland, J. (1965) 'Later adjustment of children following radical separation from family and culture.' *The American Journal of Orthopsychiatry 35*, 604–609.

Reddy, L. and Pfeiffer, S. (1997) 'Effectiveness of treatment foster care with children and adolescents: a review of outcome studies.' *Journal of the American Academy of Child and Adolescent Psychiatry 36*, 5, 581–588.

Rowe, J. (1985) *Social Work Decisions in Child Care: Recent Research Findings and Their Implications*. Department of Health and Social Security. London: HMSO.

Rowe, J., Cain, H., Hundleby, M. and Keane, A. (1984) *Long-Term Fostering and the Children Act: A Study of Foster Parents Who Went On to Adopt*. London: British Agencies for Adoption and Fostering.

Rowe, J., Hundleby, M. and Garnett, L. (1989) *Child Care Now: A Survey of Placement Patterns* (Research Series 6). London: British Agencies for Adoption and Fostering.

Rowe, J. and Lambert, L. (1973) *Children Who Wait: A Study of Children Needing Substitute Families*. London: Association of British Adoption Agencies.

Runyan, D. and Gould, C. (1985) 'Foster care for child maltreatment: impact on delinquent behaviour.' *Pediatrics 75*, 562–568.

Rushton, A. (2000) *Adoption as a Placement Choice: Arguments and Evidence*. London: Institute of Psychiatry, King's College London.

Rushton, A., Dance, C., Quinton, D. and Mayes, D. (2001) *Siblings in Late Permanent Placements*. London: British Agencies for Adoption and Fostering.

Rushton, A., Treseder, J. and Quinton, D. (1996) *Maudsley Adoption and Fostering Study: New Parents: New Children*. Report to the Department of Health. London: Institute of Psychiatry, Maudsley Hospital.

Rutter, M. (1995) 'Clinical implications of attachment concepts – retrospect and prospect.' *Journal of Child Psychology and Psychiatry and Allied Disciplines 36*, 549–571.

Rutter, M. and the English and Romanian (ERA) study team (1998) 'Developmental catch-up and deficit following adoption after severe global early privation.' *Journal of Child Psychology and Psychiatry 39*, 4, 465–476.

St Claire, L. and Osborne, A. (1987) 'The ability and behaviour of children who have been in care or separated from their parents.' *Early Child Development and Care*, Special Issue 28, 187–354.

Sampson, R. and Laub, J. (1993) *Crime in the Making: Pathways and Turning Points Through Life*. Cambridge and London: Harvard University Press.

Schofield, G., Beek, M. and Sargent, K. with Thoburn, J. (2000) *Growing Up in Foster Care*. London: British Agencies for Adoption and Fostering.

Schweinhart, L., Barnes, H. and Weikart, D. (1993) *Significant Benefits: The High/Scope Perry Preschool Study Through Age 27*. Michigan: High/Scope Press.

Sellick, C. and Thoburn, J. (1996) *What Works in Family Placement*. Ilford: Barnardo's.

Selwyn, J., Sturgess, W., Quinton, D. and Baxter, C. (2003) *Costs and Outcomes of Non-Infant Adoptions*. Report to the Department for Education and Skills. Bristol: School of Policy Studies, University of Bristol.

Shaw, M. and Hipgrave, T. (1983) *Specialist Fostering*. London: Batsford.

Shaw, M. and Hipgrave, T. (1989) 'Specialist fostering 1988 – a research study.' *Adoption and Fostering 13*, 17–21.

Sherman, E., Newman, R. and Shyne, A. (1973) *Children Adrift in Foster Care: Study of Alternative Approaches*. New York: Child Welfare League of America.

Sinclair, I. (1971) *Hostels for Probationers*. London: HMSO.

Sinclair, I. (1975) 'The influence of wardens and matrons on probation hostels: a study of a quasi family institution.' In J. Tizard, I. Sinclair and R. Clarke (eds) *Varieties of Residential Experience*. London: Routledge and Kegan Paul.

Sinclair, I. (2005) *Fostering Now*. London: Jessica Kingsley Publishers.

Sinclair, I. and Gibbs, I. (1998) *Children's Homes: A Study in Diversity*. Chicester: Wiley.

Sinclair, I., Gibbs, I. and Wilson, K. (2004) *Foster Carers: Why They Stay and Why They Leave*. London: Jessica Kingsley Publishers.

Sinclair, I. and Wilson, K. (2003) 'Matches and mismatches: the contribution of carers and children to the success of foster placements.' *British Journal of Social Work 33*, 871–884.

Sinclair, I., Wilson, K. and Gibbs, I. (2004) *Foster Placements: Why They Succeed and Why They Fail*. London: Jessica Kingsley Publishers.

Sinclair, R., Garnett, L. and Berridge, D. (1995) *Social Work Assessment with Adolescents*. London: National Children's Bureau.

Skeels, H. and Harms, I. (1948) 'Children with inferior social histories; their mental development in adoptive homes.' *Journal of Genetic Psychology 72*, 283–294.

Skuse, D. (1984) 'Extreme deprivation in early childhood 1: Diverse outcomes for three siblings from an extraordinary family.' *Journal of Child Psychology and Psychiatry 25*, 523–541.

Stein, M. (2002) 'Leaving care.' In D. McNeish, T. Newman and H. Roberts (eds) *What Works for Children*. Milton Keynes: Open University Press.

Stein, M. (2004) *What Works With Young People Leaving Care*. London: Barnardo's.

Stein, M. and Carey, K. (1986) *Leaving Care*. Oxford: Blackwell.

Stein, T., Gambrill, E. and Wiltse, K. (1978) *Children in Foster Homes: Achieving Continuity of Care*. New York: Praeger.

Taussig, H., Clyman, R. and Landsverk, J. (2001) 'Children who return home from foster care: a six-year prospective study of behavioral health outcomes in adolescence.' *Pediatrics 108*, 1, E10 (electronic article).

Terling, T. (1999) 'The efficacy of family reunification practices: Reentry rates and correlates of reentry for abused and neglected children reunited with their families.' *Child Abuse and Neglect 23*, 1359–1370.

Thoburn, J., Norford, L. and Rashid, S. (2000) *Permanent Family Placement for Children of Minority Ethnic Origin*. London: Jessica Kingsley Publishers.

Thomas, C. and Beckford, V. with Lowe, N. and Murch, M. (1999) *Adopted Children Speaking*. London: British Agencies for Adoption and Fostering.

Timms, N. (1973) *The Receiving End*. London: Routledge and Kegan Paul.

Tizard, B. and Rees, J. (1975) 'Effects of early institutional rearing on the dependency of eight year old children.' *Journal of Child Psychology and Psychiatry 16*, 61–73.

Trasler, G. (1960) *In Place of Parents: A Study of Foster Care*. London: Routledge and Kegan Paul.

Triseliotis, J., Borland, M., Hill, M. and Lambert, L. (1995) *Teenagers and the Social Work Services*. London: HMSO.

Triseliotis, J. and Russell, J. (1984) *Hard to Place*. London: Heinemann.

Utting, W. (1997) *People Like Us: Report of the Review of Safeguards for Children Living Away from Home*. London: Department of Health and the Welsh Office.

Van der Waals, P. (1960) 'Former foster children reflect on their childhood.' *Children 7*, 29–33.

Vernon, J. and Fruin, D. (1986) *In Care: A Study of Social Work Decision Making*. London: National Children's Bureau.

Walker, M., Hill, M. and Triseliotis, J. (2002) *Testing the Limits of Foster Care: Fostering as an Alternative to Secure Accommodation*. London: British Association for Adoption and Fostering.

Walton, E., Fraser, M., Lewis, R., Pecora, P. and Walton, W. (1993) 'In-home family-focused reunification: an experimental study.' *Child Welfare 72*, 473–487.

Ward, H. (1995) *Looking After Children: Research into Practice*. London: HMSO.

Ward, H., Munro, E and Dearden, C. (forthcoming) *Babies and Young Children in Care: Life Pathways, Decision-making and Practice*. London: Jessica Kingsley Publishers.

Webster-Stratton, C. (1984) 'A randomized trial of two parent training programs for families with conduct-disordered children.' *Journal of Consulting and Clinical Psychology 52*, 4, 666–678.

Webster-Stratton, C. and Herbert, M. (1994) *Troubled Families – Problem Children*. New York: Wiley.

Werner, E. (1989) 'High risk children in young adulthood: a longitudinal study from birth to 30 years.' *American Journal of Ortho-Psychiatry 59*, 72–81.

Wilson, K., Sinclair, I. and Gibbs, I. (2000) 'The trouble with foster care: the impact of stressful events on foster carers.' *British Journal of Social Work 30*, 193–209.

Wilson, K., Sinclair, I., Taylor, C., Pithouse, A. and Sellick, C. (2004) *Fostering Success: An Exploration of the Research Literature on Foster Care*. London: Social Care Institute for Excellence.

Zimmerman, R. (1982) 'Foster care in retrospect.' *Tulane Studies in Social Welfare 14*, 1–119.

Subject Index

abuse 94, 134, 203, 238
  see also emotional abuse;
    re-abuse
accommodation, after leaving care
    188–90, 207, 229–30
adolescents *see* older children
adoption
    and age 30–31, 32, 93–6
    and behaviour 10–11, 114,
        117–18
    breakdowns 91
    case studies 32, 95, 103,
        110–111, 113, 116, 118,
        119, 121
    and contact *see* contact
    decisions 94–6, 99, 141, 257
    delays in 108–9, 257
    and disability 95, 96, 100
    by foster carers 100, 101,
        104, 110, 113, 182, 200,
        258
    information provision 110,
        111, 112
    and mental health 51, 96,
        101, 111, 115, 116
    of older children 96, 98–100,
        126
    outcomes 10–11, 62, 101–3
    and school adjustment 56–7
    settling in 111–12
    statistics 30–31, 33, 92, 93,
        94
    success factors 257–9
    support during 109–116
    views
        of care leavers 182, 200
        of children 97–9, 103,
            136, 138–9, 152–3
        of foster carers 97, 98,
            99
        of social workers 97, 98,
            99, 110
aftercare 144, 183, 184, 192–4,
    207, 208, 221–2, 263–4
    see also counselling; foster care,
        after age 18; relationships;
        support
age
    and placement 30–32, 73, 74,
        93–6, 131, 132, 135–6
    and stability of care 35–6,
        129, 131
Alistair
    attachment in 240–41
    foster care experiences 226–9,
        236–7, 240–41

independent living
    experiences 229–33, 243
    outcomes, analysis of 245–6
    perspective on life 245
    pre-care experiences 226, 238
    relationship with birth family
        230, 231, 232–3, 238–9
    school experiences 242–3
attachment 37, 52–5, 81, 113, 138,
    239, 240–41, 249
    see also childlike attachment;
        stoicism

behavioural problems 10–11,
    58–61, 114, 118, 139, 206,
    208
belonging, sense of 139, 157–68,
    201–2, 220, 227–8
    see also rejection; subjective
        permanence
birth families
    contact with *see* contact
    relationship with care leavers
        194, 214, 223, 224, 230,
        231, 232–3, 237–9
    returning to *see* returning
        home

care leavers
    financial support 197, 198,
        229–30
    hopes and plans 177, 196–7,
        220, 222–3
    relationships *see* relationships
    returning home 175–6, 177,
        189, 214
    views
        on adoption 182, 200
        on foster care 199–204,
            219–20
        on independent living
            176–9, 180, 182–3,
            195–8, 221
        on social workers 200,
            203
    see also accommodation;
        Alistair; employment;
        independent living;
        leaving care; Tara
care orders 88, 262
childlike attachment 52, 53, 54–5,
    61, 101, 103, 111, 134, 206
children *see* foster children; older
    children
contact
    with birth families
        and adoption 96,
            116–19, 258
        case studies 76, 77, 119,
            138

children's wishes 152,
    153
    and disruption 49–50,
        134, 256, 260
    and re-abuse 48–50, 256
    and returning home 72
    and social workers 155
    with foster carers
        after adoption 119–23,
            257–8
        after age 18 *see* aftercare
        after returning home 152
    recommendations 65, 66
counselling 87, 232, 233, 262
    see also educational psychology

disability 27, 95, 96, 100, 130,
    174, 175
discipline, in foster care 159–60
disruption
    case studies 227, 228–9
    and contact 49–50, 134, 256,
        260
    definition 33
    factors in 131–6
    and further family placement
        135–6
    and independent living
        173–4, 178–9, 180, 192
    protective factors 145–6,
        259–60
    and returning home 71–2
    statistics 91, 131, 135–6

education *see* school
educational psychology 60, 67,
    133–4
emotional abuse 45, 46, 48, 51–2,
    55
emotional problems *see* mental
    health
employment of care leavers 190–91
    case studies 191, 229, 231,
        243
    and outcomes 205, 207, 208,
        209, 210, 211–12

families *see* birth families
financial support
    for aftercare 144, 183, 184
    for care leavers 197, 198,
        229–30
    under residence orders 141
foster care
    abuse in 46, 48, 203
    adequacy of 36–8
    after age 18: 34, 140, 143–5,
        174–5, 177, 182–4, 189,
        261
        see also aftercare

case studies 161, 201, 204,
    218–21, 226–9, 236–7,
    240–41
characteristics 15–16
discipline in 159–60
effects of bureaucracy 166–8
material provision in 162–4
and mental health 51
normalisation of 140, 167–8,
    260
objectives 9, 66, 245, 247
outcomes 62, 101, 204, 206,
    208
permanence in *see* long-term
    foster care; permanence;
    stability of care
and school adjustment 56, 57
statistics 31, 33, 94, 129, 131
success factors 247–8,
    259–61
views
    of care leavers 199–204,
        219–20
    of children 136–8,
        150–51, 152,
        153–5, 157–68, 176
    see also adoption; leaving care;
        long-term foster care;
        relative foster care
foster carers
    adoption by *see* adoption, by
        foster carers
    aftercare from 192–4, 221–2,
        263–4
    contact with *see* contact, with
        foster carers
    support for birth families
        85–6, 87, 261–2
    views
        on adoption 97, 98, 99
        of children 157–60
        on leaving care 180–82,
            195
        on staying after age 18
            183–4
foster children
    abuse *see* abuse
    adjustment to care 164–6
    attachment in *see* attachment
    behavioural problems *see*
        behavioural problems
    contact with birth families *see*
        contact
    education *see* school
    hopes and ambitions 151–3
    mental health *see* mental
        health
    outcomes 62–3
    placement *see* placement
    problems 255–7

sense of belonging *see*
    belonging
sense of stigmatisation 167–8
views
    on adoption 97–9, 103,
        136, 138–9, 152–3
    on foster care 136–8,
        150–51, 152,
        153–5, 157–68, 176
    on returning home
        79–80, 152
    on social workers 155–7,
        160, 168, 170

home, returning to *see* returning
    home
housing *see* accommodation

independent living
    adequacy of 38, 39
    and behavioural problems 59,
        206, 208
    case studies 34, 182, 221–5,
        229–33, 243
    for disabled young people
        174, 175
    and disruption 173–4,
        178–9, 180, 192
    and mental health 51, 205,
        209, 211, 231–2
    move to 173–5, 176–9,
        180–83, 195–8, 206,
        210, 212, 221
    outcomes 62, 195–9,
        204–210
    problems 197–8, 208,
        230–32
    statistics 30, 31, 33, 173,
        174, 189
    success factors 247–8, 263–4
    support in 181, 185, 192–5,
        222
    see also accommodation;
        employment; relationships
information provision, on adoption
    110, 111, 112

kin foster care *see* relative foster care

leaving care 26, 256
    see also care leavers;
        independent living;
        returning home
long-term foster care 11, 31, 130,
    131, 133, 137–8
    see also relative foster care
looked after children *see* care leavers;
    foster children

mental health 50–55
    and adoption 51, 96, 101,
        111, 115, 116
    and disruption 134
    and independent living 51,
        205, 209, 211, 231–2
movements in care *see* stability of
    care

objective permanence 17, 32–6,
    129–36, 236
older children
    adoption 11, 96, 98–100,
        126
    and disruption 131, 132
    see also care leavers;
        independent living

parenting 60, 64–5, 77, 87, 134,
    235, 262
permanence 16–17
    and foster care 235–7, 252–3
    and residence orders 139–43
    success factors 259–61
    see also adoption; long-term
        foster care; objective
        permanence; stability of
        care; subjective
        permanence
personality 205–6, 224
    see also behavioural problems;
        mental health
placement
    adequacy of 36–9
    and age 30–32, 73, 74, 93–6,
        135–6
    and behavioural problems 59
    breakdown *see* disruption
    at follow-up 30–32
    and mental health 51
    outcomes 62
    plans 71–2, 79
    stability *see* stability of care
    see also adoption; foster care;
        independent living;
        residential care; returning
        home

re-abuse 45–50, 51, 52, 256
rejection 51–2, 55
    see also belonging; emotional
        abuse
relationships
    after leaving care 194, 214,
        221–4, 229–30, 231,
        232–3, 237–9, 243
        and outcomes 207, 208,
            209, 210, 211

relationships *cont.*
    children's problems with 255
    see also aftercare; attachment;
        belonging; support
relative foster care 95, 96, 139,
    166, 168, 270
research
    analysis 22–3, 24
    bias 19, 269–72
    case studies 20–21, 23
        see also Alistair; Tara
    hypotheses 15–18
    limitations 23–4
    methods 18–23
    process outcomes 13–14
    questionnaires 18–20
    response rates 18–19, 20, 22,
        270–72
    sample 18, 20–21, 22,
        269–72
    variables 15, 22, 273–7
residence orders 139–43
residential care
    adequacy of 38, 39, 41–2,
        253
    and behavioural problems 59
    and mental health 51
    outcomes 62
    and re-abuse 47
    and school adjustment 56, 57
    statistics 30, 31, 32, 33
returning home
    and abuse 46–7, 49, 50, 94
    adequacy of placement 36, 38
    adjustment to 80–81
    and behavioural problems 59,
        60–61
    case studies 63, 74, 76, 78,
        80, 81, 83, 85–6, 87, 94
    children's wishes 79–80, 152
    and contact with foster carers
        152
    decisions 94
    factors in 71–2, 73–4
    and mental health 51
    outcomes 10, 44, 62, 63,
        64–5, 74–9
    planning 71–2, 79
    recommendations 87–8
    and school adjustment 55, 56,
        57, 77–9
    statistics 30, 31, 32, 33, 44,
        72–3, 74, 93, 94
    success factors 261–3
    support 81–7, 261–3
    by young adults 175–6, 177,
        189, 214
rules *see* discipline

school
    adjustment to 55–8, 64, 68,
        77–9
    and behavioural problems 60,
        61
    case studies 61, 241, 242
    and disruption 134
    performance 102, 206, 208,
        255–6
    and well-being 242
social behaviour *see* behavioural
    problems
social workers
    and contact with birth
        families 155
    plans for children *see*
        placement, plans
    role in preventing disruption
        260
    support
        in adoption 110–111,
            112, 113, 114, 115,
            116
        after leaving care 222
        on returning home 81–4
    views
        on adoption 97, 98, 99,
            110
        of care leavers 200, 203
        of foster children 155–7,
            160, 168, 170
        on leaving care 180,
            195–6
stability of care 12–13
    and attachment 37
    factors in 34–6, 129, 131
    outcomes 102
    statistics 33, 129, 131
    see also disruption; permanence
stigmatisation 167–8
stoicism 52, 53, 61, 101, 102, 103,
    123, 126, 140, 206
subjective permanence 17, 136–9,
    147, 236
    see also belonging
support
    in adoption 109–116
    for independent living 181,
        185, 192–5
    on returning home 81–7,
        261–3
    see also aftercare; financial
        support

Tara
    attachment in 240, 241
    foster care experiences
        218–21, 236–7, 240

independent living
    experiences 221–5, 241,
        243
    outcomes, analysis of 245–6
    perspective on life 244–5
    pre-care experiences 218
    relationship with birth family
        223, 224, 237, 238–9
    school experiences 241, 242
trial at home *see* returning home

young people *see* care leavers;
    independent living; older
    children

Author Index

Aldgate, J. 10, 255–6, 268
Allerhand, M. 11, 64
Arden, N. 14
Armstrong, J. 266

Baines, B. 11
Ballie, C. 268
Barnes, H. 15
Barth, R. 44
Beecham, J. 258
Berridge, D. 11, 266
Berry, M. 44
Biehal, N. 27, 171, 172, 184, 185,
    186, 188, 210, 213, 214, 215,
    216, 253
Bohman, M. 10
Bowlby, J. 78, 240, 277
Bradley, M. 268
Broad, R. 171, 210, 214, 253
Bullock, R. 12, 27, 64, 66, 67, 89,
    238, 249, 266, 268

Carey, K. 171, 210, 253
Chamberlain, P. 26–7, 87, 262,
    267, 268
Cheung, Y. 256
Cleaver, H. 11, 49, 267
Clyman, R. 44
Collishaw, S. 10
Colton, M. 41
Cook, R. 27

Department for Education and
    Skills 7
Department of Health 9
Di Virgilio, L. 26
Dorosh, M. 266
Downes, C. 27, 245, 249, 268

Ellaway, B. 44
Essen, J. 10, 256
Evans, E. 268

Fanshel, D. 268
Farmer, E. 11, 44, 49, 64, 66, 67,
    89, 266–7
Fein, E. 14, 16, 258
Fenyo, A. 11
Ferguson, T. 252
Festinger, T. 14
Fever, F. 14
Finch, S. 268
Fisher, M. 266
Fletcher, B. 14

Fraser, M. 89
Fratter, J. 11, 126, 127, 266
Fruin, D. 27, 89
Fry, E. 214, 215

Gambrill, E. 71
Garnett, L. 12, 13, 266
George, V. 11
Gibbons, J. 11
Gibbs, I. 11, 26, 36, 41–2, 49,
    126, 132, 185, 245, 249, 266,
    269
Good, D. 12
Goodman, R. 22
Gould, C. 44
Grundy, J. 268

Hall, C. 27
Harms, I. 26
Harwin, J. 44
Haug, M. 11
Hazel, N. 11
Head, J. 10
Health and Social Services
    Committee 26
Heath, A. 256
Hensey, D. 10, 66
Herbert, M. 267
Hill, M. 11
Hipgrave, T. 11
Hobbs, C. & G. 266
Howe, D. 255, 268
Hundleby, M. 12
Hunt, J. 139

Jackson, S. 26, 256
Jenkins, S. 266

Kahan, B. 14
King, J. 10, 66
Kirton, D. 258
Kluger, M. 258
Knapp, M. 11
Knowles, J. 185
Koluchova, J. 26
Kufeldt, K. 266, 268

Lahti, J. 127, 265
Lambert, L. 10, 16
Landsverk, J. 44
Laub, J. 15
Lipscombe, J. 11
Littel, J. 89
Little, M. 12, 27
Lowe, N. 11, 13, 92, 106

Macaskill, C. 267
Maluccio, A. 14, 16, 32, 258
Maugham, B. 10

Meier, E. 14
Millham, S. 27
Minty, B. 10, 44, 66–7
Moore, A. 14
Moreland, S. 27
Moyers, S. 11

Napier, H. 11
Newman, R. 89
Norford, L. 11
Norman, E. 266

Ogilvie, K. 258
Olmstead, K. 16
Osborne, A. 10, 256
Packman, J. 27

Page, R. 14
Palmer, S. 268
Parker, R. 11, 26, 44, 64, 66, 67,
    89, 104, 108, 124–5, 267
Pfeiffer, S. 27
Pickles, A. 10
Pollock, S. 266
Priestley, M. 185

Quinton, D. 10, 64, 69, 92, 106,
    115, 216, 249, 266, 267, 277

Rabiee, P. 185
Rashid, S. 11
Rathbun, C. 26
Reddy, L. 27
Rees, J. 10
Reid, J. 27, 268
Reid, K. 27
Rosenbloom, L. 10
Rowe, J. 10, 12, 13, 16, 26, 27,
    252, 266
Runyan, D. 44
Rushton, A. 92, 106, 126, 249,
    265, 266
Russell, J. 10
Rutter, M. 10, 26, 64, 69, 92, 216,
    249, 268

Sampson, R. 15
Schofield, G. 11, 26, 27, 267, 268
Schuerman, J. 89
Schweinhart, L. 15
Sellick, C. 11, 104, 258, 266
Selwyn, J. 104, 105
Shaw, M. 11
Sherman, E. 89
Shyne, A. 89
Sinclair, I. 10, 11, 16, 26, 36,
    41–2, 49, 64, 69, 126, 132,
    185, 245, 249, 266, 269
Skeels, H. 26

Skuse, D. 26
St Claire, L. 10, 256
Stein, M. 26, 71, 90, 171, 184,
    185, 210, 253, 268
Sylva, K. 268

Taitz, L. 10, 66
Taussig, H. 44
Terling, T. 44
Thoburn, J. 11, 91, 104, 105, 126,
    127, 128, 258, 266, 267
Thomas, C. 27, 105, 125, 267
Timms, N. 14
Tizard, B. 10
Trasler, G. 11
Treseder, J. 92
Triseliotis, J. 10, 11, 268

Utting, W. 26

Van der Waals, P. 14
Vernon, J. 27, 89

Waldfogel, S. 26
Walker, M. 11, 268
Walton, E. 89
Ward, H. 26, 105
Weber, R. 11
Webster-Stratton, C. 267
Weikart, D. 15
Werner, E. 15
Williams, J. 10
Wilson, K. 11, 16, 26, 36, 49, 126,
    132, 185, 245, 249, 252, 266,
    267, 269
Wiltse, K. 71
Wynne, J. 266

Zimmerman, R. 10, 44, 66